Gregory Corso:
Ten Times a Poet

Leon Horton
Michele McDannold
Editors

ROADSIDE PRESS

Gregory Corso: Ten Times a Poet
SECOND EDITION
Copyright ©Roadside Press 2025
ISBN: 979-8-9925009-4-3
Library of Congress Control Number: 2025938487

Cover Photography: Christopher Felver

Compiled & Edited by Leon Horton
Co-Editor: Michele McDannold

Roadside Press is committed to publishing works of quality and integrity. In that spirit, we are proud to offer this book to our readers; however, the stories, the experiences, and the words are the authors' alone.

Roadside Press
Colchester, Illinois

WHAT THEY'RE SAYING ABOUT TEN TIMES A POET

"I am telling everyone that it is without doubt the most important book published on Corso thus far."—Gerald Nicosia, author of *Memory Babe: A Critical Biography of Jack Kerouac.*

"Reading the essays, memoirs, and other material in *Gregory Corso: Ten Times a Poet* widened my awareness of who he was. It's a warts and all portrait that is painted, and I'm glad about that. It would have been wrong to try to show him as perfect in any form, poet or person. The main point is that the best work will survive, as it ought to do."—Jim Burns, contributor to *Beat Scene* / author of *Modernists, Bohemians, Mavericks.*

"I love this book so much I read it three times. The great thing about *Gregory Corso: Ten Times a Poet* is the brilliant reminiscences, literary essays, explication of childhood, photographs, interviews, and obituaries that unite the wild man running through his life and the deep poet delivering his final book, *The Golden Dot.* Read it. Then read it again." —Victor Bockris, author of *The Burroughs-Warhol Connection* and *With William Burroughs: A Report from the Bunker.*

"Finally, the tribute Corso deserves. Over the past few decades we have witnessed a surge of interest in the Beat writers, with Beat studies growing into a vibrant literary field, but as he was in life, Corso remains an outsider even in death. Gregory Corso is not an easy man to write about, but thankfully, we now have *Ten Times a Poet,* a wonderful collection of essays and poems and interviews in celebration of this most remarkable of men." —David S. Wills, editor of *Beatdom* / author of *High White Notes: The Rise and Fall of Gonzo Journalism.*

This book is respectfully dedicated
to the memories of

Rosemary Manno
(1949-2021)

Jay Jeff Jones
(1946-2023)

Neeli Cherkovski
(1945-2024)

Contents

Introduction: Cheshire-Catting Across the Universe

by Leon Horton

Gregory Nunzio Corso (1930-2001) is a difficult man to pin down. A student of the New York streets, graduate of Clinton Prison, Hermean messenger-poet of the Beat Generation, Gregory was "one of the Daddies," as he liked to remind people, one of the Big Four. With Jack Kerouac, Allen Ginsberg and William Burroughs, Corso was a formative member of a nascent literary "movement" that would change the way we look at modern literature. "Four people do not a generation make," he wryly observed much later, but the impact and the reverberating shockwaves of those "angel-headed hipsters" still resonate down the line; and, as fellow poet Kenneth Rexroth observed in *American Poetry in the Twentieth Century*, Corso was "one of the best poets of his generation."

A word-slinger who delighted in surreal word combinations, a clown who danced an orphic jig, a crazed poet visionary who saw a horse-mounted Indian in the traffic of New York, who saw the spectre of Death on the Greek island of Hydra, Gregory's entry into the Beat canon—after a chance meeting in 1950 with Allen Ginsberg in a lesbian bar—came at a price. In a 1973 interview, Victor Bockris asked him if there were any mysteries. His answer was both emphatic and enigmatic: "Generally, no. Personally, one… I don't know who I am." And there lies the problem. How do you find a man in search of himself?

Gregory looked to his hero, Percy Bysshe Shelley: "A great poem is a fountain forever overflowing with the waters of wisdom and delight." It was this "delight" in the dynamo of his imagination, in the vagaries of language, across seemingly disparate fragments of thought and image, where Corso birthed his streetwise themes of life, death and re-demption. Often lyrical, often outrageous, both in his life and in his work, adjectives like chaotic and mercurial cling to Gregory's skin like tics to a feral cat. But this Lower East Side tiger has a Cheshire-Cat smile—the more you look for him, the more he fades into the ether, until only his gnomic grin remains, cadence of Little Italy hanging in the air.

Gregory's childhood, as you will discover, was a series of traumas: abandoned by his mother, then his father, moved from one foster family to another, often without his siblings, a life of trouble with the law and petty crime beckoned. In his childhood we find much of the man. But there is more to come. Three years in Clinton Prison, age 17, would be Gregory's formal education—with "books of illumination" in the prison library, and words of wisdom from an old lag: "Don't serve time, make time serve you." Prison removes a man's identity and credentials—for Gregory Corso, it was an apprenticeship.

At first glance, Corso was a mass of contradictions and contrariness. He could be belligerent, critical, explosive, cruel, kind, light-hearted, serious, very funny, sincere, and remorseful, depending on the time of day, and sometimes his errant behaviour, his drinking and his heroin addiction overwhelmed the work. But for Gregory it was more than just the words. He didn't only write poetry, he lived it, sutured to his soul, with time off for bad behaviour. "If you believe you're a poet, then you're saved," he once proclaimed. Saved from what? From the stultifying rigidities of conventional society, perhaps, since, in avoiding the bourgeois trappings of a comfortable existence, as Gregory Stephenson noted in *Exiled Angel: A Study of the Work of Gregory Corso* (Hearing Eye, 1989), "Corso's work vehemently opposes all forms of tyranny and oppression, together with all agencies of repression and joylessness, as it celebrates the persistence and the irrepressibility of imagination, desire and liberty."

When William Burroughs and Allen Ginsberg both died in 1997, Corso was briefly landed with the moniker "The Last Beat," with Gus Reininger's documentary of the same name following him, through much of his grief, around old haunts in New York, Athens, Paris and Rome, as he came to terms with the deaths of his friends and his own mortality. Although it won several awards when it premiered at film festivals, *Corso: The Last Beat* quickly ran into legal issues and has yet to receive an official release. Through Reininger's tireless endeavors, however, Corso was finally reunited with his mother, who he hadn't seen since he was a child, a truly emotional sense of closure captured on film. But the time for celebration quickly passed when Gregory learned he had inoperable prostate cancer. He moved in with his daughter, Sheri Langerman, who nursed him through his final days and fought off too many visitors.

"Open this book as you would a box of crazy toys," cajoled Allen Ginsberg in the Introduction to Corso's 1958 collection *Gasoline*, "take in your hands a refinement of beauty out of a destructive atmosphere." I think that holds equally true here. Among the essays, memoirs and previously unpublished material in the pages of this book, you will hear many voices: friends, family, fellow poets. New facts emerge. The more you look, the more Corso morphs into view—"I am become more vivid," he observed in the poem "Power"—squaring up and backing down, joyful, full of laughter, seeing all, acerbic, profligate, and drunk… There he goes again, Cheshire-Catting across the universe.

In 2001 the last "Daddy" of the Beat Generation left us for an undisclosed address. He was cremated, his ashes later buried in Rome, at the feet of his beloved Shelley. Corso's star didn't shine as high as Ginsberg's, Kerouac's or Burroughs'—something he complained bitterly about, but was really of his own doing. His output was spare, for one thing, averaging one collection of poetry a decade, and with his burgeoning heroin addiction, publishers such as James Laughlin at New Directions found him difficult to work with. There was no biography in his lifetime either, despite several abortive attempts. But the Beat goes on. Since *An Accidental Autobiography: The Selected Letters of Gregory Corso* (New Directions, 2003), interest in Corso and his poetry has been steadily growing, and with the publication of his last collection of poetry, *The Golden Dot* (Lithic Press, 2022), and work progressing on a biography by Kurt Hemmer (a chapter from which I am delighted to present here), we are beginning to see more clearly the motive powers and the connective tissue that holds this remarkable poet together.

I hope *Gregory Corso: Ten Times a Poet* is a candle to that.

The outpouring of love for Gregory in the pages of this book, in the memoirs, the poetry, even the essays, took me back at first. To know Gregory, it seems, was to love him. How do you find a man in search of himself? You ask the people who knew him.

Spirit

Spirit
is Life
It flows thru
the death of me
endlessly
like a river
unafraid
of becoming
the sea

—Gregory Corso

Page from the *Geometric Poem*, published by Ettore Sottsass and Fernando Pivano, 1966. From the collection of Raymond Foye.

Corso: A Most Dangerous Art

by Raymond Foye

> This is how it happened:
> At the end
> everything that was
> dwindled into a dot;
> the dot exploded into the void
> and the beginning began again—
> —Gregory Corso, from *The Golden Dot*, circa. 1998

Time, cosmic and terrestrial, was one of Gregory Corso's great subjects. He saw the decades as distinct parcels, the centuries as larger ones, and millennia more so. Throughout the 1990s he had been eagerly awaiting the arrival of the millennium, exploring in his poems themes of Armageddon and apocalypse, ecological cataclysm, Revelations, and the promise of a New Age. But as the momentous date approached, personal tragedies mounted: the death of his closest friend and literary champion, Allen Ginsberg, in the spring of 1997, followed four months later by the death of William Burroughs, his second-oldest friend and the person he considered most incorruptible in life. In 1998 his oldest friend Anton Rosenberg, model for Kerouac's hero in *The Subterraneans* (and "the true hipster" in this book), passed away. Then came news of liver, heart, and lung disease, and finally inoperable prostate cancer. He managed to see the new millennium, but only just. He left his beloved Greenwich Village for the care of his daughter's home in Minnesota late in 2000, and died there shortly thereafter, on January 17, 2001.

Corso had struggled with his final manuscript, *The Golden Dot*, for the last twenty years of his life. It went through countless visions and revisions, both textual and conceptual. He knew it would be his poetical last will and testament. It had to be precisely on the mark, a summation of the many literary and philosophical themes that preoccupied him in life. Even more daunting than the personal hardships (which were nothing new to him), he had changed his fundamental approach to the poem, casting off an elaborate stylistic toolkit that no longer served his purpose. The rudiments of the poem were what mattered now, a direct and elemental relationship with the Muse. Frustratingly, throughout the 1990s, the project continually collapsed under its own weight, until...

Following Ginsberg's funeral at New York's Shambhala Meditation Center, Corso returned to his small apartment at 26 Horatio Street in the West Village and composed "Elegium Catullus/Corso, for Allen Ginsberg." It is modeled on a funeral ode by the Latin poet Catullus, who sits next to and addresses the "unspeaking ashes" (*"alloquer-er cinerem"*) of his brother. Corso lightens Catullus's famous final line, *"Ave atque vale"* ("Hail and farewell"), with the salutation he and Ginsberg always used on each other, "Toodle-loo"—a bit of '50s camp silliness they often shared. With this short and simple poem, the floodgates opened. Over the next three and a half years Corso rewrote the entire manuscript of *The Golden Dot*, beginning that evening with the "Elegium."

The Golden Dot is framed by Ginsberg's death on one end and Corso's own death on the other. It is, among other things, the story of a lifelong friendship between two of the greatest poets of the twentieth century. Corso is now alone, left to argue with his mentor and rival, pleading his case and making amends. His insecurities led him to question the very reasons Allen befriended him in a Greenwich Village bar: was it just his good looks and street smarts? But he comes to trust and accept Allen's estimation of his work, so succinctly stated on the dedication page to *Planet News* (1968), some of the only serious recognition he ever got for his poetry in his lifetime: "Dedicated to the Pure Imaginary Poet Gregory Corso," and once again in Ginsberg's *Selected Poems 1947-1995*: "To Gregorio Nunzio Corso, Wisdom Maestro, American Genius of Antique and Modern Idiom, Father Poet of Concision." Allen always told anyone who would listen that Gregory was the greater poet, and often lamented the lack of serious critical studies of Corso's work.

Corso did not like to overpublish, and by the 1960s one book per decade became his general rule, usually at the turn of the decade, with each book expressing something of what he felt to be the zeitgeist of the moment: *The Happy Birthday of Death* in 1960; *Elegiac Feelings American* in 1970; *Herald of the Autochthonic Spirit* in 1981. Another rule was that the books should be brief: these were 92, 120, and 66 pages respectively. But by the time 1990 arrived, Corso chose not to publish. He turned sixty that year, and while his reasons for not publishing were never clearly stated, profound changes were taking place in his life and work since "Hitting the Big 5-0," as he called it in a poem marking his half-century. Corso's relationship to poetry had been a trajectory from intensely private to famously public, sometimes reading to audiences of a thousand or more. He complained to me often, "I began writing poetry alone, after midnight, just me and the poem, by candlelight. The next thing I know I'm on stage reading to hundreds of people. It messed me up." This predicament led Corso to favor humorous poems, crowd pleasers with punchlines. He'd come to see himself as a performer, a clown even, in his own words. He had been on the reading circuit for twenty-five years, often touring with Ginsberg—they were public poets in a way that is almost unimaginable today, and they both took that role very seriously. But Corso's brash persona and drunken antics at readings masked a painful shyness, and he longed to escape that grind. As he so memorably put it in a poem of the time, "I feel like an old mangy bull crashing through the red rag of an alcoholic day." He'd come to see this public face of poetry as a routine, a job, an act. And while he may have had many shortcomings, failing to be honest with himself was not one. Slowly he withdrew, first to Rome (where he always felt most at home) and then to the neighborhood where he was born and raised, Greenwich Village.

These had been hard years. The drinking itself was no longer sustainable and that necessitated a separation from society. More profoundly, the half-century mark awoke in him the need to confront the many traumas that haunted his adult life: abandonment by his mother shortly after his birth due to domestic abuse by his father; five cruel Catholic foster homes, four orphanages, and seven arrests, with frequent prison time in the Tombs. The orphanages and prisons had always been part of his personal mythology, but until this point the painful details had never been publicly examined or revealed.

And once that door was opened in his writing, it could not be closed. Sharing these details with his readers makes for an unprecedented intimacy, one that could never be revealed in public readings.

Corso was a native New Yorker, born on the corner of Bleecker and MacDougal Streets. Gangsters frequented the cafés and restaurants and the culture of organized crime was hard to resist. From individual acts of petty theft, Corso eventually became the ringleader of his own larceny gang, whom he organized with walkie-talkies. At the age of seventeen he was sentenced to three years in upstate New York's brutal Clinton Correctional Facility, known as Dannemora. Ever the prodigy, he often noted that he was the youngest inmate to enter that prison and the youngest to leave. [1]

There's a remarkable film of Corso on a return visit to Clinton Prison (Danneemora as he always called it) two years before his death, speaking with prisoners about writing poetry. He recounts the advice an old inmate gave him the day he arrived: "Don't serve time, make time serve you." The prison library held few books but they were choice: *The 1905 Webster's Illustrated Dictionary of the English Language*, the *Bible, the Encyclopedia Britannica* (eleventh edition), *Bulfinch's Mythology*, and a 1925 anthology titled *Ideas and Forms in English and American Literature*, edited by Homer Watt and James Munn. I recently obtained a copy of the latter for a few dollars, after finding Corso's reference to the book in the manuscript of *The Golden Dot*. It's a fascinating selection and explains a great deal about his penchants for early epics such as *Beowulf* and *Sir Gawain and the Green Knight*, and for the ballads of the British Isles, such as "The Twa Sisters" and "Sir Patrick Spens." Running through all of Corso's work is a healthy mistrust of literacy and the written word, which he considered latecomers to his profession. The stories and beliefs handed down orally from ancient times were his true guides, and he always said his favorite author was Anonymous. He loved Sanskrit and Akkadian epics, chronicles of dynastic Egypt, the myths of ancient Greece. His sense of history was synchronous: ideas, events, and subjects all connected inside his head like the gears of a clock.

I first encountered Gregory Corso in April 1973 at a Jack Kerouac symposium at Salem State College in Massachusetts, where he was a featured guest along with Ginsberg and Peter Orlovsky. That weekend, with velvet suit and silver flask of cognac, Corso was on the attack against everyone: Ginsberg, the academics, and Kerouac himself, or at least the myth of Kerouac. (The witches of Salem seemed to be the only people he had any respect for.) But then something remarkable happened: the event concluded with an evening poetry reading, and I saw Corso take all of the hostility he had created and suddenly polarize it. (Later I would see performers like Nina Simone and Miles Davis do the same thing.) After ninety minutes of poetry and chanting by Ginsberg and Orlovsky, Corso took center stage and read what I still consider to be his greatest poem, "Elegiac Feelings American (for the Dear Memory of John L. Kerouac)." Suddenly a hushed silence fell on the auditorium as Corso cast his spell; the poem was profound, eloquent, and ravishingly beautiful. At the end of the reading, many in the audience (including many Kerouac family members) were weeping, as was Corso himself. There was no question who the heavy was on that stage.

One of my favorite things about hanging out with Gregory over the years was watching how he dealt with fans. He had a lot of them, and since he always looked like Gregory Corso, they often approached him on the street. Depending on his mood he might be gracious, but was more often flatly dismissive or downright confrontational, accusing them of pandering and vicariousness—*they* were the source of his pain. "Mister Corso, I just want to say how much your work has meant to me down through the years," someone would say in a heartfelt manner. "Do I bother you with my problems?" he would reply curtly. Other times he was more practical: "Oh that's great, gimme $5." I can't count the number of people who came up to him to say that his poem "Marriage" was read at their wedding—a true epithalamium for our times if there ever was one. (The poem is heavily anthologized; Gregory once told me he estimated he'd made over $100,000 from "Marriage"—"Not bad for one poem.") Especially surprising to me was the number of people who quoted back to him the line "Standing on a street corner doing nothing is power." Written in 1953, that line somehow represented the quintessentially Beat challenge to authority. And as Gregory often said, one great line is worth an entire book of poems.

Corso did not reveal his inner nature casually. Those who met him once or twice only saw a theatrical personality. For this reason the many outrageous stories that abound may be accurate in their picaresque details, but they are also terribly superficial. Underneath it all he was a figure of great warmth and caring, as his closest friends will attest. It seems strange even to me, but when I look back on my life most of the truly important pointers I got—about human nature, self-preservation, and other life lessons—came from Gregory.

Whether Gregory was home alone, playing pool in a bar, or sitting in a cafe, there was never a time when he wasn't *with* the poem, turning a line or image over in his head, speaking it aloud to test the sound and cadence, or questioning its inner logic. His poetry was an argument with himself. I never knew anyone who worked harder than he did, although if you asked most people they would probably say he never worked at all. A scholarly issue was always on the table, he was familiar with them all. In a barroom one afternoon he suddenly slammed the table with his fist and shouted, "It was all because of that damn swan!"—and I knew he was back onto the Trojan War.

In 1997, his sixty-seventh year, as he labored over his final book, startling news arrived. A documentary filmmaker had discovered his eighty-year-old mother: she had not returned to Italy immediately after his birth, as he had been told, but had merely fled across the river to Trenton, New Jersey, where she raised another family. Their reunion was captured on film, and a few days later they made their first excursion, to an Atlantic City gambling casino—which seemed to establish matrilineal proof beyond doubt. But joking aside, though initially joyous, the reunion only re-exposed painful feelings of abandonment. Corso told me a few years later that he wished the filmmaker had left well enough alone. "I lived sixty-seven years without a mother—how can all that be made up for now?" (He always claimed Demeter to be his true mother.) Meanwhile, his father was dying. Corso had hated and feared the man all his life, but he made the effort to visit him, only to find that Alzheimer's disease had turned his father into a gentle and kind-hearted soul. They had a poignant reunion, but the encounter ended on a painful and embarrassing note: his father called him Dominic. These and other remarkable events are recorded in *The Golden Dot.* Life now seemed a daily succession of bewildering events.

One positive development in these years was the emergence of a patron, Hiro Yamagata, a successful visual artist from Japan. His monthly stipend allowed Corso to move out of the apartment of Roger and Irvyne Richards, proprietors of the Rare Book Room on Greenwich Avenue, who had taken him in several years earlier after learning he'd spent the previous night on the subway. When an apartment came vacant next door, Corso had his own living space for the first time in many years (or practically ever). There's no doubt this helped with the work. Those of us who visited him will recall the floor covered in typed poems, often stained with wine, coffee, blood, and god knows what else. The space also allowed him to begin making art again, which brought in a little money. He was a skilled draftsman with a charming style and a deep knowledge of art history. He had his visitors and admirers and a calm domesticity prevailed. The one vexation was his addiction. A heroin user since the 1950s, now alternating with methadone, he told me it had been almost twenty years since he'd actually gotten high from the drug—it was simply a matter of maintenance. Veins had collapsed and he was losing use of both arms. Infections led to visits to nearby St. Luke's Hospital. He recounts these events in several poems, always referring to heroin as "the dirty nurse."

Corso often spent years revising a poem, and in many respects a poem of his was never finished. Friends who gave him lodging would later find his books in their libraries extensively rewritten. Poetry readings, especially in later years, often consisted of glosses on the poems; he always seemed to be having a running argument with himself, or the poem (they were the same thing). But as the end drew near he seems to have realized these endless revisions would not do, and suddenly we have the rarest of things in his oeuvre: poems written all at once, a single stream of thought and inspiration from start to finish. This is sometimes indicated to the reader by the date of composition, and often even the exact time (always in the middle of the night). Corso called these "diary poems" and he was extremely unsure about them. To me they are the capstones of his career, the works that most show off his extraordinary powers as a poet. To read a poem such as "Melted Parchment" (dated 4/26/98) is to fully enter his mind, and to witness the very act of the poem's coming into being. In these last poems he has gone back to the candle, at midnight, writing to himself and the solitary reader. For much of his life, poetry was connected in his mind with youth: not only the teenage spirit of Chatterton or Rimbaud, but the child spirit prior to that. Keeping that spirit alive had a lot to do with how he lived, and it took its toll. Now wisdom and old age come to the fore. The level of intimacy is exquisite and the effect ethereal. The conviction he had for the poem was absolute.

Another unusual characteristic of *The Golden Dot* is how very few poems have titles —perhaps only half a dozen out of a hundred or more. I don't know why this is, except clearly titles were superfluous. One is left with the sense that these are not literary "products" but a kind of unnameable issuance or outflow. It also facilitates Corso's wish, stated on page 1 of the manuscript, that this work be seen as a "shuffle poem," with a random, nonhierarchical configuration, or, if one were more occult-minded, a method of divination like the shuffling of the tarot or the throwing of the I Ching. Such a book as this may exist somewhere, but I know of none like it.

The reader may ask why, if this book was completed twenty years ago, is it only being published now? After the poet's death the apartment was cleared out and the manuscript was gathered into a paper shopping bag. In his will, Corso left the rights to the book to his friends Roger and Irvyne Richards, for their faithful support in his final years. Roger Richards, a legendary figure in New York's rare-book world, died at home on his seventieth birthday, December 18, 2002. In less than two years, Irvyne had lost her two closest companions in life, and she gradually became a recluse. I called numerous times, hoping to obtain a copy of the manuscript, but she always demurred, saying she wanted to edit the book herself—which I knew would never happen. Irvyne was a chain smoker and for years I lived in fear the apartment would burn down and the manuscript with it. Eventually she stopped taking my calls. The original work remained in her possession, a talisman to a life that no longer existed, and she guarded it against the outside world. When I learned of her death, in September 2020, I called her stepdaughter Hillary and soon the manuscript was in hand. Although pages had been copied and circulated among Corso's friends over the years, those were clearly fragments and drafts, and bore almost no resemblance to the carefully shaped final manuscript, with the author's intentions everywhere evident, the concluding chapter of a profound career.

Source Notes

(1) There were five convictions in NYC Children's Court for larceny between the ages of 13 and 16. A grand larceny charge in Bennington, Vermont, brought a 2 to 3 year sentence at the Weeks School, a prison for juvenile offenders in Vergennes, VT (from which he briefly escaped). In NYC at the age of eighteen further charges of Grand Larceny and parole violation sent him to the Clinton Correctional Facility in upstate New York.

(This essay was originally published by Lithic Press, 2022. Reprinted by kind permission of Raymond Foye.)

The following is an excerpt from a work in progress: *My Task Is the Poem Human: A Gregory Corso Biography.*

Never Knowing a Mother's Kiss: The Childhood of Nunzio Corso

by Kurt Hemmer

Gregory Corso's spirit triumphed over a dreadful childhood and a traumatic juvenescence. Of the twenty-four poets of the so-called "Silent Generation," those born between 1928 and 1945, represented in the third edition of *The Norton Anthology of Poetry* (1983), where I first encountered his work, Gregory is the only one not to have attended college. He is also the only one to have been raised by multiple foster families and to have served significant prison time. Nevertheless, he created an indelible self-identity and became one of the most significant poets of his generation.

Used by permission of the Allen Ginsberg Estate

One of the great retellings of his childhood was a letter he wrote to Jack Kerouac describing his youth, explaining himself after feeling distraught over his portrayal as the character Yuri Gligoric in Kerouac's novel *The Subterraneans* (1958). Jack thought it was better than anything he himself had written and compared it to Neal Cassady's famous "Joan Anderson Letter" that had inspired the first draft of Kerouac's *On the Road.*[1] After reading the letter, which made him cry, Kerouac wrote to Allen Ginsberg, "Poor great

Gregory, and Jesus how he suffered!"[2] Later, Jack and Allen wanted to publish the letter in an anthology they were working on that never came to fruition.[3]

We can only grasp Corso's success by understanding the trauma of his childhood. I will attempt to piece together a version of that childhood assembled from a handful of official documents and fragments of his memory from poems, essays, interviews, and letters. A completely accurate depiction of his childhood is an exercise of futility. Believe me, I've tried. Reinventing his childhood would be a common pastime for him. Memories formed and reformed in a kaleidoscope of pain and healing. The number of foster parents and families he lived with became an amorphous blur that evaded exactitude. The amount of misinformation and contradictions in his retellings of his youth are enough to drive any biographer to despair, but I think I can provide a rough portrait that provides the gist.

Nunzio Corso, no middle name given, was born in New York City on March 26, 1930 to Fortunato "Sam" Corso, a twenty-year-old laborer, and Michelina "Margaret" Corso, née Colonna, an eighteen-year-old housewife, at 190 Bleecker Street. The child was named after his maternal grandfather, Nunzio Colonna. Little Nunzio was his parents' second child. His brother, Joseph, had been born on April 10, 1928.[4] Nunzio's Certificate and Record of Birth was handwritten by the midwife, Margherita M. Lapadula.[5] The 1930 United States Federal Census enumerated that April says that his father, though misnamed as "Anthony," was a twenty-one-year old doorman at a restaurant and that his mother, "Margaret," was a nineteen-year-old housewife. They had both added a year to their ages. The couple were listed as having two children, Joseph, listed as one year old but soon to turn two, and Nunzio, not even a month old, living with them at 190 Bleecker Street. According to the census, his parents were able to read and write English. The document said they had been married when Sam, a first-generation Italian American, was eighteen-years old and Margaret was sixteen.[6] This was false.

Nunzio's mother had been born in Miglianico, Abruzzo, Italy. When she was nine years old, Michelina, the second youngest, accompanied by four sisters (Lucrezia, Francesca, Carmela, and Maria), immigrated to America with their mother, Antonia (née

Antoinette Allegretti), on the *S. S. Italia* from Naples.[7] The ship docked on January 22, 1921, and the family was admitted into the United States on January 29. Michelina's father, Nunzio, having previously immigrated to the United States was living on Carmine Street in New York. The family moved to 190 Bleecker Street, where Michelina lived with her parents. She married Sam Corso, occupied as a printer and living at 146 Sullivan Street, on October 7, 1926.[8] Anna, Sam's mother, was a widow who had come to New York in 1909 from Cannitello, Calabria, Italy.[9] Her husband, Giuseppe, had died in 1922. Sam had been born in New York on February 5, 1910.[10] Though his marriage certificate listed him as eighteen years old, he was only sixteen. Michelina was born on December 23, 1911.[11] Though she was listed as being seventeen on the marriage certificate, she was not yet fifteen years old. They had their first son, Joseph, when Fortunato was eighteen years old and Michelina was sixteen. The newlyweds were living at 190 Bleecker Street (the same address as the Colonnas). Michelina decided to leave her family in January 1931 when her second child, Nunzio, was nine months old.

It is believed that Sam had knocked some of Michelina's teeth out, so she devised an escape. All Michelina knew was that she had to get out and soon. No longer able to take the physical abuse, and with a great deal of anguish that would haunt her for the rest of her life, she disappeared where Sam would not think of looking for her. Unable to deal with the situation, Sam took the children to The New York Foundling Hospital and moved back in with his mother at 64 Suffolk Street.[12] The Foundling Hospital was a red brick building taking up the block from 68th to 69th Streets between Lexington and Third Avenues. Nunzio and Joseph would return there between stints in foster homes. Parental rights were not terminated by Fortunato, he always planned on taking them back, so the brothers could not be adopted. While in the care of a foster family, on March 10, 1931, Nunzio was baptized at the St. Vincent Ferrer Church.[13] He would later receive the Sacrament of Confirmation at Lincoln Hall, a Catholic boys' school, perhaps when he was sent there after being found guilty of burglary when he was fourteen.[14] It was there that he probably took *Gregory* as his confirmation name. At first, when he was old enough, Nunzio would be told by his father that his mother was dead.

When he was seventeen his paternal grandmother, Anna, told Nunzio that his mother was a whore who had returned to Italy. His father later told him that his mother had left the family for another man.

Nunzio would have five different foster families.[15] He was placed in his first foster home on February 14, 1931. The middle-aged couple were forced to give up the child when the mother became ill, and he was transferred from this home on June 15, 1931, less than a half year later, without any memory of them, since he was only a baby. He stayed with his second foster family until September 14, 1934, three years and three months, when he was transferred to a third family to be with his brother at the age of four. It was his second foster mother, who was taken with the child, that he initially believed for some time to be his birth mother. The mother and father of his third foster family were in their sixties, so the care of the children fell to their daughter. Nunzio was with this family for three years and six and a half months, from the time he was four until he was eight years old. Though he was considered charming, he was accused of stealing several small items from school. He started kindergarten at P.S. 3, where his work was excellent, but, when he was promoted to the first grade, he became disruptive and was reported for theft, which he denied. He was then transferred to St. Angela Merici School, where he was also found unruly. Unable to handle his behavior, he was transferred, along with his brother, to a fourth foster family on April 1, 1938. They lived in the Bronx at 1856 Tomlinson Avenue.[16] This family consisted of two middle-aged parents, a daughter in her twenties, and two teenage sons. He attended P.S. 83, and, though he was considered likable, he was also disobedient. He would spend a total of two years and four months with this foster family. Though described as having "an appealing personality, was friendly, alert and talkative," again Nunzio's behavior resulted in a request for a transfer.[17] He was first placed in a temporary home for the summer of 1938. This was his fifth foster home, consisting of a young couple and their teenage daughter. They lived in the country, and Nunzio enjoyed swimming and playing in the woods. His fifth foster mother found him to be "disobedient," "sloppy," and "sneaky."[18] His behavior improved, credited to the strict discipline of his fifth foster mother, and he returned to his fourth foster family after spending only two months away from them on September 6, 1938. His bad behavior resurfaced, and his father began weekly visits and often took his children on day trips. According to foster records, Fortunato's mother, Anna, "stated she had raised ten children of her own and she was not going to raise grandchildren."[19] Since his mother was not an option, Sam finally took the boys back. On November 6, 1940, Nunzio and Joseph were discharged to the care of their father, who had married Florence Kaufman on July 18, 1936, and lived at 190 Clinton Street in Brooklyn. Nunzio was now ten years old.

Having never experienced a mother's love, he found it difficult to express love to others. He wrote, "Never knowing a mother's kiss / nor cradling arms / I was a deformity of love."[20] Struggling with the lack of a mother's love would be a defining theme in his poetry. It was a weight from under which he was never fully able to emerge. He recalled, "See, I had a double whammy laid on me. When she left, they gave me to another mother, all right? Now, I thought she was my mother, and then they took me away from her. So that's like a double whammy. That was before I was two years old."[21] He actually had three mothers by the time he was two years old.

He recalled when he first learned of death, "I didn't know anything about death and all of that, and I must have been about four years old and I had a little turtle. I didn't know how to feed it and I carried it around in my pocket. Then suddenly it started smelling. It was dead, but I didn't know. So I kept it in my pocket until other people told me. I buried it."[22] The imminence of death would become one of his major preoccupations as a poet.

Though he seemed to reject the Catholicism of his youth throughout most of his life, his religious upbring played a major role in how he saw the world. In 1958, he wrote, "Anyway I don't regret my Catholic upbringing. There is something in me that is still very Catholic . . . ."[23] He was prone to visions and interested in rituals. Yet, bad experiences with religious adults made him distrustful of authority figures. He remembered, "The nun who punished us by pulling our ears, she was the worst of all our fears, all who attended her Sunday school during our raw early years—I was nearly lifted off the floor, both ears in her fat hands, ouching like mad . . . for having done what I thought God would have wanted me to do—which was to put a cross, made of ice cream pop sticks, on a dead cat, and say a prayer for it."[24] After burying the dead cat and placing a cross over the burial and saying a prayer, he had been scolded by his Sunday school teacher for having sinned and ordered to remove the cross: "I love cats I've always loved cats / 'But don't cats go to heaven?' I cried / 'thou shalt not worship false idols!' she replied—."[25] Corso would start developing his own spiritual values inspired by but separate from the Catholic church.

God came to him in a vision. He saw God in the sky with one black and one white book to record all the bad and all the good things he had done, as had been explained to him by a priest. "I was crossing the bridge under which trains ran," he wrote, "which separated the street on which I lived and the grocery store where I had shopped, I think it was salt I was told to buy. On that bridge, a very small one, in the Bronx, I saw in the sky, seated behind a desk of cloud, God, huge and silken-haired, rosy and smiling, and on each side of Him were the books."[26] He knew it was tricky business determining which actions went into which of God's books.

He took the vision of God in stride because he believed in God, but another event left him with a great fear: "It happened at Sunday mass. I was sitting next to a boy my age. During the mass he slyly showed me a glass elephant, a little charm he had cupped in his fist. And then he suddenly keeled over and sagged to the floor."[27] The boy was carried out by two big men. He reported, "I never knew if the boy died or merely fainted; I do know that I never saw him again."[28] The two men who had carried the boy out subsequently sat next to Nunzio. This caused him to think that he might be next.

He remembered hearing about a stranger who gave a piece of chocolate to a little boy and that the boy was later found dead, and "how a barber, instead of cutting little boys' hair, cut their throats and dumped them in his narrow alleyway."[29] Branded as having a "vivid imagination" by a teacher, he remembered imagining the next time he got a haircut "an alleyway heaped with bones and razors and scissors and bloody barber cloth torn and hanging on stark posts, a windy gloomy gray scene, awful."[30] Without any type of family, he was forced to wrestle with these fears in isolation.

Unfortunately, he was unable to find solace with his brother. After Michelina left, Nunzio and Joseph would often be separated and never emotionally connected. Later, Sam managed to form a bond with Joseph, but Nunzio remained an outsider. He recalled, "My brother was a very quiet sort of fellow, you couldn't tell if he was sulking or disinterested—nothing ever excited him, and he hardly ever smiled. We were like night and day. He could never understand me, and I think he regarded me as being downright nuts."[31] This lack of a connection with his brother was painful. He added, "He was always much stronger than me, in fact he prided himself on his strength—it sort of made up for whatever else he lacked, specifically—intelligence . . . the learning kind. Though he was two years older than me I passed him in school grades. He just couldn't learn to read or write—not that he couldn't, he just didn't want to. My brother was deeply disturbed and angry about something, I never knew what exactly."[32] We can imagine that his brother manifested the anxiety he also must have felt being motherless in ways that were unfortunately foreign to his brother.

Though his father wasn't there to console him, Sam did show up to dish out punishment. Corso revealed, "I had it real bad, truly got the worst end of it, when it came to the doling out of punishment—not only did my foster family punish me, not only did God put it in His black book, not only did the priest have me recite many Hail Marys and Our Fathers, but when my real father came to visit me every three months he too would punish me, with his hands."[33] It seemed to him that he was the only one to have to face his father's wrath. "He never hit my brother," he wrote, "not because my brother hardly did anything, wrong or good, but that he saw in my brother shades of himself—I was more like my mother, the wife who left him because she couldn't stand him—no wonder he took those pot shots at me—at the face that looked like her."[34] As time went on, it was his absent mother with whom he would most closely identify.

He recalled that when he was five his previous foster mother visited him while he was living with his new foster mother. The previous foster mother gave him a quarter, which he cherished. When he lost it, he began wetting his bed, which made his youth miserable. His new foster mother humiliated him for wetting his bed and refused him ice cream and movies because of it. Corso said he didn't stop bedwetting until he was twelve. When his father brought him back to live with his new wife, his stepmother rubbed his face in the piss when he wet his bed.

Most of his childhood memories were mixed with trauma. "I was six years old," he recalled, "and lived right next door to a Borden's milk factory. . . . I was living with foster parents and they were in the habit of locking me up in a dark room for days on end. . . . I lived in that dark room . . . windowless, and never a sign of light."[35] He became friends with the milkman, whom he called a "good father of my choice."[36] It was the milkman who was concerned about his whereabouts after he was locked in his punishment room. To help the child get over his misery, the milkman gave him a present. It was a round silver watch that didn't work. It was broken. Corso recalled, "I think it was the first thing I loved in life."[37] Watches would become another obsession.

Used by permission of the
Allen Ginsberg Estate

The first thing that he could recall stealing was a watch when he was eight years old. He stole and broke his foster father's watch, and his teacher reported him to his foster parents. She knew something was up when a kid who did not have five cents for weekly milk showed up to school with a fancy watch: "I received a series of stinging slaps, the stigma of being a crook at eight, no supper for the night, no dessert for the week, and a distrustful teacher and foster family evermore."[38] Thinking of himself as a "crook" became easier and easier as he matured.

The 1940 Census of the United States listed Nunzio Corso and his brother, Joseph, as "inmates" of The New York Foundling Hospital.[39] Nunzio had completed the third grade, but his brother, who was almost two years older, was listed as not having completed a full year of school. They were both listed as having lived with a family named Giammichele in the Bronx in 1935.[40]

His father tried to make Nunzio and Joe part of his new family. Corso wrote, "[My father] took me back in 1940, aged 10 . . . I lost all belief in mothers. . . . [My father] never showed me or gave me love (merciless beating to cite the most common) and being that he and I only lived together for a matter of 1 ½ years (the Navy took him anyway), I must conclude that he is or rather was, a stupid man."[41] One of the things Corso was determined not to be was someone like his father. "He was worse than any foster-father," believed Corso, "and he cared not for me as did the fosters. . . . In my tenth year began 'hell,' though the obstinate uneducated Italian mind of my father felt that I was grateful to be finally 'home.'"[42] On his eleventh birthday he received a cheap wristwatch from one of his father's friends. The man took advantage of Nunzio's joy by sexually molesting him a few days later. Corso later discovered that his father knew the predatory nature of this man. He felt it unlikely his father believed he could fend off the man "because my father considered me a sissy, not at all tough like himself and my brother, just a skinny frightened sissy who probably was given him by mistake at the hospital when I was born, this I clearly recall him having said."[43] Finding ways not to have to engage physically but simultaneously not be seen as a "sissy" would be challenging. Educating himself became one of the ways that would help him in his confrontation with others.

He remembered his father bringing him to the American Museum of Natural History at 200 Central Park West when he was nine. He said that he returned to the museum when he was eleven years old with fellow students of P.S. 42 from the Lower East Side.

He would write of P.S. 42, "When I think back to grammar school / I am overcome with breathlessness and sweet feeling—."[44] He claimed, "[T]wo years later [when he was 13] I ran away from home and used to spend most of my lonely cold winter days there [the American Museum of Natural History]. I'd sleep in the subway and in the morning the train would stop at the Museum and without having to go out into the street the station led directly into the Museum. And once in there I'd hurry to the men's room and wash my face and with my hands comb my hair . . . ."[45] Learning to live on the streets became a matter of necessity.

His memory of his childhood became synonymous with his memory of defying authority. He wrote, "It was the year 1943, and 1943 was a bad year for the whole world. I was thirteen years old, my father in the Navy, my mother long since gone; I was homeless, and lived with the alley cats in the wild and wonderful New York City streets."[46] On July 29, 1943, he was found guilty of petit larceny and ended up at the Youth House for Boys at 331 East 12th Street: "I was arrested for kicking in a neighborhood tailor-shop window and helping myself to a couple of suits many sizes too big for me; I sold one, and wore the other, cuffs rolled up. It wasn't much of a coincidence the tailor spotted me wearing the crime."[47] According to Corso, "The tailor pressed charges against me—thus my first involvement with the law, and it started off a time of shuffling back and forth, between the Youth House (a detention home for juvenile delinquents) to the courts, to one day of freedom (I asked the judge to send me back to my foster parents, he complied, but they declined me), and back to the Youth House."[48] The Youth House was run by Black gangs who thought Corso must have belonged to an Italian gang. "I got involved in terrible fights," wrote Corso. "Not the kind I was accustomed to in school—one against one. Here you had to fight for your life; and when I went down, that's when the feet started to fly—like a flock of blackbirds. It wasn't Gregory they were fighting though—it was White Boy."[49] Corso also learned the speech of the Black gangs: "From them I learned, beside anguish and fear, a new language—the Negro jargon, now spoken by all hipsters, black or white."[50] There was always something to be gained, even from bad situations.

Feeling he had to escape, he claimed he stole a key from a guard and made his way to the roof with five Black kids. He helped the others get down with a fire hose but was left alone without a place to tie the hose and was eventually found. He recalled, "They took me back downstairs finally, back down to more beatings and woe. One day I just flipped, putting both hands through a huge windowpane when a bunch of [gang members] began to attack me. They all backed away, and there I stood, screaming at them with my skinny arms bleeding galore. That 'mad' act got me sent to the Children's Observation ward at Bellevue Hospital."[51] After harmlessly hitting an instable inmate with a ball of bread, he was sent to the rough part of the hospital—Ward D. He recalled, "They grabbed me and put me in a straightjacket and threw me up to a room on the fourth floor where old women were screaming, where men were peeing in each other's mouths. The ball game was over, the whole thing was over already . . . ."[52] In the violent ward at Bellevue, he remembered, "Men in sheets sitting hunched in corners their skin peeling off; men in sheets squeaking like mice; men in sheets peeing on other men; 'he butchered his wife and three kids' is all I can remember being told by one of them."[53] Violence toward children became something he abhorred. He wrote to Kerouac about Bellevue, "I stood by the window, the sun was very bright; through a little slit in the window I could see and hear children playing in the street, that, and the sun, and the screams the night before seemed all at once to gather into my heart and burst forth into sobs. . . . I would like to think it was there I became a poet."[54] He admitted to Jack, "my poems always have traces of mother in them, a mother that I have never known."[55]

In his fourteenth year Corso had his tonsils removed. The doctor gave him some ether and asked him to count to one hundred. He recalled, "I cried out, scared as all hell, when the most terrible thing that ever happened to me, up to that time, happened. The doctor asked me: 'What's the matter? What's wrong?' This seconds before I blanked out. . . . Ever since then I have had the greatest fear of *going out*; death claiming the most fear."[56] To the end of his life, his poetry would wrestle with this fear of *going out*.

On May 2, 1944, he was found guilty of burglary and sentenced to time at Lincoln Hall Boys' Haven in Lincolndale, New York.[57] First he would spend some time in the Tombs. Corso recalled, "I kicked in a restaurant window, went in and took all the food that I wanted, and while coming out I was grabbed."[58] He was sent to the free-standing Manhattan House of Detention for Men at 125 White Street, one of four towers, the other three connecting towers at 100 Centre Street, that made up the New York City Criminal Courts Building. The tower Corso was in was known as the Tombs. Recalling his time in the Tombs, he stated, "All they wanted to do was fuck and of course I saved my virginity by fighting back. The lucky thing was that I was Italian; when the other Italians saw me fight back, they came to my defence [sic]. If you don't fight back then they call you a 'free-hole' . . . ."[59] In retrospect, he could view the violence he suffered more objectively. He stated, "I realize when I got the shit beaten out of me, they [the Black kids] had been fucked around."[60] He could certainly sympathize with people who found themselves mistreated by the law.

Despite the brutality of the Tombs, it was also a place of revelation. It was here that he began his self-education behind bars. Another inmate wheeled around books from which the inmates could choose reading material. He remembered, "and wanting to learn English good / I got a book on rhetoric / —in it I saw my first poem."[61] In a moment of satori, he realized he'd already been writing poems without knowing what to call them as a kid to fight against the loneliness he encountered in foster homes. Poetry was his best friend, and it helped him endure the trials to come.

He was paroled on November 15, 1945, and left Lincoln Hall when he was fifteen.[62] He often lived on the streets and by the age of sixteen he would sleep on rooftops and in cellars. He liked school, got good grades, except for conduct, but claimed to only make it to the sixth grade. In a posthumously published poem he wrote, "I was born a poet / because I wrote a poem / never having heard the word POETRY."[63] There are several versions he would tell about writing his first poem, "Sea Chanty," which was one of the poems he enjoyed reciting most at readings throughout his career. At one time he said,

"1946. I was 16 years old . . . . I spouted it on the rooftop of the Educational Alliance on East Broadway, thereon wobbling a sea chanty!"[64] At another time, regarding "Sea Chanty," he claimed, "My first writing—pen to paper—was done in that same Astor Library on 42nd Street and 5th Avenue, the biggest library in New York City."[65] In the poem he wrote, "My mother hates the sea, / my sea especially."[66]

He lived at 1496 St. Marks Avenue in Brooklyn at the end of World War II after his father returned from the Navy, but he ran away. On June 26, 1946, he was found guilty of burglary, only this time he was not in Children's Court but in the General Sessions.[67] He was given probation. On September 30, 1946, he was convicted for petit larceny.[68] Once more he was given probation after returning to the Tombs for several months.[69] Nunzio was no longer a child; in less than a year, he would be serving time in Windsor Prison in Vermont—a prison for men.

Source Notes

(1) Jack Kerouac, Jack Kerouac: *Selected Letters, 1957-1969*, ed. Ann Charters (New York: Viking, 1999), p. 150.

(2) Kerouac, Jack Kerouac: *Selected Letters, 1957-1969*, p. 150.

(3) Gregory Corso, *An Accidental Autobiography: The Selected Letters of Gregory Corso*, ed. Bill Morgan (New York: New Directions), p. 171.

(4) Windsor Prison Case File, Vermont State Archives & Records. Copy in possession of the author. Courtesy of Nile Corso.

(5) Certificate and Record of Birth for Nunzio Corso, 26 March 1930, Registered No. 9993, The City of New York Department of Health. Certified copy in possession of the author. Courtesy of Nile Corso.

(6) "Nunzio Corso in the 1930 United States Federal Census." Ancestry.com.

(7) Gustave Reininger, director. *Corso: The Last Beat*. 2009.

(8) Fortunato Corso and Michelina Colonna Certificate and Record of Marriage, October 7, 1926, Donna Stillo/Gus Reininger Archive, copy in possession of the author.

(9) Anna Corso Petition for Naturalization, August 7, 1925, Donna Stillo/Gus Reininger Archive, copy in possession of the author.

(10) Anna Corso Petition for Naturalization, August 7, 1925, Donna Stillo/Gus Reininger Archive, copy in possession of the author.

(11) "Margaret DeVita in the U.S., Social Security Death Index, 1935-2014." Ancestry.com.

(12) "Anna Corso in New York, U.S., State and Federal Naturalization Records, 1794-1943."

Ancestry.com.

(13) Nunzio Corso Certificate of Baptism, March 10, 1931, Donna Stillo/Gus Reininger Archive, copy in possession of the author.

(14) Sister Cecilia Schneider letter to Gustave Reininger, June 16, 1997, Donna Stillo/Gus Reininger Archive, copy in possession of the author.

(15) Information about Corso's foster families comes from Sister Cecilia Schneider letter to Gustave Reininger, June 16, 1997, Donna Stillo/Gus Reininger Archive, copy in possession of the author.

(16) Windsor Prison Case File, Vermont State Archives & Records. Copy in possession of the author. Courtesy of Nile Corso.

(17) Sister Cecilia Schneider letter to Gustave Reininger, June 16, 1997, Donna Stillo/Gus Reininger Archive, copy in possession of the author.

(18) Sister Cecilia Schneider letter to Gustave Reininger, June 16, 1997, Donna Stillo/Gus Reininger Archive, copy in possession of the author.

(19) Sister Cecilia Schneider letter to Gustave Reininger, June 16, 1997, Donna Stillo/Gus Reininger Archive, copy in possession of the author.

(20) Gregory Corso, "Don't tell me crocodilians head for the hills," in *The Golden Dot*, ed. Raymond Foye & George Scrivani (Fruita, CO: Lithic Press, 2022), pp. 154-55. 155.

(21) Robert King, "'I'm Poor Simple Human Bones': An Interview with Gregory Corso," The Beat Diary, ed. Arthur and Kit Knight, *the unspeakable visions of the individual* pp. 5, 4-24. 16.

(22) Romy Ashby and Foxy Kidd, "Roger Richards: The Underground Saint," *Goodie Magazine* 18 (2003): pp. 4-18. 9.

(23) Corso, *Accidental Autobiography*, p. 118.

(24) Gregory Corso, "When I Was Five I Saw a Dying Indian," *Evergreen Review* 11, no. 48 (August 1967): pp. 29-30, 83-87. 30.

(25) Gregory Corso, "Youthful Religious Experiences," *Four Poems* (New York: Paradox Bookshop): np.

(26) Corso, "When I Was Five," p. 83.

(27) Corso, "When I Was Five," p. 83.

(28) Corso, "When I Was Five," p. 83.

(29) Corso, "When I Was Five," p. 83.

(30) Corso, "When I Was Five," p. 83.

(31) Corso, "When I Was Five," p. 84.

(32) Corso, "When I Was Five," p. 84.

(33) Corso, "When I Was Five," p. 84.

(34) Corso, "When I Was Five," pp. 84-85.

(35) Gregory Corso, "The Times of the Watches," *Cavalier* 14, no. 138 (December 1964): pp. 36-37, 92-94. 37.

(36) Corso, "The Times of the Watches," p. 37.

(37) Corso, "The Times of the Watches," p. 92.

(38) Corso, "The Times of the Watches," p. 92.

(39) "Nunzio Corso in the 1940 United States Federal Census." Ancestry.com.

(40) "Nunzio Corso in the 1940 United States Federal Census." Ancestry.com.

(41) Corso, *Accidental Autobiography*, p. 379.

(42) Corso, *Accidental Autobiography*, p. 378.

(43) Corso, "The Times of the Watches," p. 92.

(44) Gregory Corso, "P.S. 42," in *Long Live Man* (New York: New Directions, 1962), pp. 85-87. 85.

(45) Gregory Corso, "Moschops! You Are a Loser!," *Nugget 7*, no. 5 (October 1962): pp. 52-53, 66. 53.

(46) Gregory Corso, "Notes from the Other Side of April: With Negro Eyes, with White," *Esquire 62*, no. 1 (July 1964): pp. 86-87, 110. 86.

(47) Corso, "Notes from the Other Side of April," p. 86.

(48) Corso, "Notes from the Other Side of April," p. 86.

(49) Corso, "Notes from the Other Side of April," p. 86.

(50) Corso, "Notes from the Other Side of April," p. 86.

(51) Corso, "Notes from the Other Side of April," p. 86.

(52) Gavin Selerie, "The Interview," *The Riverside Interviews*, 3: Gregory Corso (London: Binnacle Press, 1982), pp. 21-47. 22.

(53) Corso, "Notes from the Other Side of April," p. 87.

(54) Corso, *Accidental Autobiography*, p. 126.

(55) Corso, *Accidental Autobiography*, p. 122.

(56) Corso, "When I Was Five," p. 84.

(57) Nunzio Corso Notice of Criminal Record, May 7, 1948, Donna Stillo/Gus Reininger Archive, copy in possession of the author.

(58) Selerie, "The Interview," p. 21.

(59) Selerie, "The Interview," p. 21.

(60) Michael Andre, "An Interview with Gregory Corso," *Unmuzzled Ox 2*, no. 1/12 (1973): np.

(61) Gregory Corso, "I believe people are born," in *The Golden Dot*, ed. Raymond Foye & George Scrivani (Fruita, CO: Lithic Press, 2022), p. 49.

(62) Nunzio Corso Notice of Criminal Record, May 7, 1948, Donna Stillo/Gus Reininger Archive, copy in possession of the author.

(63) Gregory Corso, "I believe people are born," in *The Golden Dot*, edited by Raymond Foye & George Scrivani (Fruita, CO: Lithic Press, 2022), p. 49.

(64) Victor Bockris, "Humor, the Butcher: An Interview with Gregory Corso," *The Whole Shot: Collected Interviews with Gregory Corso*, ed. Rick Schober (Arlington, MA: Tough Poets Press, 2015), pp. 89-92. 90-91.

(65) Selerie, "The Interview," p. 25.

(66) Gregory Corso, "Sea Chanty," in *The Vestal Lady on Brattle and Other Poems* (Cambridge, MA: Richard Brukenfeld, 1955), p. 7.

(67) Nunzio Corso Notice of Criminal Record, May 7, 1948, Donna Stillo/Gus Reininger Archive, copy in possession of the author.

(68) Nunzio Corso Notice of Criminal Record, May 7, 1948, Donna Stillo/Gus Reininger Archive, copy in possession of the author.

(69) Windsor Prison Case File, Vermont State Archives & Records. Copy in possession of the author. Courtesy of Nile Corso.

Grand Larceny in Vermont: Undisclosed Early Misadventures of Gregory Corso

by Gregory Stephenson

Recently, I was surprised and intrigued to read in a posthumously published autobiographical poem by Gregory Corso, titled "I Was Born in 1930," the following lines: "I lived on the streets until 15 / I spent 6 months in Windsor Prison, VT / read *Les Miserables* there." [1] I was, of course, familiar with Corso's having been incarcerated in "The Tombs" (The Manhattan House of Detention) and in Clinton (Dannemora) Prison, both of which experiences the poet has made reference to on many occasions, but this was the first allusion I had encountered to what seemed to have been an earlier prison sentence. For the poem goes on to state: "Spent three months free / and was sent back to prison / Clinton at Dannemora / Plattsburg, New York." [2] Corso in Vermont—the Green Mountain State—how unexpected and incongruous! What, I wondered, was young street-smart, consummately urban Corso doing in Vermont—so far from the Big Apple? And what had he done in Vermont to warrant a sentence of six months in prison?

State Prison, Windsor, Vermont

My curiosity aroused, I contacted the archivist at the Vermont State Archives to ascertain whether inmate records for Windsor Prison were accessible. I received in return a reply from Ms. Mariessa Dobrick informing me that "Except for records pertaining to individuals who have been deceased for at least 50 years, records of individuals in the custody of the Department of Corrections are exempt from public inspection." Alas, a deadend. But Ms. Dobrick very kindly advised me that Vermont newspapers often reported on major and minor court cases and that these newspapers were available online. Following her advice, I subscribed to *newspapers.com* and searched the Vermont newspapers for the year 1947, seeking court or criminal reports concerning Nunzio Corso. (It should be remembered that Corso's official birth-name was Nunzio and that he later changed his name to Gregory, his confirmation name.) Corso's sentence to Clinton Prison began in 1948, so if he had served six months at Windsor Prison and then three months later entered Clinton Prison, his sojourn in Vermont was likely to have been in 1947. In the archives of *newspapers.com* I quickly found eighteen news items from ten local Vermont newspapers concerning the crimes, arrests and sentencing of Nunzio Corso, a youth of seventeen from New York. Indeed, sometimes the stories of Corso's criminal exploits appeared on the front page of these small-town newspapers; his misdeeds high drama, it would seem, in tranquil rural Vermont. In the following, drawing on these various news accounts, I will attempt to relate the sequence and nature of the events that transpired between July and September of 1947 in the life of the as-yet-embryonic young poet.

The first newspaper story concerning Corso appears in a journal called *The Bennington Evening Banner* on the 22nd of July 1947. The press report states that Nunzio Corso, "who has been arrested twice in New York on burglary charges," was sentenced in a local municipal court on the 21st of July "to serve a term of two to three years at Vergennes on grand larceny charges." The charges of which he is reported to have been convicted are "having stolen money and clothing from a boarding house in Manchester."[3] Vergennes refers to the Vermont Industrial School, known also as the Weeks

School, a reform school (that is, a penal institution for minors) located in Vergennes, Vermont. But what was Corso doing in Vermont?

Vergennes, Vt. - State Industrial School

Vergennes, Vermont, State Industrial School

As to why he was in Manchester, Vermont, a clue occurs in a letter that Corso wrote to his publisher, James Laughlin, many years later, in mid July of 1961. Commenting on a reference to a ski-lift that Laughlin made in an earlier letter to him, Corso remarks: "great about your ski-lift, worked on one in Manchester, Vermont, when I was sixteen."[4] A further clue can be found in another article in *The Bennington Evening Banner*, appearing one month later, which describes Corso as having been "employed in Manchester."[5] Apparently, then, working on a ski-lift in some capacity was the nature of his employment and the reason for his presence in Manchester.

Only a month after this single mention of his crime and conviction for grand larceny in the *Bennington Evening Banner*, there is a sudden flurry of interest in Nunzio Corso in several other local Vermont newspapers, as on August 20, 1947, in the company of a fellow-inmate named Melvin Hill, he escapes from the Vergennes Industrial School.

A search for the fugitives by local police is initiated and on the morning of the 21st of August, according to *The White River Valley Herald*, they are spotted "on the outskirts of the city" (presumably Vergennes) but they elude capture "by disappearing into the woods near the highway."[6] The same account goes on to mention that in the wake of the two boys' escape a dozen automobiles in the area have apparently been tampered with and that two break-ins have occurred. Soon hereafter, *The Battleboro Reformer* reports that on the 22nd of August, "Mr. and Mrs. Wayne Hill of Starksboro and members of their family woke from a sound sleep to find that thieves had ransacked the house, helping themselves to liberal supplies of food and items of clothing."[7] The intruders, we are told, "left behind them a pair of pants and a pair of shoes which authorities have identified as belonging to boys who recently escaped from the Weeks School."[8]

Corso's bid for freedom was short-lived. At 3 a.m. on the morning of August 23rd, according to a report in *The Barre Daily Times*, the Vermont state police placed him under arrest, "after a number of Hinesburg residents had apprehended the youth about two hours earlier."[9] In his possession were found "a 63 dollar watch and clothing, allegedly stolen from two homes."[10] *The Burlington Daily News* for August 23rd states that Corso was "apprehended after he was found in the living room of a Hinesburg family."[11] The young fugitive reportedly told the arresting officer that he had hidden out in the woods near Hinesburg all of the previous day. Indictments against Corso were now to include, the article states, a new charge of grand larceny together with a charge of escaping from Weeks School. (Apropos of the 63 dollar watch, it will, perhaps, be remembered that watches for the young Corso held a particular fascination, as the poet himself has described in an autobiographical article titled *The Times of the Watches*.)[12]

Initially, justice was swift and relatively lenient. As reported in *The Burlington Free Press*, on the 25th of August, in municipal court, Corso pleaded guilty to a single charge of grand larceny and was sentenced to serve "the remainder of his minority" (that is, until his 21st birthday) at the Weeks Industrial School, from which he had, of course, only recently escaped. In imposing the sentence, Judge John J. Deschenes told the youthful offender: "I am giving you a break by returning you to Weeks School. The law gives me the power to send you to Windsor (i.e. Windsor Prison) for this crime. By behaving yourself and co-operating with Weeks School Authorities, you may be released before you reach 21 years of age."[13]

Weighty as they now were, Corso's woes were, however, far from being over. As ordered by Judge Deschenes, he was returned for confinement at the Weeks Industrial School at Vergennes. A bad break for the forsaken seventeen-year-old, to be sure. But, Judge Deschennes had pronounced sentence on Corso for one count of grand larceny (the housebreaking in Hinesburg during which he had been caught by the residents of the home he had unlawfully entered) and there was as yet a separate charge pending for an earlier criminal act, also committed during the course of his flight from the Industrial School. This charge, for an offence committed in a separate jurisdiction and still awaiting trial, was for the forcible entry and burglary (on 21 August 1947) of the house of Mr. and Mrs. Wayne Hill of Starksboro, in which food and items of clothing had been stolen.

"Weeks School Escapee to Serve Prison Term" was the headline of the news story on *The Vermont Journal* for 11 September 1947, echoed in news stories in the pages of *The White River Valley Herald, The Bennington Evening Banner, The Barre Daily Times*, and *The Burlington Daily News*. The newspapers reported that Nunzio Corso, 17 years of age, of Brooklyn, N.Y. had been brought up before Judge Samuel Fishman in municipal court in Middlebury to face a charge of breaking and entering "the home of Wayne Hill in Starksboro on August 21." Found guilty by the court, he had been "given a sentence of from four to six months in the state prison here" (i.e. Windsor Prison.)[14] On the basis of Corso's reference in the poem cited above, it would appear that he served the full six months of his sentence in Vermont State Prison, Windsor, Vermont.

It's curious that Corso seems never to have mentioned these sad episodes of his early life, neither in the interviews he gave nor in the candid autobiographical essays he wrote. I suspect that his motive for this omission was not shame, but rather to lend a more dramatic coherence to his transformative experience at Clinton prison.[15] Corso did, however, in one instance, make imaginative use of his misadventures in Vermont.

A poem titled "The Last Warmth of Arnold," appearing in *Gasoline* (1958) includes the following lines: "Arnold warm with God / hides beneath the porch / remembering the time of escape, imprisoned in Vermont, shovelling snow." In the light of Corso's ordeals in Vermont, these lines—though no less evocative and resonant in the context of the poem—seem now to be more poignant, more potent and more compelling.

Source Notes

(1) Gregory Corso, *The Golden Dot: Last Poems 1997-2000*, ed. Raymond Foye & George Scrivani (Fruita: Lithic Press, 2022), p. 30.

(2) ibid.

(3) *The Bennington Evening Banner*, 22 July 1947, p.1.

(4) Gregory Corso, *An Accidental Autobiography: the Selected Letters of Gregory Corso*, ed. Bill Morgan (New York: New Directions, 2003), p. 287.

(5) *The Bennington Evening Banner*, 25 August 1947, p. 1.

(6) *The White River Valley Herald*, 28 August 1947, p. 4.

(7) *The Battleboro Reformer*, 23 August 1947, p. 4.

(8) ibid.

(9) *The Bennington Evening Banner*, 22 July 1947, p.1.

(10) ibid.

(11) *The Burlington Daily News*, 23 August 1947, p. 1.

(12) Gregory Corso, "The Times of the Watches", *Cavalier*, December 1964, pp. 37-38 +.

(13) *The Burlington Free Press*, 25 August 1947, p. 2.

(14) *Vermont Journal*, 11 September 1947, p. 4. Also *The White River Valley Herald*, 11 September 1947, p. 4; *The Bennington Evening Banner*, 4 September 1947, p. 5; *The Barre Daily Times*, 5 September 1947, p. 7; and *The Burlington Daily News*, 5 September 1947, p.1.

(15) See Gregory Stephenson, "Poetic License: The Crime & Hard Time of Gregory Corso", *Empty Mirror*, January 2019 (online), reprinted in *The Ragged Promised Land*, Ober-Limbo, 2020.

Per Gregorio

by Ryan Mathews

How many steps
From womb to The Tombs,
Then onto all those wombs
And, finally, the tomb?
Is the distance measured
In inches or iams, miles or meter?

Before he sent you to strangers
Fortunato told you the absent
Madonna Michelina was a whore
Who deserted her only begotten son.
Which one did you pray to,
All those years ago,
All those wombs ago,
All those tombs aglow,
The Vestal Lady or the debased street child?

She named you Nunzio,
The messenger, Hermes of the hip.
You renamed yourself Gregory, Gregorio
The self-baptized alert and watchful.
She was right.
You were wrong.
You were born to carry the message of the Muse.

Was it her you saw in the face of your savage Hope
Whom you said you would die loving,
And maybe did, but lost track of
In the shadows of the slopes on Mt. Neverrest?
What were you watching for?
Didn't you know
Hope abandoned can never be reclaimed?

Your father lied.
Michelina, she who is like God,
Was in Trenton, not Tuscany.
In the end you beat her back to Italy
To a tomb at the feet of Shelley.
Leaving her alone
To search for you among the stars.
You weren't paying attention.
Or maybe nobody ever told you
Un bambino non muore
Mai nel cuore di sua madre.

Between Childhood and Manhood

"At such a moment, at that point, a child becomes a man, or a rebel, a flip, a poet, a saint, a jerk, a madman, a suicide, a monk, a bum, or a replica of his father and mother—"

The point of contact between time and eternity is: Death.

The point of contact between childhood and manhood is: Reality.

As we all die differently, with different thoughts, non-thoughts, religions, hopes of heaven, fears of hell, resignations of nothingness, beliefs of re-birth, reincarnation—so do we all leave childhood and become adult differently; some become so with enthusiasm and adventure, some with hesitation and fear, others with doubt and incomprehensibility—

I liken the two points of contact for a number of reasons, but mainly for that reason which says, The bridge between childhood and manhood is as vital and difficult and important a bridge as is the bridge between life and death.

I feel it is Memory connects childhood to manhood; Memory that joins the dream to the real—

You sleep you dream you wake . . . if you have Memory of your dream then you have joined it to the real, to the waked mind. But if you do not have recall, if you cannot remember the dream, of that you had dreamed at all, who's to say you dreamed? The same for childhood; it is like a dream, but one that you remember, one that you must remember; it is this Memory of childhood that you take into manhood; it is the man remembers the child; not the child the child. The child has no need of memory. Time to a child is eternal; why remember yesterday when today is eternal?

Yet time makes mortals of us all.

It makes a child a man.

That connection between childhood and manhood is immeasurable, it is a time of crisis, of danger, of fear; an unnoticeable time, a sudden time; to know you are gong through the process of such contact is to become aware, is to experience a rare occasion seldom experienced—

There is doubt, self-doubt, the dream is going through a change to become a strange thing, a real thing, different and unfamiliar.

The child is becoming a man, he feels the suddenness of it, he has no idea the result of it, doubt and fear both drive hard, they'll either awaken him, or madden him, or create him, or destroy him—

The church-going boy becomes a man/ on his own he is unable to keep the Sabbath; he needs a mother and father to take him or demand him he go; he sits in a little dark place, stunned and cold, suddened in a stark realization that "It's their Sabbath, their God, not mine! My mother's God is not my God, she's been taking me to her God, I've no God my own, O God!"

Some grow out of religion hard, some easily, some with relief, some with no thought at all, some with continuous respect, yet all grow out of it when they leave home, supposedly, men.

The surprise. That's why it is, a surprise, like the surprised look of a heart-attack; the look of sudden fear, moments before shock—the discover, the realization, that surprises and oft suicides; like the famous movie beauty who tremblingly discovers she's a mortal body—(I would divert here to express something I thought of when Marilyn Monroe died: They die, movie stars, by sleeping pills, it is a clean unugly nearly-romantic way out; yet if all sleeping pills were suppositories . . . would they then so an absurd death commit?)

How overnight the youth and age of a homosexual: First a boy for men, then a man for boys. When does he know he's no longer a boy for men . . . when he's no longer desirable?

Fear unto doubt is panic is insanity is death. A stark realization invokes doubt; a sinking identity invokes fear; helpless, caught in air, they bring out the police and fire depts by actually dangling in air, some from the tops of bridges, others from

BY GREGORY CORSO
As it appeared in *Cavalier* (Vol. 15, No. 139, 1965)

forty-story hotel windows—Some dip their heads in gas ovens, some dye their bath waters with flowing red wrists; and those not for death stand in asylums in bed sheets facing walls squeaking like mice their eyes vacant, their minds stational, ther are either truly flipped or goldbricking it out on life . . . the life one must face to know as best one could to work and to suffer and enjoy—

What a terrible introduction it is for some this entering manhood, this discarding the dream of childhood and putting on the reality of manhood. It drives mad, it despairs, it kills.

Yet there is in man, or that which is manly in a child, enough elasticity of mind to comprehend the reality confronting it, and to accept it, not on its terms, but on his own terms.

Reality, that brick wall which hits you after you open the last door of childhood. Ever-changing reality. What is so now shant be so tomorrow. Though you can't fully understand why, you can't not understand why, and that is the armor of practicality . . . most men learn to wear.

The first great challenge for a human soul in life comes when the child is old and the man is young. Will he be made aware because of this change, or will he totter on the brink of it?

The aware are those thinkers like Columbus pondering the unchartered ways—these thinkers ponder the sea of consciousness, either as poets, or statesmen, or national leaders, or creators, mothers, saints . . . they are the ones who have learned from crossing such a bridge; and those who have not learned, who totter, and may fall, they too can know a poetry, an empire, a magic, a child, a piety, if they take much of the child along with them. There is some truth in what the philosophs [sic] say "A genius has much of the child in him"—

The dreamer naked in the alien real. The lacker of God. The movie queen of fame who deems herself a freak. The struggle of children not wanting to become men, like the condemned gangsters not wanting to die in the electric chair. The authors who dote on childhood and damn adulthood—all weep a cruel and unfair vision of mature life. Life of allotted time. They are ready to bypass that point of contact between childhood and manhood and take that other point of contact, death.

They damn reality with a sense of high purpose, of ideality, of purety, beauty, ethereality. After the child, death. Anything else is an insult, is ignoble, and degrading.

They contend manhood the hell of life, childhood the heaven.

Manhood the Reality the Ghost of Childhood . . . the Mortality of Immortality.

It is a strange and sensible deduction this logic which deems childhood immortality and manhood mortality, for it is so . . . thus the point between immortality (childhood) and mortality (manhood) is, of course, death.

The cause of death is birth. This is a holy truth. The born do not know this until they reach manhood . . . thus a man dies twice, he dies once in life, in that gap between childhood and manhood; and he dies lastly in that gap between time and eternity.

There is no set time that first death (the realization that there is such a thing as death) plus (the transformation of child into man)—it can happen overnight, or take countless years. It can happen in fractions, or in entirety, suddenly or prolongedly.

The calendar falsely tells how long a child is to be a child. Come the age of 21, unless you happen to be a Jew, you're on your own. At 21 they let you out of boys home, you get your inheritance; all that's due you according to law—At 21 you're a man, son.

"What is he *saying?* Who cares?! It's said."

by Jay Jeff Jones

> "Poetry is great; it's the poets who fuck it up"[1]
> —Gregory Corso

It was never easy knowing Gregory Corso. So many accounts, even those writ heartfelt in loving memory, feature his mercurial moods, the rapacious mooch, grifter, and conscienceless cocksman, as much as they tell of a fallen angel genius. "Gregory's other rare gift is his voice. This is not always an endearing gift," growled William Burroughs in his "Introductory Notes" to *Mindfield*, the 1989 retrospective of Corso's poems. If that wasn't clear enough, he added, "Gregory has grave flaws of character," before getting to the upside, "Poetry is made from flaws." So true, Bill, but from what else?

During Corso's three year stretch in Clinton Prison, his orphan heart found succour in the prison library, the archaic dictionary became a book of spells that he swallowed whole, the ancient poets were spirit guides leading him to believe he might also open his inner ear to the atavistic realm. Allen Ginsberg, a motherly glint in eye, directed Corso towards both the spontaneous word-bop of the moment and the poet gangs of yore. To Corso's tone were blended rays from the new avant-garde, as the hierarchies of value in literature and the arts were being overthrown. Assemblages, happenings, the psychopathic NOW would be mystically spun from street trash, culture junk, pop ephemera, and the deviant underworld by New York's relentless neoteric dynamo—against the backdrop of Establishment America's outrage at the whole Beat venture which was, in most important ways, a criminal enterprise in itself.

Corso summarized the state of mind from which he began to write, "Though I learned much in prison… I had not learned how to live in the world; and thus, when I found myself alone, lost, hungry, I became almost afraid, almost like a pregnant rat with a broom over it, and so I struck."[2]

In the introduction to *Gasoline*, the Corso collection that he successfully hassled Lawrence Ferlinghetti to publish, Ginsberg explained Corso as perfectly as anybody ever would: "scientific master of mad mouthfuls of language... But what is he *saying*? Who cares?! It's said."

Initially less impressed, Jack Kerouac typecast Corso as beggar and despoiler in *The Subterraneans*. "I'm in it as a kind of guy who gets in there and is fucking up the scene with dopey actions,"[3]—and in the movie version, he is parodied by goof-face Roddy McDowell. At a time when Hollywood's new stock comedy character was the "kook," Corso was kookiness on wheels, his default often a sneer or a Little Italy punk put-on: "... the entire American social revolution to come, was very real before my eyes... but being that I was truly a hipster, the only hip thing to do was to laugh that silly vision straight in the face..." [4]

He was more than happy to play Beat buffoon for TIME magazine (February 1959), seeing nothing to gain being diplomatic or unctuous, pandering to the armchair thrill-seeking petite bourgeoisie. Instead of uber-cool putdown hipness, black transcendence, he chose inverted mockery, proclaiming, "me, I'm still considered an unwashed beatnik commie dope fiend."[5] "Luce Publications, having built the public image of the Beat Generation from scratch in the public mind, naturally lost no time in giving it the treatment for which they had set it up. Corso's surrealism was an easy target."[6]

Confirmed through a vision, "Gregory the Poet!" was perpetually unshakeable, even after the Beat ethos was auctioned off, its underground hedonism precooked and home delivered, the loft-look gentrified, and the liberation narrative hijacked to leisure pursuits. Corso continued his drift and hustle, with lurid tales of how he got by, often off girls—rich girls with trust funds, poor girls with hearts (like any boy raised by wolves, Gregory emanated primal enzymes), loans from fellow poets—to be repaid in eternity, thefts from friends—Allen's furniture, Lawrence's bookshop petty-cash, anybody's pill stashes and pillaged bathroom cabinets, fake manuscript scams on trusting well-wishers.

> Rather: Nothing is mine, a Prince of Poetry
> made to roam the outskirts of society
> taking, if I needed a coat, what was taken
> from the lamb"[7]

And where did the money go? Casinos, junk and alcohol. "Why do I goof with the people I love?" he once said, when paying his debt in tears at the feet of Harold Norse[8] But wasn't it character building, redemptive, all that adulation? Ask in the bars that banished him for life, for mayhem and bad checks.

In "Marriage," his most reprinted poem, Corso slyly wondered, "Should I be good?"— not faithful and true, but how best to wreak subversion against the whole Square sad-sack, till-death-do-us-part deal… and as a lover he was already betrothed in blood to his Muse. Even on her, he chose to mess around with smack, and, in spite of his pledge to "expiate all that's been sadly done," his Muse moaned, "O Gregorio, Gregorio, you'll fail me, I know."[9]

"I am a creature of Power / With me there is no ferocity / I am Fair careful wise and laughable,"[10] reads his poem "Power," wherein Ferlinghetti detected a whiff of loony Fascism. Nonetheless, it is an inspiration to the Haight-Ashbury Diggers, who renounced the use of money and the necessity of leaders. According to the non-leader Emmet Grogan, "the relationship between poetry and revolution has lost its ambiguity. Gregory Corso's poem "Power" was the sole reason behind the concept of the Diggers: autonomy."[11]

"Gregorio, Nunzio, Corso," was translated by the poet himself as "The Watchful One, The Announcer, The Way."[12] In making his voice, he absorbed everything, met a million people. "I claim to know all there is to know / because there ain't that much to know,"[13] and he rejected ideologies, a messenger that didn't play to the partisans and protestors. "Poetic reality has nothing to do with political or social reality," Burroughs had said in apolitical Corso's defence.[14]

Corso renounced the mechanics of cut-up because his random juxtapositions came ready-scrambled directly from the divine tuner in multiple streams of consciousness. At their strongest, said Kenneth Rexroth, the poems are "metaphysical whirlwinds."[15] They used "the logic of imagination."[16] Why be logical when there is a transcendent and funnier Logic?

And, of course, none of the above is wholly true. Corso also wrote poems of heightened plainness, many of them observations of Corso-hood, a crumbling face in the mirror, or the hangover, "Last night was stained with fear / I or the world was all wrong."[17] And he had perfect grasp of the convictions and purposes of the Beat Generation: "…they did not know when they created that stupid name what the vast extent of the future demand would be,"[18] he wrote in "Variations on a Generation," a long essay that laid it down in stark detail.

Ultimately, he was more than the last Beat in the bar, he was the one that persevered, remained more unrooted and indignant, utterly undomesticated, beyond preservation as iconic culture artefact, some beloved, village idiot (a job he volunteered for in Amsterdam), of toothless grin and scrambled silver mane.

While the counterculture became grown-up and serious, Corso stayed anti-culture, always more the protopunk than well-preened Burroughs, even as it became harder and harder to raise a storm or lay down a fine line, working a fulltime shift on the booze, the smack, so much easier to keep pissing on the establishment's clubroom floors. "The language geyser was almost dry,"[19] thought Iain Sinclair when he visited a fading Corso six years before his death. But it seems Spirit was not quite done with Gregory Corso. Towards the end, he went back to work, perhaps as a more ghostly messenger whispered, "We all gotta go, man, but you don't have to go quietly… make a fuss, leave an echo. Those other Daddies of the Age are right here, listening."[20]

Source notes
(1) Lest anyone think Corso was out there on his own in misbehaviour, the poetry hustle is hardly a tea-party as Aram Saroyan, one who would certainly know, reminds us: "… the tiny, vituperative sandbox of American poetry. In that ill-appointed domain, you had the fortunate few sitting on little perches—castles in the sand indeed—and, otherwise, endless lunatics with

pails and shovels, erupting water and sand fights, booze, blood, piss and mucous, carrying on 24/7, bitching, yelling, punching each other, crying, marrying their students, bragging, getting knocked unconscious by their younger wives, and soiling themselves. Did I leave anything out? This is simply the American literary life, sub-genus Poets. Gregory Corso, an outlander, said it beautifully I think: Poetry is great; it's the poets who fuck it up." http://thenervousbreakdown. com/asaroyan/2013/06/rods-lonely-night/

(2) Max Nelson, "The Branded Man," *The Paris Review*, March, 2016.

(3) *Jack's Book*, ed. Barry Gifford and Lawrence Lee (New York: St. Martin's Press, 1978), p. 180.

(4) Gregory Corso, "Note on My Play" (*In This Hung-up Age*), in *New Directions* 18 (New York: New Directions, 1964), p. 161.

(5) Walter Raubicheck, "Gregory Corso" in *The Rolling Stone Book of the Beats*, ed. Holly George-Warren (London: Bloomsbury, 1991), p. 316.

(6) Chris Challis, *Quest for Kerouac* (London: Faber, 1984), p. 192.

(7) Gregory Corso, "Dear Villon," *Mindfield: New and Selected Poems* (New York: Thunder's Mouth Press, 1998), p. 181.

(8) Harold Norse, *Memoirs of a Bastard Angel* (London: Bloomsbury, 1990), p. 395-396.

(9) Gregory Corso, "Columbia U Poesy Reading—1975," *Mindfield*, pp. 161-165.

(10) Gregory Corso, "Power," *Mindfield*, pp. 87-92.

(11) www.diggersdocs.home.blog

(12) "Note on My Play" (*In This Hung-up Age*), in *New Directions* 18 (New York: New Directions, 1964), p. 161.

(13) Gregory Corso, "Dear Villon," *Mindfield*, p. 181.

(14) William Burroughs, "Introductory Notes," *Mindfield*, p. xv.

(15) *Snapshot Poetics, A Photographic Memoir of the Beat Era* (San Francisco: Chronicle Books, 1993), p. 89.

(16) Walter Raubicheck, "Gregory Corso" in *The Rolling Stone Book of the Beats*, ed. Holly George-Warren (London: Bloomsbury, 1991), p. 316.

(17) Gregory Corso, "The Saving Quality," *Mindfield*, p. 110.

(18) Gregory Corso, "Variations on a Generation," in *The Penguin Book of the Beats*, ed. Ann Charters (London: Penguin Books, 1992), p. 182.

(19) Iain Sinclair, *American Smoke* (London: Hamish Hamilton, 2013), p. 149.

(20) Gregory Corso, *The Golden Dot*, ed. Raymond Foye & George Scrivani (Colorado: Lithic Press, 2022).

Word Bomb: Turtles Exploding Over Istanbul

by Westley Heine

Why does the poet laugh in the face of death? To feel more alive? Does the poet antici-pate immortality? Is the poet truly unafraid?

Gregory Corso completed his volume of poetry *The Happy Birthday of Death* in 1960, which included "Bomb," a landmark in black humor. Here, at the height of the Cold War, Corso decided to write a tongue-in-cheek ode to the A-bomb. Meanwhile his peers were writing protests against this ultimate symbol of man's self-destruction.

I sing thee bomb   Death's extravagance   Death's jubilee

When Corso read "Bomb" at Oxford the campus was steeped in Ban the Bomb demonstrations. He was booed and students hurled shoes at him.

Toy of universe   Grandest of all snatched sky   I cannot hate you
Do I hate the mischievous thunderbolt   the jawbone of an ass

There's always plenty to fear. We can protect ourselves from danger only so much. We can prepare. We speak out against evil. We draw a line. We state the obvious, and try to be on the right side of history. But after common sense is clear, what about poetry?

Gregory sarcastically celebrates the bomb as the culmination of man's ambitions throughout history. He sings of all the phallic weapons that lead to it. He sings of all forms of death reminding us that despite how death arrives the result is the same and inevitable. Ironically, the more he glorifies the bomb the better he damns it.

Bomb mark infinity a sudden furnace
Spread thy multitudinous encompassed Sweep
set forth awful agenda
Carrion stars   Charnel planets   carcass elements

Battle forth your spangled hyena finger stumps
along the brink of paradise

"Bomb" demonstrates that inside us all is a secret fascination with destruction. Corso shows how absurd we are: children holding the powder of god. By praising the bomb he shows us by example that this horrible blast *is* human nature. Einstein's Theory of Relativity unlocked the secrets of the universe. That there are vast amounts of energy locked away in every atom! That matter and energy are one! What did we do with this knowledge? We built a bomb so big it could vaporize cities. With existential threats such as nuclear war or Global Warming, it's sometimes hard to know where the frontline is. Perhaps the enemy is in the mirror.

O Bomb I love you
I want to kiss your clank   eat your boom
You are a paean   an acme of scream
A lyric hat of Mister Thunder

Flowers will leap in joy their roots aching

Listen to enough political poems preaching with righteous indignation one might wish the end of the world would just come already… once and for all. But by using a sly wit "Bomb" becomes etched on the funny bone, stuck in the gut shaking with belly laughs. The effect is that we remember the joy of being alive and why life must be protected. Why does the poet laugh in the face of death? The poet laughs because the poet is full of life.

When the Beats and the Surrealists famously met at a party in Paris in 1960, Gregory reached for Marcel Duchamp's tie and clipped it in half with a scissors. Still unknown in France, Corso was saying that he had arrived. Reportedly Duchamp loved the beat poets ever since.

Being so lively, a poet such as Gregory Corso runs the risk of his life overshadowing his work. It's important to judge art by the work itself and not the life of the artist, which inevitably has its warts. Human beings are imperfect. The art they leave behind is what approaches grace. With Corso I'm tempted to say that I enjoy his antics, his life, as much as his work. In any Beat documentary I perk up when I see Gregory coming. He's going to say something cantankerous and hilarious. Stop reading your poems, Gregory, I want to hear you rant off the cuff, make the room awkward with your cutting wit, please contradict boring old common sense.

Yet Corso the man was genuinely close to his myth. His angst was not a persona, not a character in the writing that people confabulated with the author. By all accounts he really was like that. Corso was as fiery, razor tongued, and brazen as his writing, often more so. He actually lived the life of a streetwise hipster, excess and all. Corso really was everything the mainstream media feared about the Beat Generation.

> *I do not know just how horrible Bombdeath is I can only imagine*
> *Yet no other death I know has so laughable a preview   I scope*
> *a city   New York City   streaming   starkeyed   subway shelter*

Today, nuclear war is still a threat, though it seems we are all used to the idea. There's always a new grab bag of existential doom. Whether it's creativity or destruction our culture is only concerned with what's new. Perhaps we can learn something from *Bomb*. We need not laugh ourselves numb in nihilism. We need not throw all caution into the wind. But we can take a note from the poet and surrender to death, and therefore live fearlessly.

That I am unable to hate what is necessary to love
That I can't exist in a world that consents
a child in a park   a man dying in an electric-chair
That I am able to laugh at all things
all that I know and do not know thus   to conceal my pain
That I say I am a poet and therefore love all man

Gregory Corso made peace with the bomb long before the rest of us. Why? The answer can be found, perhaps, in a line Gregory wrote in his latter years: "Death is a rumor spread by life." It's all illusion. Even death. There is nothing to fear.

Mapping Corso: Yaks, Bombs, Revolutions of the Spirit

by A. Robert Lee

"Gregory Corso is the last voice of the original Beat rebellion."

—Lawrence Ferlinghetti, *Woodstock Journal* (September 2000)[1]

Corso long has been assigned supporting-player status: Beat's fourth Beatle. Ginsberg was not alone in recognizing that so lowered an estimate did serious disservice. In his "Introduction" to *Gasoline* he wrote, "Open this book as you would a box of crazy toys… Such weird haiku-like juxtapositions aren't in the American book."[2] Ted Morgan, author of *Literary Outlaw: The Life and Times of William Burroughs*, takes a leaf out of Alexander Dumas: "If Ginsberg, Kerouac and Burroughs were the Three Musketeers of the movement, Corso was their D'Artagnon."[3] From either vantage-point Corso gives reason to occupy his own ground. His poetry carries shelves of often extravagantly inventive image, devotion to Shelley, penchant for the visual arts (notably Uccello, Botticelli, Vermeer and Rembrandt), a keen sense of historic place, long commitment to Thomist Catholicism, and always genuine reaches of wit. It can hardly surprise that Ginsberg's Introduction, written in evident affection and with flourish, goes on to call him "a scientific master of mad mouthfuls of poetry."[4]

Ginsberg goes on to give laudatory mention to "a refinement of beauty out of a destructive atmosphere." On the book's blurb William Burroughs speaks of Corso as "a gambler" and of his life's "reverses"; Jack Kerouac invokes the Lower East Side "tough young kid" yet also "the one & only Gregory the Herald." These all supply further cross lights through which to remember Corso's bow into poetry. In one sense Corso has always appeared the junior partner, with New York's reformatories and jails his Harvard or Columbia. In fact he was quite the equal of the others in originality, his poetry full of rare contrariety and arresting dissonance.[5]

Given that the fuller repertoire is to be met in *Mindfield: New and Selected Poems* (1989) the best-known collection remains *Gasoline* (1958), thirty-plus pieces in all and not out of print since its first issue as No. 8 in the City Lights Pocket Poets Series. Corso's other collections, starting from *The Vestal Lady on Brattle and Other Poems* (1955) and extending through *Happy Birthday of Death* (1960), *Long Live Man* (1962), *Elegaic Feelings American* (1970) and *Herald of the Autochtonic Spirit* (1981), indubitably yield their returns. *Gasoline*, however, and as Ginsberg highlights it, carries Corso's especial flavor, his talent for situating the world within loops of unique Beat-Dada observation.

The two epigraphs that introduce *Gasoline* hold both for the poems within and for the wider arc of his other poetry collections. The one epigraph gives acknowledgment to prison library reading, Dostoevsky to Stendhal, Chatterton to Shelley ("books of illumination"), which he says saved him during cell-time served in New York's Clinton Prison. The other echoes Gary Snyder's celebrated short poem "How Poetry Comes to Me" ("It comes blundering over the / Boulders at night"). For Corso, the poetic process resembles mysterious collage, a species of alchemy: "It comes, I tell you, immense with gasolined rags and bits of wire and old bent nails, a dark arriviste, from a dark river within."[6]

This double emphasis holds throughout the writings, the poet's hallmark. "The Mad Yak"[7] offers an absurdist yet unmistakably compassionate vision of death ("I am watching them churn the last milk they'll ever get from me, / They are waiting for me to die"). The milk signifies a she-yak, one from whose bones buttons will be made and whose "sisters and brothers" have previously gone to their deaths. The executioners are not mad Nazis but a single likely Mongolian monk, accompanied by his muffler-wrapped student who loads up the yak-speaker's tired yak-uncle. The closing couplet ("And that beautiful tail! / How many shoelaces will they make of that?") might conjure Hamlet's Yorick or lines from Samuel Beckett. A near Buddhist compassion holds the yak as gallows-humor secret sharer. Yak milk, bones and tail succinctly conjoin as fantasy, Corso's engaging but also disturbing contemplation of mortality.

In "I am 25"[8] the "I" is all impatience with the establishment turn of older poets ("Especially old poetmen who retract / who consult other old poetmen / who speak their youth in whispers"). The fear of losing edge, his own necessary vitality of contra-stance, runs throughout. The pitch is kept playful, both fond and unfond ("I HATE OLD POETMEN!"). The speaker, Hermes-like, even assumes the role of messenger-burglar out to renew the force of poems discarded or renounced by their begetters: "Then at night in the confidence of their homes / rip out their apology-tongues / and steal their poems". The duty of true poetry, runs Corso's implication, is to de-familiarize, un-settle agreed norms. "What you once were, thru me / you'll be again" runs the insistence.

A jazz tribute like "For Miles"[9] with its "Your sound is faultless / pure & round / holy / almost profound" confirms his agility in having the verse reenact the measure of a late-night riff between Miles Davis and Charlie Parker ("some wondrous / yet unimaginable score"). "2 Weird Happenings in Haarlem"[10] ("Four windmills, acquaintanceships, / were spied one morning eating tulips") and "Paris"[11] ("Childcity, Aprilcity / Spirits of Angels crouched in doorways, / Poets, worms in hair, beautiful Baudelaire, / Artaud, Rimaud, Apollinaire") typically envision creative inner as much as outer city landscapes. It would be hard to escape the Beat rowdy-ism and drugs, the many fissures and collisions in Corso's life—but there can be no mistaking the better challenge of his poetry, the contrary wit, the invention behind line and image.

A brief selected sheaf of poems from across his range does further duty. "The Whole Mess ... Almost,"[12] first published in *Herald of the Autochthonic Spirit* (1981), offers a key Corso paradigm: his symptomatic penchant for play, for his seeming extemporization. The operative metaphor is one of cleaning out his apartment ("I ran up six flights of stairs / to my small furnished room / opened the window / and began throwing out / those things most important in life"). "Out," repeated throughout, twice capitalized, several times with exclamation marks, acts as an initial hinge. "Those things," however "important," are serially given mock-notice to quit. The impact as the piece unfolds is that of a near pattern-poem yet cannily varied by each droll interjection or commentary.

"Truth" is first to go, "squealing like a fink." "God" follows, "glowering & whimpering in amazement." "Love" is dispatched "on her fat ass" while "cooing bribes." "Faith Hope Charity," however plaintiff and "all clinging together," come next. "Beauty" falls under accusation of being murderous ("Beauty kills") even as the speaker runs downstairs and catches her fall. "Money," if diligently searched for, is noticeable only by its absence. Death, "hiding beneath the kitchen sink," gets the heave ("Kitchen sink and all"). The final "all that was left" is "Humor" which elicits the elliptical turn-about of "Out the window with the window." Engaging to a fault the poem gives funny-sardonic resistance to thinking Big Themes always make Big Poetry. Corso indeed wants a clear-out, a winnowing, of heavy-duty abstraction. The ludic impulse as voiced in his poem brings just the right subversion to bear, antic yet deftly serious.

"Bomb," [13] written in Paris at the Beat Hotel, printed as a City Lights Broadside in 1958, and included in the collection *The Happy Birthday of Death* (1960), stirred controversy from the outset. [14] Could Corso actually be endorsing atomic warfare? From the bomb-shaped opening lay-out, through to the four or so pages that follow, Corso positions himself as serious jester. He takes up the unexpected stance of situating the bomb within the larger trajectory of human life and death. A challenging thesis is so built into the poem, namely that however gravid the A-bomb it serves as but one more increment in the cycle of historic violence and warfare that runs from the Stone Age (and behind it the Big Bang) through to Hiroshima and Nagasaki. It includes diseases ("it is no crueler than cancer"), capital punishment ("a man dying in the electric chair"), still births, and all military "bomb death."

Corso calls the bomb "the final Pied Piper" and recognizes that "all man hates you." But he also suggests that other modes of death have been quite as momentous. The poem thereby assaults the standard piety about thermo-nuclear destruction, neither advocating nor simply condemning its place in humanity's generic fear of death's darkness. In reality the Bomb indeed may act as a "budger of history" and "a brake on time," but its blast is also to be imagined stirring a surreal aftermath—"turtles exploding over Istanbul," a "flying jaguar," "penguins plunged against the sphinx." The Bomb so almost beckons as apocalyptic love affair ("I sing the Bomb / Death's extravagance / Death's jubilee"). It invites being thought "The spitball of Buddha," "Planetarium Death." Within the galactic sum of things there might even be life-after-bomb, a kind of bomb cemetery where "more bombs will arise." The imagery could not be more provocative, the violent, and quite arguably inevitable, zigzag of life's entrances and exits. When Corso read the poem at Oxford in 1957, a shoe was thrown at him by anti-nuclear campaigners, no doubt without an ear for the fuller irony being put before them.

"Marriage," [15] the other best-known poem from *The Happy Birthday of Death*, carries a full menu of tease, a shyness at society's presiding institution. The opening lines leave no doubt of the riffs ahead: "Should I get married? Should I be good? / Astound the girl next door … Don't take her to the movies but cemeteries / tell all about werewolf bathtubs and forked clarinets". The speaker can imagine himself called to bourgeois right behavior and couture ("hair finally combed, strangled by a tie"), a fright to prospective parents-in-law ("He wants our Mary Lou"), and bound for the cliché of a Niagara Falls honeymoon ("I'd sit there the Mad Honeymooner / devising ways to break marriages, a scourge of bigamy"). He parodies himself as model spouse ("God what a husband I'd make"), drooling paterfamilias ("For a rattle a bag of broken Bach records"), lover bemused by love ("I see love as odd as wearing shoes") and, finally, aged bachelor ('all alone in a furnished room with pee stains on my underwear'). Corso himself, belying this persona, in fact had three marriages. The closing refrain ("Everybody else is married! All the universe married but me"), however, hints of a frame of reference wider than domesticity. The poem, figuratively and with the usual Corso loops of metaphor, shies away from all forms of fixity, the closing down of life-appetite, spirit, openness.

His Jack Kerouac obituary in the extensive title poem of *Elegaic Feelings American* ("Alas, Jack, it seems I cannot requiem thee without / requieming America"), [16] with its affection for his "dear friend, compassionate friend" summons comparison with Whitman's eulogy to the slain Abraham Lincoln in "When Lilacs Last in the Dooryard Bloom'd." An accompanying work of serious fellow compassion in *Elegaic Feelings American* lies in "Spontaneous Requiem for the American Indian." [17] Throughout, Corso gives compendious historical and geographic sweep to the "Indianic earth"—Muskegee to Iroquois, Mohawk to Choctaw—and the settler dislocations visited on the tribes. To his credit he avoids Vanishing American mawkishness but rather celebrates energy, survival against odds, closing with the Beat counter-image of a very much alive motorcyclist Blackfoot barreling down the highway. The "spontaneity" of the poem reminds not only of Beat poetics, but the enduring spoken and chant legacies of the Native American tribal tradition.

Few Corso poems better summarize his Beat calling-card than "Columbia U Poesy Reading—1975" [18] in *Herald of the Autochthonic Spirit*, in which, with typical bravura, he identifies himself as belonging to the "Revolutionaries of the Spirit":

> 16 years ago we were put down
> for being filthy beatnik sex commie dope fiends
> Now—16 years later Allen's the respect of his elders
> the love of his peers
> and the adulation of millions of youth...
> Peter has himself a girl so that he and Allen
> Hermes willing might have a baby...
> Bill's ever Bill
> even though he stopped drugging and smoking cigarettes
> Me. I'm still considered an unwashed beatnik sex commie
>   dope fiend ...

Beat poetry at times could risk solemn, bardic mission statements close to tripping over themselves. The unique tilt of Corso's poetry keeps matters on the right side of pretension; play of voice, flair of invention. We are still learning his full map.

Source notes

(1) Lawrence Ferlinghetti, *Woodstock Journal*, Vol. 6, September 2000. This essay draws from, and revises, two previous accounts I have given of Corso. See *Modern American Counter Writing: Beats, Outriders, Ethnics*, (New York: Routledge, 2010) and *The Beats: Authorships, Legacies* (Edin-

burgh: Edinburgh University Press, 2019).

(2) Allen Ginsberg, "Introduction", in Gregory Corso, *Gasoline*, Pocket Books Series, Number 8 (San Francisco: City Lights Books, 1958).

(3) Ted Morgan, *Literary Outlaw: The Life and Times of William Burroughs* (New York: W.W. Norton, 2012), p. 242.

(4) Allen Ginsberg, "Introduction", *Gasoline*, p.13.

(5) Key accounts are to be found in Kirby Olson, *Gregory Corso: Doubting Thomist* (Carbondale: Southern Illinois University Press, 2002); Michael Skau, *"A Clown in a Grave": Complexities and Tensions in the Works of Gregory Corso* (Carbondale: Southern Illinois University Press, 1999); and Gregory Stevenson, *Exiled Angel: A Study of the Work of Gregory Corso* (London: Hearing Eye,1989).

(6) Gregory Corso, *Gasoline*, frontispiece.

(7) Gregory Corso, "The Mad Yak", *Gasoline*, p. 48.

(8) Gregory Corso, "I am 25", *Gasoline*, p. 42.

(9) Gregory Corso, "For Miles", *Gasoline*, p. 50.

(10) Gregory Corso, "2 Weird Happenings in Haarlem", *Gasoline*, p. 24.

(11) Gregory Corso, "Paris", *Gasoline*, p. 54.

(12) Gregory Corso, "The Whole Mess…Almost," *Herald of the Autochthonic Spirit* (New York: New Directions, 1981), pp. 48-9.

(13) Gregory Corso, "Bomb," *The Happy Birthday of Death* (New York: New Directions, 1960), interleafed and folded into pages 32-3.

(14) Gregory Stephenson offers the following pertinent summary: "The poet suggests that much of the modish opposition to the bomb has its origins in the fear of death which is an inevitable component in the human situation. He enumerates other forms of death which he sees as far more likely and equally or even more terrible… In the fiery wind of thermo-nuclear blast all human vanities will be revealed in their ultimate triviality, and surreal, absurd juxtapositions and metamorphoses will occur." *Pilgrims to Elsewhere* (Roskilde: EyeCorner Press, 2013), p. 88.

(15) Gregory Corso, "Marriage," *The Happy Birthday of Death*, pp. 29-32.

(16) Gregory Corso, "Elegaic Feelings American (for the dear Memory of John Kerouac)," *Elegaic Feelings American* (New York: New Directions, 1981), pp. 3-12.

(17) Gregory Corso, "Spontaneous Requiem for the American Indian," *Elegaic Feelings American*, pp.13-17.

(18) Gregory Corso, "Columbia U Poesy Reading—1975," *Herald of the Autochthonic Spirit*, pp. 1-2.

(The main parts of this essay were originally published in *The Beats: Authorships, Legacies*, 2019. Reprinted by kind permission of the author.)

Memories of Gregory

Ed & Miriam Sanders

Memories of Gregory

by Ed and Miriam Sanders

Gregory Corso's impact on Miriam's and my life began not long after we started dating after meeting in Greek class at NYU in 1958, and Miriam's purchase of Corso's poem "Bomb," published by City Lights Books. The poem was memorably written in the shape of an a-bomb blast, with riveting sections such as:

O Bomb I love you

I want to kiss your clank   eat your boom

You are a paean   an acme of scream

a lyric hat of Mister Thunder

O resound thy tanky knees

BOOM BOOM BOOM BOOM BOOM

BOOM ye skies and BOOM ye suns

BOOM BOOM ye moon   ye stars BOOM

nights ye BOOM   ye days ye BOOM

BOOM BOOM ye winds   ye clouds ye rains

go BANG ye lakes   ye oceans BING

Barracuda BOOM and cougar BOOM

Ubangi BOOM   orangutang

BING BANG BONG BOOM bee bear baboon

ye BANG ye BONG ye BING

Ed remembers a reading at the Living Theater around 1959, where Gregory called out for support from Allen Ginsberg.

Kerouac's definition in *The Subterraneans* of his friends being un-selfconfident egomaniacs comes to mind. Ed: "Some people would be humiliated upon being interrupted or heckled during a reading, but it was honorific when Gregory did it to me during my years giving poetry readings."

We followed Gregory's career in the 1960s, including his taking a principled position against the New York loyalty oath requirement.

Around the time of the Spring Arts Festival of April '65 the bard Gregory Corso was required to sign the so-called Feinberg certificate certifying that he was not then a member of the Communist Party & if he had ever been, to fess up to the University.

The Feinberg text reads:

"Anyone who is a member of the Communist Party or of any organization that advocates the violent overthrow of the Government of the United States or of the State of New York or any political subdivision thereof cannot be employed by the State University. Anyone who was previously a member of the Communist Party or of any organization that advocates the violent overthrow of the Government of the United States or of the State of New York or any political subdivision thereof is directed to confer with the President before signing this certificate. [...] This is to certify that I have read the publication of the University of the State of New York. 1959, entitled Regents Rules on Subversive Activities together with the instructions set forth above and understand that these rules and regulations as well as the laws cited therein are part of the terms of my employment. I further certify that I am not now a member of the Communist Party and that if I have ever been a member of the Communist Party I have communicated that fact to the President of the State University of New York."

Less than a month after the Spring Arts Festival, Corso was fired by the University because he refused to sign the loyalty oath.

In response, there was a protest picket held by the Faculty-Student Committee for Academic Freedom, as reported in the University of Buffalo student newspaper.

Friday, April 9, 1965

Gregory Corso Firing Protested; Picket Staged at Crosby Hall

Monday evening from about 8:00 until 9:30 p.m. the Faculty-Students Committee for Academic Freedom staged a picket in which over 70 people participated, to protest the firing of Gregory Corso for his refusal to sign the Feinberg disclaimer certificate. The committee, after meeting for a half hour in Norton, proceeded to Crosby Hall where Mr. Corso's class was scheduled to meet.

The marchers, under the leadership of Kim Darrow, Henry Simon and Jeremy Taylor, student members of the executive committee, carried signs calling for the abolition of the Feinberg Certificate and condemning Corso's dismissal. The group sang such songs as "My Country 'Tis of Thee" and "Oh Freedom" and raised such chants as "Feinberg must go."

For a time, a small group, not participating in the picket, dis-

Student-Faculty Committee Picket Outside Crosby Hall

played a sign which stated the following: "Private, autonomous, independent picket in behalf of Gregory Corso, poet and educator, offered in protest **not by any means** to champion the right of a Communist to teach at UB, but by virtue of the inherent and universal apoliticality of the poet."

The pickets increased in number throughout the demonstration. To climax the picket the demonstrators marched around Hayes Hall, past Diefendorf Hall to Norton Union, chanting loudly most of the way. A letter of protest was sent to Dr. Robert F. Berner, Dean of Millard Fillmore College.

A spokesman for the group expressed satisfaction with the picket and indicated that there would be an accelerated program of action against the Feinberg law and certificate.

"Without a Drop of Blood" 1975

At the New Year's Reading at St. Mark's Church in 1975 Gregory said, of his friends in the Beat movement, "We created change without a drop of blood."

An inspiring comment by Gregory!

1977 at Naropa

We arrived at Naropa on June 14, and stayed at Allen and Peter's duplex the first night, until we checked in to receive the key to our apartment in the same building, unit # 230.

There was a note from Allen Ginsberg, "Ed—here's our key, take it to your room 230 and only give it to my nephew Peter [who was staying in Allen and Peter's duplex] not anyone (Will Royster especially) else—Allen."

Will Royster, as I recall, was a filmmaker involved in a love triangle with Gregory Corso and the woman, on hand at Naropa, with whom Gregory had had a child, Max, who was also on hand.

Royster apparently had recently stabbed Jocelyn, the mother of Max. Royster was banned from the apartment building where we lived in Boulder; Max and his mother were in one of the apartments in our building.

This was all playing out when we arrived at Naropa to begin the Investigative Poetry group.

The next morning, June 15, I ran into Gregory Corso, who was also staying at the Varsity Townhouses. He was attired in shorts, and no shirt which revealed the ancient Egyptian word for scribe, "Sesh," tattooed on his shoulder. He recited four poems, the last one being

four lines from Shakespeare's "Under the Greenwood Tree." One of the poems, I recall, went something like, "I can disappear before your eyes…
(pause) killing you."
which was accompanied with a slight lunge of pretend knifewieldhood in my direction. He said his wife was here, and their young son Max, also known as Orpheé, in diapers. Michael Brownstein also stopped by. He said Naropa was "quieter" this year than last summer. Brownstein mentioned Corso's plight. He arrived three weeks early, and Corso himself has been caring for Max. The mother, said Brownstein, is from a branch of the Rothschild family, or had been married into it, and apparently receives checks, as I noted, "of moderately big bucks." But she keeps running away with someone Brownstein described as "a killer outlaw type," who is in town, but banned from the Varsity Townhouses.

June 28—Allen Ginsberg said that today the Secret Service had been to the Varsity Townhouses regarding Will Royster. Royster, said Allen, apparently claims to be a cousin of President Carter, and part of the movie which Royster is trying to peddle apparently features back-yard chat footage of Carter. Allen told me that the rumor was that, in addition to Carter celluloid, the movie had porn-segs; and that Royster probably had thrown Carter's name around a lot during his recent incarceration for stabbing Jocelyn.

Allen further said that Gregory had driven Jocelyn and Royster to the airport today, for a flight to Paris. Allen referred to him as Jocelyn's "demon lover." She apparently has $50,000 in Paris, apparently her last money, which they're going to blow. Allen said that her former husband (last name Stern) had cut her off, apparently to check if Royster were only attracted to her because of the moolah she could offer.

Miriam recalls the recently stabbed mate of Gregory, Jocelyn, sitting on the couch of our apartment at the Varsity Townhouses

She also remembers the incident when a large piece of pegmatite granite someone had

brought from the mountains above Boulder and placed on a high shelf
above the bed of William Burroughs fell down suddenly and bloodied his nose.

Here it is from Ed's journal:

"July 15,
in the morning William Burroughs was lying in bed at the Varsity Townhouses, thinking about his class and class lectures, when a shelf above the bed fell down, tossing a rock residing upon it, down onto Burroughs' nose, possibly breaking it. Bill later told me, 'It seemed to inspire me, so I jumped up and did ten pages' on his lectures."

Miriam also recalls discussing Sabbatai Zevi and other historical false Messiahs with Gregory. She said, "I was impressed with his knowledge of the subject." She had learned about Sabbatai Zevi, the Jewish would-be Messiah, in the 1950s studying at the Yeshiva of Central Queens.

And Miriam also recalls Burroughs placing a freshly-baked pot roast on his balcony, and then Gregory leaping from a nearby balcony onto the balcony outside Burroughs' apartment, to get at it.

Ed performed with Gregory on a number of occasions, including the time in 1994 when Gregory told him how the parents of Beat generation young women sometimes put them into asylums and even gave them shock treatment, in order to de-Beat them. Ed wrote a poem about it:

Gregory Said

We talked
at Town Hall backstage

Corso & I (Ginsberg & Vosnesensky were standing nearby)

Gregory said
one of the hidden tragedies of the beat era
was how some parents seized their beat daughters and sent them
to mental hospitals for shock therapy.

—something like $50 a day

the parents thought
it was good to do.

Seized, locked, shocked—a hidden
scandal
of the time

The years went by, and Gregory became ill. On August 9, 2000 Ferlinghetti wrote Ed in Woodstock, suggesting Miriam and Ed publish a Tribute to Gregory in our newspaper, *The Woodstock Journal.* "How about covering Gregory with glory," he suggested, "before he croaks? I talked to him yesterday, and he's still kicking!"

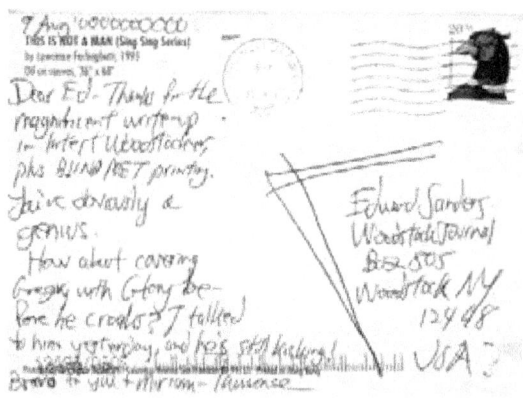

After that card, Ed put together a Salute to Gregory that was spread across three successive issues of the Journal.

The Journal printed salutes to Corso in the issues for September 1, 2000, September 15, and November 24. Featured were poems and commentary by Ferlinghetti, Robert Creeley, Bob Rosenthal, Joanne Kyger, Michael McClure, Roger Richards, Patti Smith, Andy Clausen, Oliver Ray, Diane Di Prima, Chuck Pirtle, Janine Pommy Vega, Rosebud Feliu-Pettet, Raymond Foye, Ira Cohen, Anselm Hollo, Donald Kennison, Anne Waldman, and Bob Holman. Ed inadvertently left out of the Salutes one by Gary Snyder.

Ed's opening salute in the Journal stated "Miriam and I first saw Gregory read at the Gaslight Cafe in the Village in 1959 when we were still in NYU, and subsequently we have been onstage, backstage and on the poetry circuit with him on many occasions.

"He's the real stuff. I've seen him pull a crumpled note sheet from his pocket just before heading out to a podium to thrill a crowd with a few hot-off-the-mind lines. I've seen him at a packed Town Hall in NYC literally being begged by the audience to read his famous 'Marriage,' hesitating for a few seconds, then reciting it as freshly as if it had been just written that morning."

Gregory was cared for by long time friend Roger Richards and his wife Irvyne, in a building where Gregory and the Richards resided on Horatio Street. Gregory's daughter Sherry Langeman, a cardiopulmonary nurse in Minnesota, came to NYC to take care of him during his final weeks.

Going to Gregory's Funeral
by Ed Sanders

I set out now/in a box upon the sea
—Charles Olson

What does it mean
to have been Gregory Corso?
Secure yet insecure, ferocious yet friendly a bit cruel on occasion & usually apologetic

He was banking
on his sequence of vowels
& consonants to carry his legacy

a presentation of poems frail & strong
in Olson's box on Olson's sea

1-24-01
6:50 am
on the Trailways bus to NYC from Kingston

All hail to the memory of Gregory Corso!!

The Beat of Silence: An Interview with Kirby Olson

by Michael Limnios

The following interview with Kirby Olson, Professor of Philosophy, Literature and Creative Writing at SUNY-Delhi and author of *Gregory Corso: Doubting Thomist*, is extracted from a longer interview. Reprinted by kind permission of the interviewer.

MICHAEL LIMNIOS: Why did you think Gregory Corso continues to generate such a devoted following?

KIRBY OLSON: He took the American line that William Carlos Williams developed out of Imagism and "married" it to the longer loopier lines of the surrealists. He also set this on top of his familial Catholicism combined with the traditions of the Bohemian seekers. It's a fascinating blend of cultures that one finds in his writings. Corso has no natural group. In American culture the ecological people have Gary Snyder, the gay groups align with Allen Ginsberg, and the drug addicts with William Burroughs. Corso has no natural group, but everyone feels drawn to his humor. He defies groups, and group orientation. He expresses a need for individualism. This aligns him with American individualism and people who feel like individuals relate to him. He is also very popular in Europe, where the socialist impulse is stronger, but where there is also a natural affinity for Bohemian individualism going back many centuries. Corso offers a blend of Dionysus and Jesus. In his own life, it was mostly Dionysian pleasure, but in his writing we also see how much of childhood Christianity was retained. Reading him one takes a communion wafer that unites readers with the entire history of the Bohemian individualism. You can become a cat while you are reading Corso.

LIMNIOS: What characterizes the sound of Corso's poems?

OLSON: Corso loved jazz music. He grew up in a milieu where a parallel search for individual freedom was going on in the jazz world. I never knew that world and don't like the poems where he references jazz. Corso knew jazz musicians and loved them. What can't be found in Corso's poems is love toward rock music. Corso looked down on rock musicians. He explicitly denounced Jim Morrison and Bob Dylan for being false poets. He didn't accept them and was furious that they had eclipsed poetry. He hated Donovan. Ginsberg accepted Dylan and Morrison and rock singers as poets. Corso rejected them. Corso increasingly came to hate music. At one point Corso smashed all of Allen Ginsberg's jazz records from the fifties. He told Allen that jazz music was a prison for him, and he needed to liberate Allen. This was in 1977 at Naropa Institute. I don't think Allen felt liberated, but Corso really did feel he had helped Allen.

LIMNIOS: Are there any memories from your book *Gregory Corso: Doubting Thomist* which you'd like to share?

OLSON: A scenario that haunts me is talking with one of his friends Roger Richards or Richard Rogers, a bookseller that Corso lived with. This man (I can never keep his name straight because both names are first names) was very high on heroin. He didn't make sense. He told me that even on his deathbed Corso used heroin. Since the publication of my book on Corso many of Corso's friends have sent very short anecdotes. These are in an online blog called Corso Biography. I have only put up about a tenth of these, as I am lazy. It's amazing how many friends he had, and how many people loved him. These were mostly drug-addicted poets. One that I personally like is the poet Michael Andre. We have argued and corresponded for many years. He's a liberal and I am an arch-conservative. I am what is called a classical liberal. Most of Corso's friends were socialists or Marxists. Most of them think Cuba is cool. I see Cuba as a military dictatorship. The penalty for being gay is four years in prison. The penalty for opening the internet is four years in prison. But people think that because it's a state controlled economy that features equality of income it's a good thing. Everyone in Cuba makes one hundred dollars a year. Corso has a poem "Upon My Refusal to Herald Cuba," which I think links him to the classical liberal tradition. He defied the general trend toward equality. He thought some poems were better, and some people were better, and that he was the best. Like me, he saw equality as evil. He liked capitalism, but not always capitalists. He thought some of what's sold was shoddy goods. He thought much of poetry and art was lousy. He thought good poetry should make money. He liked to get paid. He thought he had a beautiful profession. I'm also proud of my profession. I like to make money on poems. I see poetry as work for a community and that the community should pay. I also like working and helping young people with their poems and what I like best is when some- one pays them! Roger Richards died from drug abuse a few years ago. Drug use reminds me of the world of the Lotus Eaters in the Odyssey. It's a waste of time, and time is living money.

LIMNIOS: Do you miss him? What is your favorite Corso motto?

OLSON: I didn't actually like Gregory Corso. He was too crazy. His wife was crazy. His girlfriends were crazy. I like his definition of poetry as "risked and fevered thinking." He said to me, when in doubt between two things, "choose both." I think this is funny. It's a way to cut the Gordian Knot of indecision. Ginsberg had more sensible mottoes. He said for example, "Discretion is the better part of valor," which I think comes from Shakespeare's Falstaff. Ginsberg also had initiative and follow-through. Corso was rarely sober. He was shy and insecure and used drugs to fuel himself up for contact with others. So he was a mess in real life. He wrote only when he was completely sober. He told me he couldn't write otherwise. So when we're reading Corso we're reading the sane and quiet man, not the public drunk. Ginsberg used drugs to write later on and his later writing was horrible. But he kept himself off drugs when meeting the public. So he was sane in public and that was his valuable part.

LIMNIOS: Did you ever meet him?

OLSON: I met Corso probably hundreds of times at Naropa Institute. He lived across from me in a townhouse complex in Boulder, Colorado. I saw him every day for two whole summers. Much of this ended up in my book, *Doubting Thomist* in the early chapters. Every once in a while Corso was sober. He read my poems and told me which ones were best. He was unerringly correct. Corso had taste. If you saw him early enough in the morning he would make sense and he was spot on genius. By late afternoon he was a lunatic. By evening he was a full-on cyclone. He had hundreds of girlfriends. Most said he did things like ask them to jump on a bed with him then he would fall asleep and snore. He was fifty years old at the time.

LIMNIOS: What connects Corso with the legacies of Homer and Percy Bysshe Shelley?

OLSON: Corso is a classical poet. He took the classics seriously and understood them. He could quote entire poems by Shelley even when he was completely stoned. He could recite his poems. He could even quote entire poems of minor poets such as John Suckling or John Cleveland (Cavalier poets from the 1600s). He knew Frank O'Hara's poems by heart. He had been to Harvard and was the favorite of now forgotten poets such as Archibald McLeish, who was a very famous poet in about 1970, and a full professor at Harvard. Randall Jarrell loved Corso. Jarrell was a big poet in 1970. Corso was almost certainly the most brilliant man I have met within the poetic milieu. His mind was so powerful that it was eerie. Half drunk and in a stupor, he would begin to discuss a poem by Edgar Poe and relate it to algebraic equations. He wasn't trying to impress anybody. These were his natural thoughts. I've never met anyone who could make strong clear synthetic connections such as he could so simply and easily but he was lonely because no one really understood what he was saying. He would talk about hieroglyphics and jazz. Or about the pyramids on the backs of dollar bills, and about haloes and smoke rings. Because he had no backup in terms of family, I think he felt profoundly insecure, but had learned to talk to himself. He was lost and without drugs he would have to hide in a so-lipsistic realm. So when he came out of his house he looked so often like a fool. We had a guy in America who killed all kinds of people named Ted Kaczinsky. He was called the Unabomber because he blew up university academics with bombs. He got sent to prison for life. He had an IQ of about 190 but had all his own ideas, and wrote terrific papers in his youth but no friends. I think Corso and he would have had terrific conversations about math. The two of them would have understood one another. I never understood Corso. I wrote *Doubting Thomist* to try to piece together what on earth he had been say-ing.

LIMNIOS: Random question: how you would spend the day with, say, Zeus, Peter Sellers, Captain Beefheart and Gregory Corso?

OLSON: I am not a fan of Zeus, and would prefer Hermes. Zeus was so full of himself! Hermes was the messenger god. Corso often put Hermes into his poems and thought of the poet as the "nuncio," which apparently means "messenger" in Italian. It was also his middle name. Let's leave Zeus out. I imagine that Corso would shun Sellers and Beefheart. He had no respect for rock so I doubt he would accept him. Did Sellers write well? If Corso didn't like you, he didn't even look at you. I don't think Corso accepted actors. He did accept painters. Many of his poems reference paintings and I think he had painters as friends. He threw a fit when he met other poets especially if he felt they were fraudulent. Some of this was jealousy. Some of it was contempt. He hated Anne Waldman's poems, but she was beautiful so he accepted her. Waldman's poems weren't his thing. He was a classicist. He liked classically beautiful women even if they were stu-pid (Waldman was not stupid, but I'm not sure he understood her more prosaic aesthet-ic). I was embarrassed by how he dismissed people. He hated Larry Fagin. He hated rock musicians. And his hate was not something he tried to hide. If he didn't think you were beautiful or deep he would not even look at you but would scream curses at you and tell you to drop dead in a million different ways. He was a snob who looked and smelled like a bum who lived in a dumpster. He liked Bohemian men, and if you had some kind of poetry in you, he accepted you, but could turn on you any second. He thought he was better than everyone even with no teeth and vomit on his sweater. He hated me at times and terrified me after two hours of conversation. He kept yelling at me, "Stop asking why!" I asked, "Why?" He laughed and then would slam out of my apartment, knocking over my bookshelf as he left and spitting on the floor. I do think he was cleverly analytical. He read poems well, and understood art. He could talk well. He also saw an easy mark either in a woman or in someone with money.

LIMNIOS: What mattered to Corso?

OLSON: I think women, drugs, poetry mattered to him. Humor mattered. Remember that in his poem "I Threw Out" it is humor that he is last to toss. When he was young he was not on drugs and everybody liked him. As he got older he began to disintegrate. He saw the Beat label as a meal ticket. He saw his fame as a meal ticket. He saw that people could be used. He was shameless but underneath that was a ferocious shame. He was totally ashamed of his childhood and how his mother had rejected him. He drank to overcome the shame, and the shame of his self-taught background. Most people don't know what a poet is in America, and so he lived in a remarkably small world here— Greenwich Village, San Francisco, and college campuses. Within those places, he lived and breathed literature and art. He could only swim in that rarefied aquarium. But if he liked you, and was in a sane moment (earlier in the day), he was a congenial and incorruptible human being.

Where Marble Stood and Fell:
Gregory Corso in Greece

by Leon Horton

"Homer!" Gregory Corso stands on Mount Parnassus at Delphi and cries out to his Muses: "Euripides! I am your friend Grigorie! Eumenides!" It is the late 1990s and Corso, still grieving over the recent deaths of his friends and fellow Beat stalwarts Allen Ginsberg and William Burroughs, has returned once more to Greece, retracing many of his previous visits for Gustave Reininger's documentary *Corso: The Last Beat.* He seems happy, bolstered no doubt by the alcohol concealed in an orange juice bottle, as his words echo back at him. "Heraclitus!" [1] It will be the last time he ever sets foot on Hellenic soil.

The Beat Generation was, of course, a decidedly American phenomenon, and yet almost from its very inception, thanks in no small part to the extensive world travels of its respective players, its influence and reach developed into a truly international literary movement. Greece has been no exception, and anyone wishing to study in depth the cross-pollination of Greek and Beat culture would do well to read Eftychia Mikelli's superlative paper "The Greek Beat and Underground Scene of the 1960s and 1970s" (available through the Purdue University Press, *CLCWeb: Comparative Literature and Culture*, Vol 18, Issue 5) and Maria Nikolopoulou's "The Transfer and Appropriations of the Beat Generation in Greece" (published in *Beat Literature in a Divided Europe*, 2018). Following in the footsteps of Byron, Greece is a natural draw for poets; and as Bill Morgan stated in *The Beats Abroad*: "Of all the Beat poets who had an interest in the classical world, no one was more captivated by Greece than Gregory Corso." [2]

Some flew east, some stayed west, a descendant flew over a cuckoo's nest, but of the original Beats—Kerouac, Ginsberg, Burroughs and himself—the "Daddies" as he liked to call them—Gregory Corso was as well-travelled as the next; especially if he owed the "next" money, or found it prudent to borrow more and quickly move on. From Paris to Venice, Amsterdam to Rome, the often destitute and starving poet-messenger raced through a series of misadventures, fated love affairs, and endless begging letters to publishers, friends, and anyone else willing to finance his itinerant lifestyle.

Corso's life was Greek drama, comedy and tragedy writ large; punctuated, it has to be said, by more than his fair share of *deus ex machina*. A kid from the New York streets, deserted by his mother before his first birthday, abandoned to a foster home by his father, then homeless, though still attending school, Gregory Nunzio Corso nurtured a deep-seated desire to visit, breathe in and exhale an ancient classical past; not from Harvard or Columbia University, as had his contemporaries, but from the books he read in prison. After breaking into a tailor shop to steal a suit for a date, aged 17, he was sent to Clinton State Prison in Dannemora, and was taken under the wing of the mafia inmates, who saw his potential and encouraged him to take advantage of the prison library. In his second book of poems, *Gasoline*, Corso wrote: "I dedicate this book to the angels of Clinton Prison who, in my 17th year, handed me, from all the cells surrounding me, books of illumination." [3] Corso would credit Clinton for making him a poet—with all the truth, pain, ecstasy and deprivation that entails.

Corso first visited Greece in September 1959, but three months earlier, in a letter from New York to Allen Ginsberg and his lover Peter Orlovsky, May 29, he was anticipating a far earlier departure and arrival: "I am off really honestly and truly yes to GREECE this here Friday…" he wrote, simultaneously complaining of his dire finances and griping about a possible advance on his latest book of poetry, *The Happy Birthday of Death*. "I just don't want to get to CRETE and find that I ain't got the fare to DELOS; are you envious jealous and hateful and happy that I am going?" [4]

Writing to Lawrence Ferlinghetti only a few days later, Corso spoke of a burning desire to walk in the dust of ancient Hellenic culture: "So, Greece tomorrow; my life's dream; when first in prison I looked upon Athena's noble lovely worn away face; a grand civilization appeared; a mile long civilization becuz Delos is only a mile long, and lovely Delphi not much longer. Anyway; I extenuate no error but that of liberty and 'aggrandizement'—why not. " [5]

These were grandiose if tongue-in-cheek pronouncements, but the Olympian Gods simply weren't listening that day because, true to form, after surreptitiously selling Allen Ginsberg's furniture to part-fund his trip—"sorry about the cats, the bed, the chair, the tv, but I had to get away from USA" [6]—his plans almost immediately ran aground aboard the Greek cargo ship he had booked passage on. Writing again to Ferlinghetti, June 16, Corso sounded desperate: "Please send me as much money as you can because I am in trouble with my fare. I gave a $200 check to Hellenic Lines in N.Y. and $55 cash. Mid-sea, the check bounced. There was only 160 in bank. Woe was me. Fifteen days at sea. Stopped at Genoa—they held my passport—it cost me 65 dollars for telegrams to banks and Hellenic Line. I can't go to Greece now." [7]

He was, in fact, writing from Venice, and while he may have sounded desperate, he failed to mention to Ferlinghetti that he had been rescued by his old friend Alan Ansen; something he was all too happy to celebrate in a letter to Ginsberg: "By some quirk which I shall later explain, I have stopped in Venice and have resumed the dream—hectic ways of Ansen and Venice. I am staying with Alan, and we shall go to Spoleto, then in August I shall go to Greece." [8]

It isn't possible to write of Corso's Greek adventures without acknowledging the huge role Alan Ansen played. Ansen was a notable associate of the original Beats; a poet, playwright and collector of art; former secretary and research assistant to W. H. Auden. A flamboyant character known for his colourful outbursts such as "Shit on God!" he is Rollo Greb in Kerouac's *On the Road*, AJ in Burroughs' *Naked Lunch*, and Dad Deform in Corso's only novel *American Express*. Thanks to a small trust fund, Ansen (who would move permanently to Athens in the 1960s) could afford to be generous to his friends. Not for the first time, tumbling Corso had landed on his feet.

Dionysus (god of wine and ecstasy) aside, Greece would just have to wait its turn, for time spent with Ansen and his eccentric expatriate friends was too good an opportunity to miss. For the next few months, Corso drank, caroused and generally misbehaved in the company of such luminaries as the actor Sir John Geilgud; the publisher and co-founder of Black Sun Press, Caresse Crosby; and most famous of all, the wealthy art collector and socialite Peggy Guggenheim. Corso had enjoyed a brief affair with Guggenheim only a year before, when they had planned their own visit to the Greek islands. "Ah, how nice Greece will be with Alan and Peggy!" he had written to Allen Ginsberg at the time. "Crete, Rhodes, Minos! What future poems!" [9] The plan was scuppered, however, when Gregory insulted Guggenheim's daughter Pegeen.

Following a brief sojourn to Germany, where he read at the University of Munich, slept rough with the rabbits in an English garden, and cadged money from the poet James Merrill, Corso scraped together the fare to return to Venice and some further rounds of partying—"got drunk with [Willem] de Kooning last night" [10]—all the while firing off missives requesting money from various friends and patrons. He could no longer stay with Ansen, however, who now had other guests, and perhaps sensing his welcome was wearing a bit thin, Corso turned his attention once more to Greece. "I go to Greece tomorrow on a Yugoslav boat," [11] he wrote to Allen Ginsberg circa September 12.

He stayed true to his word. After setting off from New York some three months earlier, fleet-footed Gregory Corso finally arrived at the destination he had so long craved: the cradle of civilisation, the seat of democracy, the city of Athena. He celebrated his arrival in the short poem "First Night on the Acropolis", collected in *Long Live Man* (1962):

> The night was right
> All the plugs of heaven seemed in
> The night was black was white
> And the moon like a woman's breast
> Nippled the Parthenon full

Corso was clearly smitten by his first taste of this ancient city, writing to Lawrence Ferlinghetti, "Well I'm finally here! On the Acropolis with wind and storm—hear old Triton blow his weathered horn" [12] and to Ginsberg, "I am filled with Athens and know well its tower of winds Acropolis Agora stoas etc." [13] Here was a land where he could stand and stare for a time since, as Bill Morgan observed in *The Typewriter is Holy,* "he could indulge his passion for the classics on a tight budget. The low cost of living in Greece made it more practical for him to survive on the occasional kindness of wealthier friends. He used all the Greek museums and archaeological sites as his classroom and continued his own private study of mythology and the ancients." [14]

To anyone who has visited Athens (myself included), who has stood in the sun-stretched shadow of the Temple of Olympian Zeus, reflected among the ruins of the Theatre of Dionysus, clambered up the Areopagus Hill, and climbed the steps of the Propylaea to the Acropolis—to marvel at the Parthenon, the Caryatid sculptures, the Erechtheum (temple of Athena)—it is easy to understand how Corso felt when he gazed at the Ancient Agora (where Socrates held court) and wrote in "Reflection in a Green Arena": "Where marble stood and fell / into an eternal landscape / I stand ephemeral."

Piecing a life together, especially one as itinerant as Gregory Corso's, is like trying to fit different jigsaw puzzles together. While a precise date has been impossible to establish, shortly after arriving in Greece, Corso (with Caresse Crosby's "surrogate" son, an aspiring poet and actor called Bill Barker, and his common-law wife Diane) played a bit part in a film based on the 1938 novel *Eroica* by Greek writer Kosmas Politis. The film, directed by Michael Cacoyannis (*Zorba the Greek*) was released in English as *Our Last Spring* in 1960. He isn't easily identifiable in the finished print (not, at least, to this author), but as Corso enthusiastically wrote to Crosby: "Bill & Diane here very dear to me—we are the most handsome irresolute starvelings in Athens—On drunken nights we transform into Spartan laurel wreaths—The 3 of us are 3 centuries of joy… Life here in Athens good—we are in a film called "Eroica" being made now—much fun." [15]

When he wasn't making films, Corso continued to visit the ancient archaeological sites—taking road trips to Mycenae, Olympia and Delphi (no doubt in Crosby's car, which Barker had driven down from Venice)—and making connections with the Athenian literati through his new friend, the surrealist Greek writer Nanos Valaoritis.

It wasn't long before he got into trouble. In the company of Valaoritis, American writer and director Conrad Rooks and his wife, actress Zina Rachevsky, Corso agreed to be photographed by the noted *LIFE* photographer James Burke in and about Athens. In *Half the Perfect World: Writers, Dreamers and Drifters on Hydra, 1955 - 1964*, Paul Genoni and Tanya Dalziell wrote: "Exactly how the connection was made is unclear, but in September 1959, Burke photographed Beat poet Gregory Corso in several locations around Athens including at the Parthenon, at a poetry reading and having lunch at the home of aspiring American filmmaker Conrad Rooks, who would go on to make the acclaimed Beat-influenced films *Chappaqua* (1960) and *Siddhartha* (1972)." [16] Burke's photographs are readily available on the internet, and remain the most significant visual record of Corso's Greek adventures.

The day itself did not go well. Not for the first time, Corso's mercurial nature got the better of him. As Genoni and Dalziell in *Half the Perfect World* revealed, "in one intemperate and alcohol-influenced incident, he flung a glass at the unfortunate Burke" [17]—something Corso readily confessed in a letter to Don Allen, editor at Grove Press: "Was bothered so much yesterday by a *LIFE* photographer that I got drunk on ouzo and threw a glass at him. Missed (thank God) and ran out crying into the gymnasium of Diogenes." [18]

> Gymnasium of Diogenes lost in you
> all made up like a scarecrow
> a refugee from the grape festival
> I am bleeding
> having been stabbed ceremoniously by the Vine-Rat

Diogenes the Cynic—the philosopher who legend has it slept in a large ceramic jar, who heckled Plato's lectures, and made a virtue of poverty and begging to show his disdain for a corrupt society—would doubtless have applauded Corso's outburst. Gregory, however, was still trying to justify his errant behaviour in another letter to Don Allen dated October 8:

I thought it'd be nice to have my picture taken on the Acropolis, but they also wanted a "group" picture; so to a tavern they led me and there the photographer starts calling me names all to get up my anger, that he did, I threw a glass at him and ran into the street crying, ran into a car my leg all black and blue and he the photographer comes after me and says "All right Corso we're alone you can stop the act." I ran from him but he kept on coming after me and I stopped and wept hysterically to him that I was a poet and not a freak. [19]

Corso was so unhappy about the incident that he fled Athens for the island of Hydra. "I got up at six this morning and saw the sun come over the Peloponnesus," he wrote to Don Allen. "This is really an extraordinary lovely island. And what fun watching the fishermen sell their fish. Am writing a long poem called, of course, *Greece*." [20] Unfortunately, he ran into trouble with some of the locals after drinking too much whisky: "was crying all night putting down the Greek peasantry for having chased Poseidon away etc. etc., almost got killed." [21]

Hydra, just off the Argolis peninsula in the Aegean Sea, was at that time a remote, idyllic, underdeveloped island with no cars or bikes (only donkeys), no running water (only a well), and no telephones (only the local grapevine). With a horseshoe curved harbour, and ramshackle, whitewashed, sun-bleached houses dotting the hills above the main town (also called Hydra) like an Ampitheater, it had attracted many Greek artists in search of light and inspiration. When the author Henry Miller visited in 1939 and wrote about it in *The Colossus of Maroussi* (1941), his enraptured descriptions brought the island to the attention of the international literati—it seemed the perfect retreat for any writer or artist seeking to escape from the modern world. For good or ill, Hydra would never be the same again.

In 1955, Australian husband and wife writers Charmian Cliff and George Johnston arrived on the island, looking to escape from the drab realities of post-war London. In their wake, came many others: the eccentric Russian Lily Mack, the Russian-French artist Mark Chagall, the English painter Anthony Kingsmill, American poet Kenneth Koch, English writer Patrick Leigh Fermor, Norwegian novelist Axel Jenson (soon to separate from his wife Marianne Ihlen)—and, most memorably, a then unknown Canadian poet by the name of Leonard Cohen.

As Clift wrote in her memoir *Peel Me a Lotus:* "It is a diverse and tantalising collection of human beings sprawled about these rocks and ledges on a hot cliff far from their native lands, insurgents all who have rebelled against the station in which it pleased God to place them. What devious roads brought them to this island, what decisions and indecisions, what drifting, what moments of desperation and hope? And what are they looking for?" [22]

There is little evidence that Corso was part of Clift and Johnston's circle, but on such a tiny island it seems doubtful that their paths did not cross. In an oblique reference in an essay titled "Old Acquaintance be Forgot" collected in *The World of Charmian Clift* (1970), Clift wrote: "There was an American poet of some beat renown who drugged himself into somnolence at our kitchen table and couldn't be woken up for two whole days." [23] There are others who might fit such a description (Allen Ginsberg visited in 1961) but for such a performance the award must surely go to Gregory Corso.

Somnolent, drugged or merely hung-over, it was on Hydra, while out walking with the neo-expressionist painter Norris Embry—"the most depressed soul I have ever met" [24]—that Corso experienced a powerful vision. "I actually saw Death, yes, it was the morning after the big night of sad drunk and much tears." [25] Corso had been subject to waking visions from the age of five, including an apparition of a mortally wounded American-Indian on horseback amid the city traffic, and whether they were related to his fierce imagination or to the traumas of his youth, they were part of his psyche and of his poetry, giving faculty and sustenance to both. He would relate his Hydra vision in the poem "Greece":

Hydra, only isle of my touch & sight

where came where came that skinless light
Hydra, "thy beauty which did
haunt me in my
sleep to undertake
the death of all the
world"—This my first night I dreamed
we piled in the car
each with his cigarette of Death

In a letter to Ginsberg dated October 11, by which time he had returned to Athens, Corso elaborated on his vision in detail—how he and Norris Embry had got up at six in the morning, walked to a "high deserted spot, five miles out, no inhabitants" when suddenly,

I began to see spots, I kept silent from then on, he walked ahead, out of sight around a bend, I sat down, "Do you see that black bird, Norris? Is it a vulture, Norris?" He was out of hearing distance, I screamed to him, "Do you see the vulture, Norris?" He yelled back, "No!" Then it happened, I lost my breath, fear set in but only for a second, everything became light, I say not the edges of the mountains, not the sea nor where I was sitting nor myself, just light, I was in that light, the description that it was "skinless" is only my helpless description of sight that I felt and can readily be expressed, but what I saw, ah… [26]

What he "saw" he expressed in "Greece":

Oh the brilliant lining!
What is not there is present!
Many many are the occurrences of Light!

> Overcreatures gazeless like grapes
> Wondrous unbeasts blazing crests of undercreatures
> Even one thin perched stony lion
> Ball-bellied the color of the Rat!

And:

> Behind the wheel Death, a big sloppy faggot;
> He opened the door I had to get in!
> For one whole year he sucked me off, and I always came!
> But did not come to die.
> In you Hydra I left this mistrustful light
> spotted out almost died and entered a skinless light

It is curious that Corso should couple his Hydra vision with the automobile, since (then as now) there were no cars on the island. In the 1950s, however, the motorcar, perhaps most especially to Americans, had come to represent much more than a mere mode of transport—it had taken on symbolic meaning. As Professor John Gray wrote in *Straw Dogs: Thoughts on Humans and Animals*: "Which is more important today: the use of cars as means of transportation, or their use as expressions of our unconscious yearnings for personal freedom, sexual release and the final liberation of sudden death?" (27)

In his letter to Ginsberg, Corso continued his description of his chance encounter with (the Greek god of death) Thanatos:

> Right after the blackbird that only I saw came Death with only a drop of
> human fear, I am sure that that drop of fear did not bring back my breath,
> else I would not have seen Light disrobe. Still human me when I came out of
> it I sat breathing heavily and happily and cried happily like one released from

a horrible ordeal vowing never again to hurt any man or thing or interfere with any way in Life, when Norris returned I told him half all, and badly and excitedly yet enough to blank his eyes with strange curiosity. I sat there for two hours or more after, couldn't get up, couldn't walk, very weak, and VERY CONFUSED, slight fear because of this harbouring and catering and blending of death for one whole year entered, this I thought is the beginning of death, I will not leave this spot a body; else what did Light mean? Will my breath stop again any minute? I did not wish it to, though I have been very, very unhappy of late, I did not wish to leave this mad crazy lovely world. [28]

Returning to the mad, crazy world of Athens, Corso joined playwright Tennessee Williams for an interview on air forces radio, and later some heavy carousing. "Had a nice time with Tennessee here, much drink and talk and fights," [29] he wrote to Ferlinghetti. He showed Williams proofs of his most recent collection of poetry, *The Happy Birthday of Death*, which he claimed Williams liked. Corso was still obsessing over his Hydra vision, and all his talk of death left an indelible impression on the sensitive playwright. In a letter to James Laughlin, Corso exclaimed: "Tennessee Williams looked into my eyes and said 'YOU MUST LIVE!'—death is a big thing with him":

> I tried to explain to him that the death I was going through was not suicidal but a probe. That death (its subject) at first fascinated me and I played with it (as you can see in DEATH poem) and then the sudden realization that by probing it I might well get into it and even go beyond it, and I feel I did that in Hydra—but I think he sees the kind of death I see… we had long talks about this; but I don't think he understood me because all he would say is "YOU MUST LIVE." [30]

In November, Corso ran into an old friend. Amy Mims had first met him when she was a student at Harvard in the mid-fifties, when Corso was surreptitiously living on campus, hiding in plain sight and utilizing the university's amenities to write his one-act Greek play *Sarpedon*. In part three of her *Greek Trilogy*, subtitled "Professor Helen Sullivan's Buried Treasure", Mims (referring to herself as Daedala in the text) wrote:

> It seemed to Daedala miraculous that just when she was ready to turn her back definitively on America—here was the most eloquent spokesman of the Beats—by divine "coincidence"—in Athens—"scrubbing the earth" in the country, which Daedala was about to adopt as her motherland. The fact of Gregory's presence here in Athens at this moment was indeed a wonderful surprise. For although Daedala remained geographically far from Corso and most of the other Beats, even in absentia, she belonged with them far more than she ever belonged to any other group of human beings. [31]

Mims/Daedala remembered visiting Alan Ansen at his apartment, cooking an inedible Beef Stroganoff for his coterie of unusual friends, and noting a significant work of art on the wall.

> Gregory had given Daedala a glimpse of this bizarre circle. But she never felt at ease there. Nor did Gregory, who kept pretty much to himself, in his own room a few doors away on Alopekis Street. At least, he had a more immediate connection with the group and especially with Alan himself. For example, the large triptych Gregory had painted recently became the most coveted gem of Alan Ansen's Art Collection. In fact, a triptych so dazzling that it deserves the following digression: In the right wing of the triptych, an angel is pouring a sack of gold coins into a dark river—the River of Life?—On the cloud where the angel kneels, there is a Big City full of steeples and a Grecian edifice. And there is also another small golden city near a bright golden bridge—perhaps the San Francisco Golden Bridge? Or

perhaps a Gregorian vision of Saint Augustine's Heavenly City of God?—
Whatever the vision may mean, just below the cloud, there is a huge ominous Pterodaktyl dangling in Space, as the impish angel pours the gold into
the Renaissance part of the triptych, where two figures garbed in brownish
robes stand in operatic poses inside a cavernous Church. [32]

The triptych (christened "From the Crypt to the Cradle" by Alan Ansen) had to be
rescued after Corso "suddenly became possessed and started slashing his own canvas,
howling in agony: 'No more monsters!'" [33] Ever the art collector, Ansen had the painting repaired and smuggled back to his summer home in Venice under its crazed creator's
very nose. "From the Crypt to the Cradle" would return to Athens when Ansen moved
there permanently in the 1960s; when he died on November 12 2006, his books, papers
and artwork were bequeathed to the Athens Centre, where they remain to this day.

Perhaps it was merely the joy of seeing an old friend, perhaps it was Corso having
stared Death in the face on Hydra, but Mim's narrative revealed a side to Gregory that
hasn't often been touched upon in the drama of his life: a gentle, caring, guiding nature.

When Daedala used to visit Gregory in the autumn of 1959, she was aware
of this tender side of his character. But for complicated reasons of her own,
she didn't want to let herself go. So she decided to visit him only on "profes-
sional" terms. As soon as she entered his tiny room, she started to talk about
how "blocked" she'd become with her efforts to write. She confessed that
she only felt panic whenever she had to face a blank sheet of paper. Gregory listened, without looking at her. His eyes were fixed on the little kitten,
playfully prancing up and down his jacket. But after a while he answered: "If
you have a hard time at first, just sit down and tell yourself to write a letter
to God."

Daedala was deeply grateful to the poet Gregory Corso for this gift he
had given her. As for Gregory, the human being, Daedala was only "platon-

ically" in love. She firmly believed that usually the strongest form of Love —in order to remain free of jealousy and everyday banality—is better off to remain "Platonic". That's why a few days before Gregory was supposed to leave Greece, she accepted his invitation to meet at the Parthenon for a midnight rendezvous. Those were the days when—even in the cold depths of winter—the Acropolis remained open until very late, to celebrate the Night of the full moon. Nevertheless, Gregory did not show up for that rendezvous. To tell the truth, Daedala hadn't really believed he'd be there—he always did everything in his own way—and at that time, although disappointed, she didn't really take it too seriously. But in retrospect, she wondered what might have happened if Gregory had come to their "tryst". [34]

On December 15, Corso witnessed the very first state visit to Greece by a sitting US President, as Dwight Eisenhower passed through Athens in an open-top Rolls-Royce with King Paul of Greece: "saw Ike pass by today, was a nice feeling to see him amid flags and crowds." [35] He would commemorate the occasion in "Some Greek Writings":

WHEN PRESIDENT EISENHOWER
came to Athens
he got a helicopter
and flew over the Acropolis
and looked down at it
    like only Zeus could

I told that to a sharp Englishman
who replied:
He's fortunate he did not fly over it
    like Icarus

Sharp Englishmen and Presidential visits aside, after yet again receiving a much needed financial boost from Lawrence Ferlinghetti (and enjoying a drink with the Italian World Heavyweight Champion prize fighter Primo Carnera—"what a strange experience, his hand is ten times the size of mine!"[36]) Corso finally left Athens for a return visit to Paris and the Beat Hotel. In "European Thoughts—1959" published in *Long Live Man*, he mused:

> And Greece was a marvellous country
> but of course I was not marvellous in it
> because man is made to suffer in a happy place
> when he has been happy all too happy
> in an insufferable place.

Writing to James Laughlin from Paris, circa December 25, Corso sounded happy to have left Greece: "These last three months in Greece affected me very much, my last shakings of Death-probe, with the result of a ordinary stage prop illumination on Hydra; I was broken up after that because I went into Death and came out of it with a creation of invisibility, with a Hollywood powder-puff vision, if it were any vision at all." [37] In another letter to Laughlin, dated a day later, he conceded that he had owed rent to his Greek landlady who had, so he claimed, threatened to "go to the American embassy." [38]

It was almost a year to the day that Corso returned to Greece. In the interim, he had flitted across Europe—Paris, Florence, Paris, Geneva, Venice, Berlin, Paris… but by December 18, 1960, he once again found himself on Hydra. "I am here, all is wonderful, and if you could send me an advance on book I'd be very happy," he wrote to James Laughlin. "I am wishing to obtain a small room on the isle of Hydra, and here rest and work." [39] The book to which he referred was his collection of poetry *The Happy Birthday of Death*; the "work" would be his freewheeling novel *The American Express*, which would be published by Maurice Girodias' Olympia Press in Paris later that year.

After the disturbing, visceral vision of his previous visit, Corso wanted to see if he could once again summon a supernatural appearance. On this occasion, however, despite his optimism, and his somewhat comical idea of taking binoculars, there was no illumination, hallucination or "Death-probe" visitation, as he explained in a letter to Allen Ginsberg:

> God knows why, but I had to return to Hydra, and did. I went to the exact spot where it all happened. It's a long walk to it and this time I went with no sorrow but with heavy breath. And excitement. The place is the only truly deserted enclosure of the whole island. A ship grave yard in the crack of two mountains. Nothing happened. I looked for the black bird—no bird. The light was the light I had always known. [40]

If he was disappointed by this corporeal experience, Corso had little time to dwell on it.

> I hurried back to the main part of the island—where all the people lived. It was seven in the morning. Raining. I turned the bend—and lo! a Norwegian girl dove into the sea. She had been drinking and was upset about her child. "Suicide! Suicide!" cried the fishermen and the whole town rushed to where she had jumped. I was standing over her—where she dove from very shallow. She hit her head, she came up and held her head, "My head hurts." "Grab the iron rail," I said, as she swam to it and held on. Boats came to get her. "Great! Wonderful! Beautiful!" I cried, as she looked up at me in amazement. "I'm sorry, but I couldn't jump in after you because I would have been an embarrassing casualty as I cannot swim. [41]

Corso made no further mention of the "suicidal" Norwegian girl, and her identity remains a mystery. Although it is tempting to surmise it might have been Marianne Ihlen, lover of Leonard Cohen, they were not on the island at this time, having left Hydra for a short tour of Europe in November. (It has been suggested to this author that the girl might have been Dinnie Pederson, then wife of Norwegian artist Tore Pederson, who had arrived on the island in September. Dinnie, now living in the US, flatly denies this.)

In January 1961, Corso made a trip to Crete, birthplace of Zeus, where he was so taken by the archaeological ruins at Knossos that in a letter to James Laughlin, he expounded on a theory (his own) that the Cretans were directly descended from the Native Americans. "Actually, I think the American Indian started it all," he proposed. "They migrated from the Americas to all parts of the world. One place they migrated to was Crete,

> Where else can such a long black braided hair be found but in the American Indian? Also the red skin, the nose (that famous Greek nose) and the colors are very Aztec and the pillars are smooth totem poles. Yes, it is my belief that America is the cradle of all civilizations and that is why things are the way they are today. But I must do more research before I expound this fact. What a wonderful people these Cretans must have been. Also, all the designs, the rosettes etc., are just like those found on teepees. Yes, there is no doubt that Sitting Bull is descendant of Minos...
>
> You are the first one I am telling this to, as I only came upon the illumination yesterday when visiting the ruins at Gnossus. At first I was greatly disappointed... then upon studying a real fresco of a Cretan youth, I saw the American Indian I always believed there was something spooky about the American Indian. In short the whole glory of Egypt, Greece, India, China, etc. etc., is because of the vast migrations from the Americas many thousands of years ago. I will write an exact and scientific report on this (I will write it just like an archaeologist's) and will shatter all history books. [42]

He got his migration back to front, and he shattered no history books, but he did manage to write to Ginsberg—"I saw the Neolithic caves, all so wild and new, new in a way that life is so close and new, not old" [43] —and to mention the nearby village of Phaestos in his poem "Some Greek Writings":

PHAESTOS IS A VILLAGE WITH 25 FAMILIES
and one taverna
There my friend and I sat
drinking with the Tallest Greek in the world
And though he must have been close to sixty
his face and body seemed those of a strong young prince
We could not speak each other's language
but drink after drink we talked about everything

"Come to Greece," Corso had implored Allen Ginsberg and Peter Orlovsky back in December. "I have a three room apartment right underneath the Acropolis. And only a few feet away, on both sides, from the Roman Agora, and Diogenes' gymnasium." [44] Ginsberg, travelling alone, wouldn't arrive until the following October, by which time Corso was in London. He'd left his mark on the Athenian intelligentsia, however, as a letter from Ginsberg to Orlovsky in Israel, October 21, 1961, clearly illustrated: "I live across street from bar where whore boys gather. I know them all. Also hang around Zonars and Flocas cafes and see intelligent old literary men here and they like me. They're all bugged at Gregory who apparently teased everyone, threw fits etc…" [45]

Not everyone who met Corso was "bugged" as Ginsberg put it. In an email to the author, Greek poet Spyros Meimaris recalled:

I must have been around 18 years of age when I first met Gregory in Athens, an early summer morning, I think in 1961—a few months before Allen [Ginsberg] came to Athens on his way to India. I must have seen pictures of Gregory in *Time* or *Newsweek*… I immediately recognised him and approached him. He was cordial and open and invited me to sit with him at the famous Athens café and restaurant Zonar's. He ordered a Bloody Mary for himself and explained that he was coming off junk, that he needed some alcohol to taper off. We started talking about the Beat phenomenon, of which I was quite eloquent—it had occupied my mind since coming home from America and suffering from the provincial Greece of the late '50s/early '60s. Then Gregory asked me about the Turkish Baths in Athens, which I'd never visited but managed to find—they were located at Omonia Square, famous from Allen's poems. We went there and took a hot bath. [46]

Meimaris, who had lived in San Francisco and met Lawrence Ferlinghetti, would play a significant role in the Greek-Beat counterculture that would develop during the 1960s and 70s and beyond, producing Greek translations of many poetic works, as well as Allen Ginsberg's early journals, while acknowledging a direct Beat influence on his own poetry.

Corso had once again left Athens for Paris by late April, but not before Meimaris met him a second time:

> I spotted Gregory with a group of five or six other beatniks. I should say the first to be seen *en masse* in Greece at that time. I followed them and we all converged on another famous place, the Milk Shop—not the one at the Plaka, which much later on became a hangout for hippies—but the one on Omonia Square, where bouzouki players were returning after playing all night. They were recuperating from too much alcohol and hashish by ingesting hot milk, yoghurt with honey, or eggs fried sunny side up. [47]

"I live very strangely and continually without money in this merchant-drunken-happy city of Athens [48] Corso wrote to Lawrence Ferlinghetti before departing for Paris. Perhaps his first flush of enthusiasm was beginning to wane, as he wrote in "Some Greek Writings":

IN A WAY
the Greeks today
don't like the Acropolis
because
it hovers over them
as though mockingly
as though imprisoning them
in a you-can't-do-better-than-me
      abyss

By the time he returned to Greece in 1966, Corso was in bad shape. His drug and alcohol intake, exacerbated by his financial situation, was now so debilitating that it all but precipitated a permanent move to Athens, as Bill Morgan observed in *The Typewriter is Holy*, "Greece was ideal for him for several reasons, among them the availability of drugs and the low cost of living." [49] The South African poet Sinclair Beiles, an old friend from the Beat Hotel days, commented in an interview with Gary Cummiskey: "I can remember when Corso and I shared a room in Athens, and I would have to go out to the chemist at 3am to get something or other for him, in order to keep him going. Corso couldn't go to the chemist himself, he looked too wrecked!" [50]

In the previous years, Corso had continued his travels then returned to the USA, where he met, married, had a child with and split from Sally November. Returning to Europe and his dissolute ways, he alienated more and more friends through his use of heroin and his endless freeloading, and by some circuitous route he once again found himself in Athens.

Athens, too, had rung some changes. In the wake of Allen Ginsberg's visit in 1961, other beat poets had begun to arrive, to engage with Athenian poets, young and old, in cross-cultural assimilation. When they weren't throwing their money away in the tavernas, they were kick-starting an underground publishing movement, launching and contributing to small literary magazines. As Eftychia Mikelli observed in *The Greek Beat and Underground Scene of the 1960s and 1970s*: "The Beats exercised a strong appeal to controversial writer and publisher Leonidas Christakis, whose numerous publications have played a focal role in the Greek literary underground scene."[51]

In 1963, Christakis published two issues of *A Different Kind of Art*, which featured poems by Conrad Rooks and an article celebrating the arrival of poet and musician Ted Joans: "he has come to Athens to bring a 'Happening,' to wake up the dull intellectuals, and to disturb the noncreators." [52] Nanos Valaoritis followed up with *Pali (Anew)*, a much more ambitious magazine, and in 1965, Dan Richter published the first issue of *Residu*, which was notable for publishing (in English) works by Allen Ginsberg, Harold Norse and Nanos Valaoritis.

At the same time, Corso's output had dropped to near zero. James Laughlin had spent months trying to get him to finish his next book of poetry, but the publisher's pleas met with digression and, as often, cries of poverty. By now, Corso's letter writing was sporadic at best, dribbling to nothing; and gone were those exuberant descriptions of ancient Hellenic sites and Hydra visions, replaced by hubris. When Laughlin, in a last ditch attempt, suggested Corso would be forgotten if he didn't, at least, write something soon, Corso's reply was one you might expect from a heroin addict:

Dear James,

As for people forgetting Gregory Corso, since Gregory Corso is no longer in public eye, all good and well. A poet is not a movie actor whereby he needs make a picture a year thus to be remembered. Old grows a movie actor and he's had it, not a poet. I think of Tennyson who stayed from publishing twelve years and I amongst many hath not forgotten Tennyson. But I do agree that these times are quick and if a poet has what to say he best say it when said. What then has happened to eternal poetry? That verse which stands for all time? Alas—poets today are become eventful and topical, prophets indeed, merely roseate journalists, if you ask me.

He signed off: "Athens is 100 years behind the times. Something new and wonderful could happen here or something creepy and sad." [53]

With more of his friends and fellow Beats arriving every year—Harold Norse and Ted Joans in 1963; Irving Rosenthal, editor of *Big Table*, in 1964; Philip Lamantia in 1965—whether this cultural exchange was "new and wonderful" or "creepy and sad" can only be surmised, but Corso had no shortage of expat playmates to party with. The renowned science-fiction author and polymath Samuel Delany was in Athens at that time:

> The most important thing that happened to me on my first sixth-month European trip is that one afternoon, possibly in mid-March—I will never know for sure, though it may be recorded in Alan Ansen's journals—in a café neon at the foot of the Athenian Plaka, at a crowded table under sunlight and a shady tree, I got invited, suddenly and surprisingly, to lunch at Alan Ansen's Kolonaki apartment by Gregory Corso. Both Ansen and Corso were at the table, and I knew, perhaps, two others of the eight of us sitting around. "Hey, this guy looks interesting," Corso said, turning to me. "Let's ask him." Ansen said sure and gave me his address. There followed a weird afternoon running all over Athens with Gregory while he explained he was researching a version of the Bacchae—"This is a classic, and you can't fuck around with the classics!"—Which as far as I know, he never finished.
>
> One or two days later, I turned up at Ansen's, which had some original Cocteau drawings framed on the walls in the peasant-style kitchen, over a failed stew that Greg cooked and wouldn't eat because he'd misjudged the heat of the peppers: I thought it was okay, and Ansen and I both had a bowl. I'd brought a bottle of retsina, but there was already some white wine, which we all drank. ("Hey, really," Greg said, "you guys don't have to eat that shit.")
>
> One of them asked what I was writing about, and I'd explained the topic

of the new novel I was working on, back then called *A Fabulous, Formless Darkness*. There, Greg made the remark about my project, now published as *The Einstein Intersection*, recorded on page 101 of the book: "Jean Harlow? Christ, Orpheus, Billy the Kid, those three I can understand. But what's a young spade writer like you doing all caught up with the Great White Bitch? Of course, I guess it's pretty obvious . . ." Gregory, of course, had recognized me as black, and the "Great White Bitch" was Harlow herself, which is not the way I'd have described her; but I knew what he meant. [54]

Perhaps all the excitement and endless parting in Athens was becoming too much for him, or perhaps it was seeing his colleagues galvanized by this new underground scene, but something seemed to have short-circuited in Corso's mind when he wrote to Allen Ginsberg, circa June 16, and expressed a deep desire to escape away from it all.

Dear Allen,

I am going to live like a monk for a month, high up on a mount on the isle of Moni, in a German outlook post. The isle is uninhabited 'cept for peacocks and wild goats. Lovely Miranda Rochschild has secured it for me. It will take half an hour to climb up to it. I will bring with me all my work of the past four years, and shall thus put together my book. Plus I shall truly regain mine health there, I'm hopefully sure. You wouldn't think I went thru what I did these past four years by the look of me, yet beneath that look is a pretty much purged skin of blood. Still it was something I had I had to go thru with, as I first realized, and as I hoped you would have understood. [55]

This extraordinary letter reveals much about Corso's state of mind at that time, as he pours out a confession worthy of a good (bad) Catholic in a stream of battered and bloodied emotion:

I was, so I felt, that Gregory Corso, poet and bohemian, who in a matter of ten years lived a full youthtime and speedy age. God knows where I got the drive and ego (if such can be termed, being I was always living in an environ that knew not the liberty of the ego). Nor was I so desperate to "make" of my past, a present, and a future. I cut off the past, lived the present; and when the boom was lowered, I faced the future with no real history to present it with… The boom came when I realized I could not husband be, nor father. The ten year old poet could not cast off the father of my own past. Indeed I was mother and father and child, and none could trio it, a sad helpless split left mine spirit a cold and frightened thing. Thus the "filthy nurse" was secured me in the infirmary of hell, and from that hell I fell. When one gets knocked down that low, one either stays down for good, or mutates. Well, I feel that I have mutated into the only thing I could understand and live with… a thing familiar to me all my 36 years, that realistic dreamer, that stuff called "spirit"; and once I knew this to be so I thanked the Gods there be that I might yet live AND evolve. [56]

Having admitted his sins and the deprivation caused by his heroin addiction (which he often euphemistically referred to as "filthy nurse"), Corso seemed to approach something akin to salvation:

I do not say I am completely healed. For I still have to make strong my will, as I would still fall for that filthy nurse, and she is always around. Well, she won't be when I go to mine retreat. There I shall be entirely alone, except for the heavens of Zeus, and the whole of the past four years scored on paper before me. I go there not for any spiritualistic savior, but that I have not had such solitude ever, for even in prison I was yet with conditional life… I need the piece, the rest, the quiet, and the self-certainty of a clear head and soul. [56]

Corso signed off: "Ah, Allen, so it does matter all this, it does change, it does mean, and how nice to wake up to it, and feel it, and progressively, i.e. evolutionary, be. Love to you, Gregory." [57]

It seems doubtful that Corso pursued this mountaintop self-imposed exile, away from the allure of Athens and his friends, and his attempts to remove himself from the "filthy nurse" of heroin were sporadic at best. He did maintain a relationship with the country, as Bill Morgan in *The Beats Abroad* said: "Corso was frequently drawn back to Greece, where he could live affordably amid the ruins. He even tried to settle here for good, spending most of 1966 in Greece trying to find a place that he could call home, but by then his addiction to drugs was beginning to undermine his poetic (and house-hunting) efforts." [58]

"Anyone know where the Trojan horse is from? The Cassandra myth?" Corso had asked an assembled auditorium at New York University in 1995. "Big big man Mr. Homer. Homer is the daddy of all mythology. You should have read Homer, there is no excuse for it, if you haven't. No excuse for not embracing Homer. If you haven't gone through Homer…" [59]

The extent to which Greece—its mythology, literature and philosophy—played a significant role in Corso's work as a poet is clear to see and readily accessible. Even before he first visited Greece in 1959, he was incorporating his extensive knowledge of Greek mythology into poems such as "Paranoia in Crete" and his play *Sarpeden* (1954):

[It] was an attempt to replicate Euripides, though the whole shot be an original. Like the Greek masters, I took off where Homer left an opening (like Euripides did with the fate of Agamemnon). My opening was found in the *Iliad*. Sarpedon, son of Zeus and Europa, died on the fields of Troy, and Homer had him sent up to Olympus with no complaint from Hades, who got all the others who died there. Thus I have Hades complain, demanding from his brother Zeus, the dead, all the dead, from said fields. [60]

What is not so easy to ascertain, however, is to what extent Corso's relationship with Greece changed over the years. Post 1966 there are no further letters from Greece (more accurately, there are no further letters from Greece in *An Accidental Autobiography: The Selected Letters of Gregory Corso*) and from here on in we are almost entirely reliant on the reminisces, anecdotes and memoirs of those who knew him.

George Scrivani first met Gregory Corso in 1970, in Buffalo, New York, when he was studying Classical Languages (Latin and Greek). The two became firm friends, occasionally living with each other; and over the decades, George became Gregory's personal assistant, above and beyond the call of duty. There are those (including Corso himself) who regard George Scrivani as Gregory's guiding light through some of his darkest days. In 1972, he helped secure Corso a summer residence with the Athen's Centre.

> I helped him take up a teaching position on Aegina, arranged I think by Alan Ansen. By help, I mean I passed myself off as a heroin addict to a doctor and obtained enough methadone for him to balance out and travel to Greece, where I joined him a month later. When he wasn't on Aegina he stayed at a pension/apartment in the Kolonaki that I had rented. They were fun times. Gregory was less involved in my travels as he had already been to Greece years previously and had seen most of the important sites. That meant a lot of drinking in the tavernas and meeting with the émigré population in Athens at the time. We were only together there for about three months, with me running off to visit the sacred groves on my own. But I did accompany him to Aegina once for a class, and through him I did meet Alan Ansen and Mary Rogers, briefly. [61]

With Scrivani and Ansen acting as middlemen, Corso pulled himself together just enough to get on a plane and return to Greece. As Yannis Zervos, director at the Athens Centre, recounted in *Passage to Paradise: Hellenic Sketches of the Mind:*

Through Alan Ansen, we arrange for the infamous Beat poet Gregory Corso to be poet-in-residence, in addition to Katerina Anghelaki-Rooke, Sinclair Beiles and others. Gregory has a colorful background, but his poems are rapidly growing in acceptance…

I love meeting Gregory; he is always funny, sharp and personable. He is conducting a poetry workshop and giving readings, involving himself in the events and attending lectures. Gregory has tousled hair, medium height and maximum irreverence. He bears the scars of a mean upbringing, with a mind bereft of niceties and a vision of reality that has traded social acceptance with uncomfortable truths. He is so brutally himself that one cannot help but embrace him for his charm. His intellectual honesty ripples through the air, dispelling real or imagined lacunas of the mind.

At one talk on "Poetics in Modern Greece" a rather boring speaker refers to the Temple of Poseidon at Cape Sounion, mentioning that one of the columns has Lord Byron's initials carved on it. From the back of the room, Gregory intervenes: "You are full of shit. It is Byron's name, not his initials, that is carved on the column." Flustered, the speaker disagrees.

A month later, on a stormy afternoon, Willie Eliot from the American School of Classical Studies is giving his usual stunning talk and slide presentation on "Athens in the Time of Lord Byron". The room is full, with Corso in attendance. An hour later, there is a huge thunderbolt and the last slide appears on the screen. It is a column from the Temple of Poseidon with Byron's name carved in large letters. The crowd stands up and claps. [62]

There was time for play on Aegina, and Corso took the opportunity to revisit some old friends on Hydra, where he met Brian Sidaway—"I first met Gregory when he was in Athens in the winter of 1965/66? I'm a bit vague which winter it was. He was often at our favourite taverna near the Temple of Winds in Monistraki. Baba Stavros, I think it was called"—and his wife Valerie Lloyd Sidaway: "We met him again in the '70s (72?) when he was poet-in-residence at a summer school on Aegina (near to Hydra). Gregory liked to come to Hydra as there was a more 'interesting' group here in those years." [63]

In "Hydra Reflections" collected in Helle V. Goldman's *When We Were Almost Young: Remembering Hydra through War and Bohemians* (2018), Valerie wrote about a "friendly" softball challenge between Gregory's Aegina students and the Hydra expat community:

> When Gregory heard about our softball game, he challenged us to a match. Gregory was the captain of their team and he was sure of a win. It was a hot and dusty day and our rag-tag crew was keen to go. After an hour or so of play, with much bantering and haggling of scores, the Hydra team managed to pull off a win. Gregory was his usual rebellious, irascible self and not a happy loser.
>
> He and Anthony Kingsmill spent time together and tried to out-drink and out-quote each other. Quite often I took to avoiding them, especially when they were inebriated. My nickname for him was Coarse Corso. I was too young to realise that his advances and attempts to make conversation were just his way of flirting.
>
> Gregory was disgusted that I was reading a Greek comic book instead of Homer or other Greek literature. He was, after all, a Beat poet as well as a great cynic and was known to make those kind of remarks. I would have been kinder had I known what to do with the comments thrown my way. I was no match for his variable mind. Gregory, I found out later, had experienced a difficult period in Athens, when he was struggling with a serious drug problem and alcohol was a way out. My compassion missed the moment! [64]

If Corso was suffering at that time isn't known, it would depend on his supply of "filthy nurse" or his methadone, but if he was drinking that usually meant he wasn't using. Either way, it didn't seem to harm his duties as poet-in-residence, as Yannis Zervos wrote:

> There is a lot of action in the hotel Miranda gardens, where rehearsals are taking place and actors are milling around in ancient Greek outfits and masks. To fit in, Gregory is wrapped in a white sheet with holes cut out for his nipples. He looks at me over coffee and says, "All these people are *karpouzia*" (watermelons). Two weeks later, under an olive tree, he gives the best poetry reading of the season. He reads just one poem, perhaps his most famous, called *Marriage*. It is a magical moment at sunset. He reads it slowly, from his heart, and mesmerizes his listeners. Even the cicadas stay silent out of respect. [65]

After his successful stint on Aegina, there is little information regarding Corso and any further Greek adventures. Doubtless, he enjoyed many other (uncharted) visits, especially with Alan Ansen's open door policy; but without his letters, Gregory Corso starts to fade, phantom-like, from his own story… until only his Cheshire Cat smile remains. Spyros Meimaris remembered one last meeting in Athens, sometime in the late 1970s:

> It was certainly in the '70s, but it would have to be at a later date than when he was here for the Aegina School. It was a nightly visit at the apartment of one of Athens' coterie of English speaking queens—or should I say, homosexuals. I knew a few of them, but I wasn't on a very friendly basis with them, especially the one at whose apartment we were. I was with a girlfriend of mine at the time, and when Gregory was ushered in—a thing I didn't know about—I was very excited and glad to see him. I saw he came escorted by a girl who was a close friend of my own girlfriend. In fact, in the apartment and the party that was going on, were assembled some young men who

hang out with those girls. Young men who were hovering between sexual roles and attitudes and whom I didn't like, although I had met them a couple of times in Athens' dives or apartments where there was drug use.

I was amazed that Gregory recognized who I was—I had seen him around 1961 on two short occasions—and that he spoke to the assembled, sorry crowd on my behalf, something that didn't go well with them, they felt jealous. They, the young guys, had rolled a joint of hash and passed it to Gregory along with booze. Gregory, who seemed pretty much inebriated, proceeded to Bogart that joint for a long, long, long time.

He also expressed his adoration to my girlfriend and paid her many compliments, proposing, obviously not serious, if we could exchange girlfriends. I really don't remember much else of importance from that night onwards. I guess I left early because I couldn't stand the atmosphere of the old queens feeling and generating their jealous contempt for the celebrated Beat poet Gregory Corso. Wow! Gregory, sensitive to that atmosphere, at some point said, addressing the cohort of queens, "Hey, you guys, I don't have to worry giving a blowjob to someone because I am toothless, while you might bite the guy's dick!"

And you know what—all that time, Gregory *was* really toothless but charming nonetheless. [66]

There would be more returns, many doubtless lost to antiquity. In an email to the author, Yannis Zervos recalled: "Gregory returned to Greece at the invitation of USIS (the cultural center of the American Embassy) in December 1996. He gave a reading of his "Marriage" poem at the house of Bob Callahan, the Public Affairs officer of the American Embassy. He had by then risen in cultural importance. Still as charming as ever…" [67]

Corso returned to Greece two years later for Gustave Reininger's documentary *Corso: The Last Beat*, revisiting many of his old haunts in and around Athens, on the Acropolis,

at Delphi. The film won many accolades when Reininger premiered it at several independent film festivals, winning awards at Italy's prestigious Taormina Film Festival,
the Dubai International Film Festival and the Festival Litteratura in Mantua, where
it won best film. Sadly, the documentary became mired in legal issues and this significant record of Corso's final years has been denied an official release. With the death of
Reininger in 2012, it seems even less likely the film will see the light of day.

In his 1989 treatise, *Exiled Angel: A Study of the Work of Gregory Corso*, Gregory
Stephenson, author of *The Daybreak Boys: Essays on the Literature of the Beat Generation*,
described Corso's first visit to Greece as:

> a pilgrimage in homage to, and in quest of the original motive power of
> civilisation, the mythic consciousness of the ancient Greeks. Amid the
> artifacts and landscapes of the now outmoded vision of the classical world,
> he senses the imminence of a new, emergent vision. He hails a forthcoming
> "great event", a new age, and exhorts us to heed the new divine message
> and to strive to realize it: "Hear! Hermes is at the door / who will take the
> message?" [68]

That Greece left an indelible mark on Gregory Corso cannot be doubted. We have his
letters and Greek poems to thank for that. From "Reflection in a Green Arena" we learn:

> Ah good consoling Greece
> She was not the love I know
> Having crossed over into her world
> I became the sad unlove
> which separates us so

Burned out and sitting at the edge of wisdom, Corso had perhaps seen enough. He
turned more to his beloved Rome in his later years; but in his own small way, he too left

an indelible mark on Greece. During one of his Hydra visits, Corso left some permanent artwork in the home of Lily Mack, which remains there, chipped and peeling, to this day. In *How to be on a Greek Island—in Lockdown London,* Mack's granddaughter, artist and illustrator Katyuli Lloyd, recalled: "Gregory Corso, the beat poet, painted a large mural in our hallway, which still greets us every time we come back for a swim." [69]

Though he tried to destroy it, Corso also left the Alan Ansen triptych, which even now hangs proudly in the Athens Centre, a reminder of both his artistic abilities and his connection to the city.

He should also be given some credit for the Beat-Greek literary scene that sprang up in Athens in the wake of Alan Ginsberg's inaugural visit in 1961. Corso had been the first on the scene, almost two years before, imploring his friends to visit: "Hear! Hermes is at the door / who will take the message?" He was there—in on it—from the beginning.

And he left us his Greek poems: "First Night on the Acropolis," "Greece," "Some Greek Writings," "Reflection in a Green Arena"—collected in *Long Live Man* (1962), the dominant tone of which is, as Gregory Stephenson stated in *Exiled Angel*: "one of affirmation and celebration. Corso's optimism remains one that is neither naïve or facile, but of the kind which is achieved at the cost of recurrent inner-struggles and which is thus all the more ardent and genuine for having been so dearly purchased." [70]

There is a sense of unfinished business between Corso and Greece, a sense also that there is much more to know. As more pebbles are overturned, through snippets in biographies and memoirs, we might start to piece together a more precise picture of Corso's time spent in Athens and the islands, and his relationship with that country and its culture. In the meantime, we can reflect on his own words, spoken to Michael Andre in a 1972 interview for *Unmuzzled Ox* (later published in *The Whole Shot: Collected Interviews with Gregory Corso*): "I found that going back to Greece I was no longer awestruck by looking at the Acropolis and things like that. I think that's what gave me my opening when I was a kid, to see something in books, you know pictures of beautiful old stone and what not. The literature and the mythologies of ancient times grabbed me, but today no, it's more held down to what is going on, the present day. But I think it's no longer a sad thing. It's just a change of feeling I knew would happen." [71]

Source notes

(1) *Corso: The Last Beat* (2009), directed by Gustave Reininger, trailer available at Vimeo, <https://www.vimeo.com/>

(2) Bill Morgan, *The Beats Abroad: A Global Guide to the Beat Generation* (San Francisco: City Lights Books, 2015), p. 83.

(3) Gregory Corso, *Gasoline* (San Francisco: City Lights Books, 1958), p. 11.

(4) Gregory Corso, *An Accidental Autobiography: The Selected Letters of Gregory Corso* (New York: New Directions, 2003), p. 196.

(5) ibid, pp. 197-198.

(6) ibid, p. 206.

(7) ibid, p. 198.

(8) ibid, p. 199.

(9) ibid, p. 88.

(10) ibid, p. 208.

(11) ibid, p. 209.

(12) ibid, p. 210.

(13) ibid, p. 210.

(14) Bill Morgan, *The Typewriter is Holy: The Complete Uncensored History of the Beat Generation* (New York: Free Press, 2010), p. 165.

(15) Gregory Corso, Letter to Caresse Crosby, 1959 (The Caresse Crosby Papers, Special Collections, Morris Library, Southern Illinois University), Box 36, File 4.

(16) Paul Genoni, and Tanya Dalziell, *Half the Perfect World: Writers, Dreamers and Drifters on Hydra, 1955-1964* (Victoria: Monash University Publishing, 2018), p. 16.

(17) ibid, p. 17.

(18) Gregory Corso, *An Accidental Autobiography*, p. 210.

(19) ibid, pp. 211-212.

(20) ibid, p. 211.

(21) ibid, p. 211.

(22) Charmian Clift, *Peel Me a Lotus* (Sydney: Collins, 1959), p. 24.

(23) Charmian Clift, "Old Acquaintance Be Forgot" in *The World of Charmian Clift* (Sydney: Ure Smith, 1970), p.192.

(24) Gregory Corso, *An Accidental Autobiography*, p. 215.

(25) ibid, p. 213.

(26) ibid, p. 215.

(27) John Gray, *Straw Dogs: Thoughts on Humans and Animals* (London: Granta Books, 2002), p. 15.

(28) Gregory Corso, *An Accidental Autobiography*, p. 215.

(29) ibid, p. 218.

(30) ibid, p. 219.

(31) Amy Mims, "Professor Helen Sullivan's Buried Treasure" (2018). Available at: <http://arks.

princeton.edu/ark:/88435/dsp01836h467g> Accessed 29 July 2021.
(32) ibid. pp. 59-60.
(33) ibid, p. 60.
(34) ibid. p. 61.
(35) Gregory Corso, *An Accidental Autobiography*, p. 222.
(36) ibid, p. 222.
(37) ibid, p. 227.
(38) ibid, p. 230.
(39) ibid, p. 271.
(40) ibid, p. 271.
(41) ibid, pp. 271-272.
(42) ibid, p. 274.
(43) ibid, p. 276.
(44) ibid, p. 271.
(45) Allen Ginsberg, *The Letters of Allen Ginsberg* (Philadelphia: Perseus Books Group/Da Capo Press, 2008), p. 250.
(46) Spyros Meimaris, Email to the author, 20 May, 2021.
(47) ibid.
(48) Gregory Corso, *An Accidental Autobiography*, p. 280.
(49) Bill Morgan, *The Typewriter is Holy*, p. 221.
(50) Sinclair Beiles, interview with Gary Cummiskey in *Who Was Sinclair Beiles?* (Johannesburg: Dye Hard Press, 2014), p. 26.
(51) Eftychia Mikelli, "The Greek Beat and Underground Scene of the 1960s and 1970s." *CLCWeb: Comparative Literature and Culture* 18.5 (2016) Available at <https://doi.org/10.7771/1481-4374.2964> Accessed 28 August 2021.
(52) Leonidas Christakis, *A Different Kind of Art*. Volume 2 (Athens: Independent Publication, 1963).
(53) Gregory Corso, *An Accidental Autobiography*, p. 383.
(54) Samuel Delany, Email to the author, 28 June, 2021.
(55) Gregory Corso, *An Accidental Autobiography*, pp. 385-386.
(56) ibid, p. 386.
(57) ibid. p. 386.
(58) Bill Morgan, *The Beats Abroad*, p. 84.
(59) Elissa Schappell, "A Semester with Allen Ginsberg" in *The Paris Review Interviews: Beat Writers at Work* (London: The Harvill Press, 1999), pp. 241-242.
(60) Gregory Corso, *An Accidental Autobiography*, p. 405-406.
(61) George Scrivani, Email to the author, 20 May, 2021.
(62) Yannis Zervos, *Passage to Paradise: Hellenic Sketches of the Mind* (Alimos: Publications Hydroplane, 2019), pp. 163-164
(63) Brian Sidaway and Valerie Lloyd Sidaway, Email to the author, 23 May, 2021.
(64) Valerie Lloyd Sidaway, "Reflections on Hydra" in (ed) Helle V. Goldman's *When We Were Almost Young: Remembering Hydra through War and Bohemians* (Tromsø: Tipota Press, 2018), p. 130.
(65) Yannis Zervos, *Passage to Paradise: Hellenic Studies of the Mind*, p. 164.
(66) Spyros Meimaris, Email to the author, 19 June, 2021.

(67) Yannis Zervos, Email to the author, 1 July, 2021.

(68) Gregory Stephenson, *Exiled Angel: A Study of the Work of Gregory Corso* (Toronto: Hearing Eye, 1989), p. 45.

(69) Katyuli Lloyd, "How to be on a Greek Island—in Lockdown London", Available at: <https://www.katyuli.com/2020/04/29/how-to-be-on-a-greek-island-in-lockdown-london/> Accessed 29 January, 2022.

(70) Gregory Stephenson, *Exiled Angel: A Study of the Work of Gregory Corso*, p. 47.

(71) Gregory Corso, "An Interview with Gregory Corso" by Michael Andre (1972) reprinted in *The Whole Shot: Collected Interviews with Gregory Corso* (Massachusetts: Tough Poets Press, 2015), p. 54.

(This essay was originally published in the literary journal *Beatdom #22*.)

One of the most coveted artworks in Alan Ansen's art collection, the above triptych was painted by Gregory Corso in the late 1950s. According to Corso's friend, poet and translator Amy Mims, Ansen self-titled the painting "From the Crypt to the Cradle" and described it as a "Tintoretto-inspired adaptation of the Venetian history of Saint Mark and the stealing of the Saint's body from an Egyptian crypt." Ansen related how Corso suddenly became possessed and started slashing his own canvas with a knife, howling in agony: "No more monsters!"

Unbeknownst to Corso, Ansen rescued the damaged painting, had it stitched back together and smuggled to his home in Venice. When Ansen died in 2006, the triptych was repaired once more with the assistance of Belgian art historian Els Hanappe and was gifted to the Athens Centre. The triptych currently resides in the home of Yannis Zervos.

Photograph by kind permission of Yannis Zervos

The following is an excerpt from a work in progress, provisionally titled *My Ten Years at the Chelsea Hotel:*

Shadows Dancing Down the Street

by Dan Richter

I first met Gregory Corso in London at the huge Albert Hall poetry reading in 1965. I was one of the producers and read my own poetry. He was scruffy and bedraggled in a romantic poète maudit fashion. He had a permanent scowl that was a cross between an irreverent laugh and a smirk of disdain. He was completely wild and, from the first, I loved him. He was a Beat icon, and a good perhaps great poet.

"You've got to cut the fat from your poems Dan," he said after reading some of my poems. "They're good but they can be a lot better." I hung on his words. As he spoke, his whole body moved. You felt he was always a bit hungry, ready to devour whatever he could find, whether it be food, drugs, alcohol, women... In the man you could see the wild abused street kid from Little Italy who at seventeen had been sent to Clinton Prison in Dannemora for three years for stealing a suit. After prison, he had been liberated into a new life by his gift for poetry.

Gregory had been coming by the hotel room more and more. There would be the banter about poetry and the constant gossip about friends, but the main reason was food and dope. He rarely had any cash. There were stories that he would go up to Columbia to see his manuscripts in their collection and then steal some and take them down and sell them at the Gotham Book Mart for a bit of cash and then they would return them to Columbia.

He would laugh as he ate and talked at the same time. "I take back all I took," he would say with a laugh and toss his head like a pirate from Treasure Island. "Dan, do you have some bread? Let's get high. Christy has a place we can go up to on the Upper

West Side where we can get some smack."

I knew I shouldn't have, but my disease was telling me that just this time it would be OK to have another hit. Times had been tough and after all, I wasn't hooked even if I was sailing a bit close to the wind.

"In a bit Gregory, I got someone coming by with some cash to buy a few ounces of grass."

We giggled, rolled a joint, and as we smoked Gregory regaled me with the stories of his time in Dannemora prison.

"The old Italian hoods, they were Mafia guys, would look after me because I was an Italian kid. I was put in Lucky Luciano's old cell. It had books and a light switch. No one bothered me because these Mafioso guys were really tough and all the other inmates were afraid of them."

He threw his craggy head back as he toked the joint and his scraggy Medusa locks would flop about his face as he produced his gravelly laugh.

"I learned to ski," he went on. "There was this little sort of a raised area in the yard, and when it snowed, I made some skis out of barrel staves."

Later that evening with the dope deal done and some cash in my pocket we got on the 7th Avenue subway and took the Broadway local up to 34th Street and changed the express to 96th Street. We met Christy where he had told us to meet him at an apartment in a little building on Columbus Avenue just North of the Museum of Natural History called "Planetary Apartments." Excited and giggling we climbed the dim lit stairs to the 3rd floor with a combination of fear of who we would have to deal with and the anticipation of the rush and release that the shot of heroin would bring.

Christy opened the door of the apartment a crack and we could see his face looking out at us.

"Hey man, just you two, yeah?"

"Yah Christy, just us, me and Dan—let us in," said Gregory.

Christy was wiry and street rough. He had a changing face that seemed to be constantly evaluating what deceit to tell you next.

The studio apartment was dirty and devoid of any furniture, except a milk crate on the floor in the center of the room. On the crate were bottle caps whose bottoms were black with soot from the matches and lighters used to cook the junk in them. Against the walls were five or six fucked-up junkie friends of Christy's nodding out or staring into space.

"Who are all these guys Man, this is not cool. I thought you were alone," said Gregory.

"It be cool Man—relax. You want the shit or not?"

We gave Christy the money and took the little white packet.

"You got to do it here and leave me some," he said.

"Fuck that," said Gregory.

"Then give me those boots," he said, pointing to the tan kip leather Justin cowboy boots I was wearing.

Back-to-back we started moving slowly for the door trying to keep everyone in sight.

As we got to the door, Gregory said, "Go fuck yourself, Christy" and we were out the door and tumbling down the stairs without looking back.

Gregory was a true poetic genius, and it is hard to write about him during the period I knew him. Drugs and alcohol bring us all low, and as we descend deeper and deeper it is amazing what we call denial insulates us from the reality of our broken lives. Gregory and I running down Columbus Avenue, laughing and joking, exhilarated and high from our escaping intact from the shooting gallery, could not see what we had become.

Gregory, who as a youth had the potential to be one of America's most important poets of the 20th century, and I, who had starred in and choreographed the opening of *2001: A Space Odyssey*, could not see two reckless junkies whose lives and careers had been destroyed by drugs and alcohol. Shadows dancing down the street on our way to hell. The promise of our artistic gifts and our careers in shambles, our physical health decaying, and worst of all we were petty criminals who had betrayed our friends and families.

Or an Angel Come to the Door:
My Godfather Gregory Corso

by Kaarina Hollo

I was born in London on October 28, 1961, to the poets and translators Josephine Clare (1933-) and Anselm Hollo (1934-2013), and was to be baptised as a Catholic. In my parents' circle of friends and acquaintants, Catholics were scarce, and finding a godparent was proving tricky. The solution was to ask Gregory Corso. This is how my father described the situation years later, when asked to contribute to an online appreciation of Corso shortly before Gregory's death:

> Gregory performed his duties as godfather impeccably. Josephine's mother, a devout South German Catholic, would have been heartbroken if our daughter Kaarina had not been properly received into the church. At the time, GC was, literally, the only Catholic we knew. When I asked him about it, he said sure, he'd be glad to, but the next day he told me he had checked out the baptismal liturgy, and among the lines the godparent had to speak was one he wasn't so sure about: "I renounce Satan and all his works..." After all, Satan... especially Milton's take on him... But after another day's reflection, he agreed to do it, and I remember his giving the priest a tip the size of which made the fellow's eyes bulge. [1]

Corso's hesitation was non-trivial. His engagement with religion was complex and deep-rooted, and to publicly renounce Satan—particularly in his aspect of Lucifer, the rebellious angel—was something that needed some thought. As Art Buchwald reported in a 1958 interview (republished in *The Whole Shot: Collected Interviews with Gregory Corso*): "As a poet he said he's taken a vow of poverty, but he added: 'It's hard to live up to it because I like Lucifer too much.'"[2]

It seems however, that Gregory had moved on in his thinking by 1961, and that the christening marked a watershed, as he relates in an "open letter" written in March / April 1963, in response to a request by Brocard Sewell, editor of the *Aylesford Review*, for a poem for a special poetry issue. In a handwritten note on the typescript of the "open letter", Corso opined: "Yes, I feel this letter states my religious history as I would like it printed."[3] Concerning his thoughts around Lucifer and the christening, he wrote:

—and one more thing, dear fathers, now that I have the chance, I always used to see Lucifer in a silly romantic way, I saw him as a romantic figure, smart witty and wearer of cloaks, used to call him the first free thinker, the first rebel, etc; but this too back fired on me, I was not Luciferian, I was of the idea, romantically, yet I dreamed that I had given birth to a little red monster devil, it did not come from my body, yet it was on a table, and I felt that I had given birth to it, god o god I cry out against that, "This is not my Lucifer, my curly haired cloak wearing cavalier!" and so I gave him up, and had chance to redeem myself thanks to Hollo of Red Cats, I was asked to be godfather to his daughter, the priest had me recite the Apostles creed, in it I renounced Lucifer... [4]

Around this time, my father wrote an ebullient praise-poem for Gregory titled "He was here, is he where now?" A carbon copy among Anselm's paper is dated London, October 31, 1961, and I believe this to be the first time it has been published. I would imagine the original typescript was given to Gregory as a gift, although the hand-written annotation "53 lines" at the bottom (not visible in the scanned copy here) hints that it was intended for publication somewhere. It is not typical in its style of Anselm's poems of this period, and the long lines and fecundity of imagery are undoubtedly a response / homage to Gregory's work.

The poem relies on a simple and powerful rhetorical device (Is he X? Or is he Y?) with

Anselm Hollo:

--for Gregory Corso

HE WAS HERE. IS HE WHERE NOW?

            or is he the man from the Mountai
    eyes focussed on augur coals
for hundreds of nights
or was he the boy of the Boulevards
    exuding small flowers wherever he walks
among ladies
or is he the messenger all in black
    striding down a white glaring street
bells tolling tolling
mindless windless winter morning--
or is he the Sun's courtier
    making merry and tinkle amid the ice-cubes
and breasts of pure gold

            or was he the teller of truth
    in foggy and stifling Chelsea bars
cutting that air with charioteer voice
and whiplash of bitter fact
or is he the draughtsman of Clio--idle
    her pale long fingers as his crayons race centuries

reborn in a hostile land   or is he the great god Pan
    fluting his pipes on the stairs of a derelict house
on Primrose Hill
or is he the desperado hurling words bhulders rain
    hailing the black tall taxi cabs of pain in the endless
    street

                or was he the Indian
    brought back to amaze the half-naked Queen
or is he the voice to soothe both tiger and hummingbird
    mother and child and sweaty father
or is he the red flower of courage with wild burning petals
    and a warm hard mouth
for all happy lips
or is he the Angel come to the door
    the derrick lifting Blake from his grave
the Shepherd entrusted
    the Bearer of Christopher's Lamb

                or is he the hermit
furry omniscient worm in the World Mind Apple
or was he the Travellor and his Tale
    Rook Bird of Ages
and sole survivor of the City of Luz

            or was he simply the fastest
    man in the world
launching himself--
    and through the slow air--
and wheeling--
    a fiery basket through orchards
    leaving us at the roadside
    (groping glad groundsloths)
    shaking and dazed
        with a Vision of Speed-- --
                "Godspeed!"

London, 31st October 1961

an elision of the first element that plunges us into an ongoing monologue / dialogue / multilogue which takes the reader through 15 possible personas or ways of describing Corso. Gregory is represented as prophet or messenger come from the New World to the Old, as a redeemer and heir of the mystical greats William Blake and Christopher Smart. The Beats loved angels, and it is almost inevitable that this is one of the possible versions of Corso the poem offers us. The poem also contains a range of various mythological and literary allusions and references to Corso's Parisian stays. With the penultimate description of Gregory as a "fiery basket freewheeling through orchards," my father no doubt had in mind Gregory's next collection, which had the working title of *Apples*.

On a more personal note, the "derelict house on Primrose Hill" was almost certainly our own home at 80 Regents Park Road, which directly faced the park. If perhaps not strictly derelict, it was not luxurious, with a kitchen shared with at least one other family. "The mother and child and sweaty father" could be a reference to my appearance three days before the date of this poem. The Chelsea Bars section alludes to an incident related in Anselm's *Woodstock Journal* tribute, which starts in a Chelsea bar and ends up with the police having to send everyone home. The "desperado...hailing the black tall taxi cabs of pain" is of course evocative of such a night out as well.

Earlier in 1961, my father, Gregory and Tom Raworth had collaborated on *The Minicab Wars* (Matrix Press). In addition, Anselm had interviewed Gregory for Tom's planned series of poetry recordings under the label of Charge Records, which was to include "other 'first records' by Robert Creeley and Edward Dorn."A partial transcript of that interview was published in *Nomad 10/11* (1962) and reproduced in *The Whole Shot: Collected Interviews with Gregory Corso*. My father also kept a fuller version of the interview transcript, with the following previously unpublished final section, which any "young English beatnik poets" (or any other kind of poet for that matter) might find of some use:

ADVICE TO YOUNG ENGLISH BEATNIK POETS

What should they write about?

Well, there's the Zoo, they can write about the Giant Panda there-- they can write about Mini-Cabs, if they want to be social-- they can write about Days at School, if they went to a school—they can just write up their reminiscences of their teachers… They can write about what their mother does around the house—you know, like how she washes clothes, like a Vermeer painting almost—

They should really be what Keats said, God's Spies—they shouldn't spy on themselves, that is not spying, that's ratting—it's complaining, it's bugging people about them creepy selves.

A poet is supposed to See: and what he Sees, he puts within himself, and records outwardly, in Poetry. [5]

In the same letter, in which Anselm offers the interview for publication to Anthony Litten, he writes that 'Gregory C's new book, out from New Directions next spring, will be titled "APPLES" (letter from AH to AL, 21/11/61). This name was eventually abandoned, and *Long Live Man* arrived at through discussion with New Direction's James Laughlin.

I have in my possession a typescript with this handwritten note in my father's hand on the cover page: "Gregory's New Poems—APPLES copied 21.x.1961". It contains the following six poems: "Apples," "Man about to enter sea," "First Night in the White House," "Active Night," "A bed's lament" and "Nature's Gentleman". All of these poems are to be found in Gregory's *Selected Poems* (Eyre and Spottiswood, London, 1962), where they are listed as published in *Long Live Man* (New Directions, 1962). In actuality, only "Man about to enter sea" (under the title "Man Entering the Sea, Tangier"), "First Night in the White House" and "Active Night" were published in the latter collection (*Long Live Man's* "There Can Be No Other Apple For Me" is another version—differing in the last few lines from "Apples"). Somewhat confusingly, "The Bed's Lament", "Apples" and "Nature's Gentleman" are to be found under the "previously unpublished" heading in *Mindfield* (1989)—as are seven other of the *Selected* poems—and given the date 1962. For these three poems, at least, the date can be revised with certainty to 1961.

Anselm was involved in the publication of *Selected Poems*, insofar as he appears to have lent his copies of "three books by Gregory Corso" to the publisher, Eyre and Spottiswood. In a letter dated January 11, 1963, Maurice Temple Smith apologises to Anselm for the condition in which they have been returned to him, and offers to find clean replacement copies. I have two of these marked-up copies, *The Happy Birthday of Death* and *The Vestal Lady on Brattle* (which, interestingly, is inscribed "Lawrence Ferlinghetti (his copy)" in what appears to be LF's hand). Both are quite heavily marked, and reflect the changes made to "Greenwich Village Suicide" (omission of final line) and "Sea Chanty" (omission of second stanza) from *The Vestal Lady on Brattle,* and to "Notes After Blacking Out" (removal of two lines) from *The Happy Birthday of Death.*

It is not clear whether Anselm had any further hand in the preparation of *Selected Poems,* beyond loaning the books to the publisher. Anselm travelled to Paris from London in the summer of 1962 to spend some time with Gregory (and David Ball, a mutual friend), so the social side of the relationship certainly remained strong, as it did for many years after.

As a godfather, Gregory was more of an imagined and inspirational presence rather than a material one. I think I remember receiving a card from him as a teenager, and my copy of *Mindfield* is inscribed: "To my God-daughter / Gregory Corso / 1994". Some of his poems and his photo were in the poetry anthology we used in 11th grade high school English, and I think I read one aloud to the class (was it "Marriage" or "The Race"? I can't remember). I was immensely proud of having him as my godfather, and read and reread his poems many times.

As I grew older, I became more aware of the problematic nature of Beat attitudes towards women as people and as artists in their own right (see *Women of the Beat Generation: The Writers, Artists and Muses at the Heart of a Revolution*). [6] We know Gregory was aware of how women artists of his generation fared. Something my mother (who trained as an actress and is a poet and translator) told me about Gregory remains with me. She said that when Ginsberg, Orlovsky and Corso visited us in London in the early 1960s (and I think more generally), Corso was the one who really talked to her as a human being in her own right, and also helped out with tasks, e.g. clearing plates, washing up, etc. She told me this when I was much younger, but now, a day after my 60th birthday, I see how important this recognition of her humanity, of a woman's existence *in her own right*, was and is.

What do I have of or from him, as a godchild? Well, wherever it comes from I have a lifelong relationship with Catholicism, a love for St Francis and of poetry, and the knowledge that the world is eternally strange and wonderful, as are the words we use to try to express what we see in our spyings. I'd say that's more than enough.

(Thanks to Tamsin Hollo for making sure our father's papers were kept safe and for encouraging me to take this article a bit further; to Father Francis Kemsley, Prior of Aylsford Priory, for a copy of the *Aylsford Review*; and to Rick Schober for providing a copy of the *Nomad* article.)

Source notes

(1) Anselm Hollo, "Gregorio the Herald," *Woodstock Journal* (2000), http://www.woodstockjournal.com/corso6-18.html

(2) Gregory Corso, "Poetry and Religion: An Open Letter," *The Aylesford Review*, 5(3), (1963), p. 119.

(3) ibid, pp. 121-122.

(4) Gregory Corso, *The Whole Shot: Collected Interviews with Gregory Corso*, ed. Rick Schober (Arlington: Tough Poets Press, 2015), p. 24.

(5) Transcript of interview with Corso by Anselm Hollo, private collection of Kaarina Hollo.

(6) Brenda Knight, Anne Waldman & Ann Charters, *Women of the Beat Generation: The Writers, Artists and Muses at the Heart of a Revolution* (Berkeley: Conari Press, 1996), p. 141.

An Iconoclast at Naropa

by Kirby Olson

In 1977, I was twenty and had gone to study with the Beat poets at Naropa University in Boulder, Colorado. One morning my front door was open and Gregory Corso walked in.

"Whaddya got for food in here?" He asked in a growly voice.

My suite mate wasn't there. Her name was Barbara Milton. She was rarely around as she was a statuesque blonde with several boyfriends. I knew she had some eggs and there was a cast-iron pot. I had some Norwegian cheese. I asked Corso if he wanted an omelette.

"Yeah!" he said.

I made the eggs, although I didn't have permission to use the skillet. I had actually never made an omelette before, but tried to pretend I knew what I was doing. I cracked the eggs and spilled in four, added some Jarlsberg cheese and then put ketchup on it. Corso wolfed it down and then laid down on my couch.

"I heard you write poems," he said. "I will look at four of them now."

I ran downstairs and eagerly brought up four poems. I can only remember one of them, as it's the one he liked. They were all about colors. One was about lavender, and had ships and trees and other lavender things. It was the only unity. He didn't remark on it. Then there was this one:

The Beauty of the Living

I have often met the beauty of the living.
It was in the magenta sunset.
It was in the hummingbird.
It was a child reaching up to kiss his mother goodnight.

I wondered how Corso would react. Kids in all the classes were writing very destructive poems about the United States and the war in Vietnam, or about big messy sexual affairs they had had, or ranting about their parents. I had never had any experiences like those and I barely knew where Vietnam was. I was seventeen years old and lived in a self-reflexive universe that still held Jesus as the centerpiece of the universe. I loved my mom and dad, and I liked how pretty the world was. The poem seemed too simple. Corso said, "Top shot!"

He handed me that poem. I heard him use the phrase the rest of the summer. Whenever he would talk about a poet, any poet from world history, not just the students, he would try to ascertain the best poem by that writer. This, he would call the "top shot."

I asked him why he liked that poem the best. He took his glasses off his nose and stared at me as if he was about to beat me up. His face got red.

"Why? Why? Don't ask me why! Only an idiot asks why! What's the matter with you, Why?" He had a very strong New York accent. Now I had a nickname: WHY. I can't explain what it was he did. His voice would go extremely high like it was a piercing screech, and then suddenly he'd turn normal again, and his voice would rumble. To say the least, he was excitable, and could turn on you fast, and then like you again. It was very strange.

"Why?" I said, before I realized I had used the same word. He walked out of the apartment, disgusted, and never came in again.

I still wondered why Corso and Burroughs had liked the brief poem. I've never had it published, and it seems too simple. Also, Corso didn't have much of a relationship with his own mother, so maybe it was that. I loved my own mom, on the other hand. She was boss. I called her and told her about the interactions, but didn't tell her that Corso was always drunk. I read the poem he had liked to her and she said, "That's a good poem. Keep on going and meet more of the poets!"

About a week in, I was invited to a dinner party at a psychiatrist friend of Ginsberg's. His name was Steven Schoen. I had met him by the swimming pool. Ginsberg and [Peter] Orlovsky were there, as were Gregory Corso and his wife Jocelyn Rothschild, and their baby, Max. The party was in one of the Boulder Townhouse apartments. These were very simply designed. They had a circular white table just outside of a kitchen which had a counter connecting the cooking and refrigerator area with the seating area. It was crowded. I didn't know why I had been invited. The others did all the talking.

Corso was in a manic phase and talking about how he wanted to eat a cow's ocular nerve. He kept looking at me as if my shock were some gauge of his success. I expressed shock as well as I could. He dug into the beef, and talked about his love for animals as he sloppily chewed the flesh. He didn't have many teeth left, and his face was a patchwork of collapsed veins. He was an inveterate drug user, but could occasionally rise above this needle-marked life and attain elegance in diction and dress. Then he would slop back into craziness.

His wife was a genuine Rothschild. She was glamorous and skinny, with a beautiful long dress and lush red hair. She was also drunk. She kept talking about wanting to eat an ocular nerve, and kept looking at me for shock. I dutifully complied. I remembered a phrase from a book about the surrealists which said "to shock the bourgeoisie" was their whole mission. I realized I had been invited to represent the bourgeoisie.

Ginsberg was busily eating salad. He didn't know what to do with Corso and his wife, but was trying to make sure their toddler, Max, had something to eat. Corso had filled a baby bottle with red wine, and the tiny boy was sucking on the nipple. I wanted to say something, but didn't. Corso spotted my objection.

"I am a God!" He screamed. "My son is drinking ichor! What do you think, Why? Why? Why?"

I knew I had no standing at that table, but would have preferred the boy was drinking milk.

Orlovsky spoke. "Allen," he said in a very rough voice that sounded like Brooklyn. "Dja hear that Bob Hope filled an auditorium with his own money just to have listeners? He's addicted to getting laughs, Al."

This didn't sound right to me. Whatever had gotten into Orlovsky's head had been filtered through an extremely primitive educational background that was not quite capable of critical thought, but I didn't want to argue with him. He was wearing a white shirt that was twisted behind to expose his abs, which were fairly tight. His graying hair was also tied back in a bun. I think he had probably read something in *National Enquirer* or perhaps in the *Post*, and hadn't been able to figure out the truth. Ginsberg and Corso pretended that Orlovsky hadn't spoken and went on eating. Orlovsky had a large, powerful, manly body. White shorts, relatively clean, and the flip-flops, completed his outfit.

The host's wife was going to show up the following day, and he mentioned this to move us along. "Oh?" Everyone nodded out of politeness, and went on chowing down.

Suddenly, Orlovsky said, "*Star Wars* is coming on, Al. Let's go." We walked about a half mile to a cinema up near the University of Colorado bookstore, and went in. I didn't like science fiction, and never understood the *Star Wars* craze. The Beats ate popcorn noisily and offered me some popcorn. I wasn't sure that they had washed their hands, so I declined. After, we all walked back. They were somewhat excited about the film, and Corso had loved the bar scene with its exotic alien animals and said every bar he had ever been in looked just like that one.

Corso's wife may have had her own income, but she continually collapsed. She collapsed in the parking lot outside my apartment one morning and had her beautiful face stuck to the hot macadam. I went to get Gregory and he said, "Jesus Christ, Jocelyn!" He threw her over his shoulder like a sack of potatoes and carried her back to his apartment like a caveman.

"Thanks, Why!" Gregory cried.

In classes, Ginsberg spoke from memory about his life with the Beats. Corso, on the other hand, assigned books. He assigned the Sumerian epic *Gilgamesh*, as well *as At-Swim-Two-Birds*, by Flann O'Brien, and *Flatland: A Romance of Many Dimensions*. I read all of the books before the class in anticipation of his discussion of them. He never said anything about any of the books. He came to class very drunk and proceeded to insult the students. Corso's class was called Socratic Rap. He had apparently read the Plato *Dialogues* and thought that it meant he could get drunk and hold forth on any topic. Basically, he tried to go too far, and then would pull back, but it was personal. He would make fun of our haircuts or our clothing, or cite a poem, and dare anyone to place it. "No one here even knows the Flemish landscape painter Peter de Witte." Later, I looked this painter up, and there are no specific works that survive by him, but he is mentioned in the histories.

Corso was useless in front of a classroom. It was only when you got him by yourself that he made any sense. I only got confusion in his class. He seemed flabbergasted by the students, and looked around wildly at us, and yelled and whispered and ranted and raved. He tried to make us go crazy with sick images at times, but I didn't feel any logic.

I went with him later that summer to a bar in downtown Boulder. I was hanging out with my suite mate, the skinny blonde named Barbara Milton, when he had come in to my apartment, but this time to see her. Someone suggested we walk to a bar about two blocks away. At the bar, he began to talk about geometry in poetry. He discussed the poem by Jacques Prevert in which the disciples' plates at the Last Supper are said to have been behind their heads. Corso began to talk about circles, and mentioned a line by Hans Arp. "A circle amuses itself." He then moved on to a discussion of Edgar Allan Poe's poem about a moat with shadows that are infinitely deep. He said that nothing finite can be infinite. He looked at me then, and said, "You're going to ask WHY? Aren't you? WHY? WHY? WHY?"

The abuse suddenly stopped. He drank the rest of his Brandy Alexander, but the bartender cut him off. "Can you buy one for me?" he pleaded. I was only twenty, so I couldn't.

Barbara and I walked out with Corso. It was a nice, dry summer evening in Boulder. The sky was dim, at twilight. Corso took a shine to my pretty suite mate and reached up toward a quarter-moon and said, "With this gift, I thee wed." They went back to his place. I went to mine. She came back about ten minutes later and said he had fallen asleep.

Corso was an iconoclast. He attacked the feminist movement. He also attacked the Buddhists. He reminded me somewhat of what I had read about the crazy Athenian philosopher Diogenes who chose to live in a bathtub because he wanted to be as flexible as a mouse he had once seen. One Buddhist said that he thought sharing was a good idea. Corso moved in and shared the man's groceries and bed, and said that he also thought it was a good idea.

Ginsberg was big on non-attachment but he was also an inveterate collector. He collected everything and had a huge archive. One day Corso smashed a priceless collection of Ginsberg's vintage jazz records. When Ginsberg came back to his apartment and found them shattered all over the floor, he asked Corso why he had done this. Corso said, "To help you attain enlightenment! You're too attached to some things!"

The Biography I Never Wrote

by Gerald Nicosia

I first met Gregory Corso in July, 1977, at the Naropa Institute in Boulder, Colorado. I remember thinking he was an "old man," which is hilarious to me now, since Gregory was 47 then and I am 73 now! But at the time I was only 27 years old. My first real interaction with him was at the Varsity Apartments, and I was appalled at his style of parenting his young son Max, who was about a year old. Gregory's parenting style was to completely ignore his young son, who was running about naked wherever he pleased, and sometimes coming perilously close to the edge of a second-floor terrace. One of the more meaningful conversations I had there that summer was with a very pretty young woman named Lisa Brinker, who told me she wanted to marry Gregory because it would allow her to care for Max. And of course, a couple of years later that is just what she did.

Gregory was scary. He was fast-talking, with an even faster mind, and came on like an Italian gangster. Even the tough young studs were wary of him. I remember a couple of students that reminded me of Hawkeye and Trapper John (tall, self-assured, wise-cracking and dominating young men) who were trying to get the best of Gregory. They were taunting him about how poorly he dressed, how poor he looked in general—in need of a haircut and a shave almost all the time.

"You think I'm poor?" Gregory responded. "I could get a hundred grand by the end of the month, if I wanted."

At first the young guys started to jeer at this boast. But Gregory spun their heads around.

"All I have to do is send a proposal to some big New York publishing house for my autobiography, and I'll bet you I have a hundred grand advance by the end of the month. You want to bet me on this? Come on! I'll take your money."

And I watched the young hotshots turn tail with their heads down. One said to the other, "He probably COULD get a hundred grand right now, if he wanted it."

On another afternoon, I glimpsed a different Gregory, as he led a kind of Socratic poetry class in the backyard of two of Naropa's administrators, Bataan and Jane Faigao. Gregory had the students sit in a circle, with him standing in the center, and he would focus on the various students as different points came up in his conversation. Most of the students were aspiring poets, and Gregory had them all hanging their heads when he asked which of the students had memorized some of their poems. None of them had.

"A real poet memorizes at least some of his most important poems," he told them. And then he demonstrated by quoting from memory some of his own best works.

He was funny, sometimes cruelly so, as he skewered person after person, finding the weak spot in each one of them. He pointed at me, and said, "This guy looks like the Son of Sam!" My face turned red as the whole class burst into laughter. But then, as he often did, when he saw he'd gone a little too far and had actually hurt someone, Gregory tried to make it better, to lessen the blow. "But he knows about Melville and Shakespeare," he said, again looking at me, "so I think he's okay."

Gregory's talk that afternoon was far-ranging, as he quoted authors from all countries, all times. His knowledge staggered me, especially considering he hardly had any formal schooling at all. Elvis Presley had just died, and Gregory got the whole class engaged by demanding to know whether or not Presley deserved the title of "King," and what it meant to be king. I thought to myself, *This guy (Corso) seems to be rehearsing for the role of king himself.* And in a way I think he was. And I think it was one of the private bitternesses of his life that he always had to stand in the shadow of Ginsberg, Burroughs, and Kerouac, because in many ways he was their better—had a quicker intellect, and often more graceful poetic lines.

It's hard to squeeze a friendship of twenty years into one short essay, so I'm going to try to just hit the highlights.

When I moved to San Francisco in 1979, Neeli Cherkovski quickly became my best friend. Since Corso was living in Neeli's railroad flat on Harwood Alley then, I got to spend a lot more time with Gregory, and began to really get to know him. His flair for drama was always present. One of his most famous poems was "Ode to Coit Tower," and I remember Gregory leaning out of Neeli's window and pointing up toward the tower, "Keep her pure, boys, keep her pure!" I also remember his almost non-stop practical joking. One day when Neeli was talking to Harold Norse on the phone, Gregory took the handset, and began telling Harold, "I lost my fame, Harold! I don't know what I'm going to do." Harold was suckered in completely, and was prepared to rush up to North Beach right away to comfort Gregory!

I'll always remember New Year's Day, 1980. I was the only one with a car, and so I was the designated driver when we went out to the ocean to watch the movie MOLIERE at the Surf Theater. The car held me, Neeli, Raymond Foye, Corso, and Lisa Brinker (Max was probably with Lisa's mother). I'd never seen anyone that restless in a movie theater. Corso was in and out to the lobby more than a dozen times—maybe smoking pot or drinking from a flask of brandy in the cinema john. He would badger Neeli every time he'd have to climb over him to get back to his seat, and Neeli put up with that abusive treatment in a way he probably wouldn't have from someone else. After the four-and-a-half-hour movie, I remember Corso insisting I find somewhere that he could get vodka. He was like a tyrant, and we were all intimidated by him. But the funny thing was, he was afraid of my mother! I drove out to our house on 44th Avenue, and told him we could get some vodka in her kitchen. And he said, quietly, "I'm not going in there—let's go somewhere else."

The thing I most remember from that night, though, was his tenderness toward Lisa. It was a side of him I rarely saw, and it was not common in his dealings with women. I began to think he really loved her—and maybe he did. But no woman could put up for long with his lifestyle—endless rounds of booze, drugs, and manic activity—and Lisa was no exception. They separated not long after that.

One thing that never failed to surprise me was that I was almost always spared from his verbal brutality. He called me the "Owl," and would defend me if others attacked my shyness and reluctance to speak up. "Nicosia's watching everything," he'd say respectfully. Many times he referred to the fact that we were both Italian, and I began to see that

that was a bond he respected. But I think there was something else too. He would sometimes chide me for writing Kerouac's biography when, according to Gregory, I should
have been writing his. And I think he harbored the secret hope that someday I would
write his biography. But in those days it was a hopeless proposition. The way I work,
which is endless field research, it would have required a sizable advance, and at that time
Gregory's stock had nearly hit bottom in the literary world. No publisher would have
put up even five thousand dollars for a biography of Corso, and to do a good book, I
would have needed a lot more than that.

I remember so well a long evening, night, and early morning I spent with Gregory
in North Beach—probably at least eight hours, and hands down my best time with him
ever. One evening we met at Little Joe's on Broadway and Columbus—it was where the
well-known photographer Marc PoKempner took a photo of us together—for a pasta
dinner, and where he almost got thrown out for openly drinking from his pint of gold
tequila ("the ichor of the gods," he called it) at our table. After dinner, Gregory had nowhere special to go, and I told him I'd like to spend the evening with him, "to learn what
you can teach me." He told me I could be his companion for the night as long as I kept
paying the bills and bar tabs, and I agreed to that deal—probably the best educational
arrangement I ever entered into!

The night with him was magical. We kept meeting fascinating people, like Austrian
writer Jakov Lind at the Bohemian Cigar Store (a dark, dive bar). And Gregory had a
fountain of fascinating stories. He told how, though many people thought he disliked
Neal Cassady, he had spent one of his best afternoons riding around San Francisco
while Neal drove the car, and they tested each other's "check-out technique." Each one
would try to do a complex description of something they saw—for instance, "You see
that chick on the corner, she knows she's not very pretty, but she's trying to act like she
is"—and then the other one would find some other observation to try to top him with.

That night he showed tenderness toward me that I never forgot. He asked me how I
had started writing, and I told him I had started writing stories and poems when I was
eight years old. Gregory said, "I started at eight too." Intimidated, I said, "Yeah, but

you've become a great writer. I'm nowhere near where you are!" And he looked at me like a gentle Italian father and said, "Don't worry about it. Just keep doing it, and you'll get there."

True to his word, when my pockets were empty, he said goodbye and headed off by himself.

There were other nights, of course, that were not so ethereal. I remember a night at Neeli's flat when Corso was drunk as a skunk, and horny as a goat. He got mad at Neeli for something, picked up Neeli's wooden dining table, and flung it upside-down with dishes crashing on the floor. Then he opened his fly, pulled out his small, very dark, uncircumcised cock, and demanded, "Which one of you is going to give me a blow-job?" He found no takers.

There were tragic times too. One year around Christmas, Gregory, drunk as usual, got into a scuffle with some San Francisco cops, who had a notorious grudge against beatniks. Instead of backing down or deferring to them, Gregory called them every name in the book. The cops locked him up for several days, and beat him badly in his cell. I saw Gregory when he had just gotten out of jail, and his face was covered with infected red sores. People kept asking him what had happened, and he seemed too ashamed to talk about it—for once in his life, at a loss for words.

I remember so well when he was courting Kaye McDonough, a fine poet, but also someone whose finances he knew he could live off of for a while. These were the early 1980s, the days before cellphones, and Corso would monopolize the payphone in the Caffe Puccini on Columbus, coaxing her with all his poetic riffs. I didn't like it because Kaye was a good friend of mine, and I knew that in the end he would abuse her badly, which he did. There was one happy result, though; Kaye bore his last child, his son Nile. I had the honor of being the person who drove her and Nile home from UCSF Hospital, after she gave birth.

Perhaps the most meaningful talk I ever had with Gregory was in June 1995, in New York City, when NYU was holding its famed Jack Kerouac Conference. At the demand of John Sampas, Jan Kerouac had been dragged by police out of that conference before she could speak to the audience. She had wanted to tell the attendees about two major libraries that wanted her father's papers, since the Sampas family was claiming they had to sell Kerouac's papers to dealers and collectors because no library wanted them. Jan was deeply embittered that she was not allowed to speak at a conference about her father, and so I began circulating a petition asking that she be allowed back into the conference.

David Stanford, the editor from Viking Penguin, which was Sampas's publisher, was running around the room telling people not to sign the petition—and a lot of people, including Joyce Johnson and Anne Waldman, took his advice and refused to sign it.

I walked up to Gregory with my long, tattered roll of paper, and asked if he would sign it. And he said, "Sure, of course I'm going to help my friend's daughter." (I still have that paper roll, with Gregory's signature on it, if anyone disbelieves me.)

But Gregory did more than sign it. He was clearly touched, close to tears. This was only a little more than five years before his death. He told me, "The thing I regret most in my life is that I didn't do more for my own kids."

And of course, in a final irony, or maybe actually an act of healing, it was one of his neglected children, his daughter Sheri Langerman, who took care of him in the last painful months when he lay dying of cancer.

The other day, going through my archives, I found a post card from Kaye and Gregory from Paris in 1983. It was written on the back of a Louvre postcard of the Winged Victory. Most of the words were Kaye's, and she told how happy they were together, how life now seemed easier for both of them than it ever had before. I am glad Gregory had at least some moments like that in his hard life. I only wish that one could have lasted.

Poem for Gregory Corso's Ashes in the English Cemetery in Rome

by Gerald Nicosia

Dear Gregory, as long as I knew you
They were throwing you out of places
I watched Bob Levy
Normally a kind man
Give you the bum's rush out of City Lights
Yelling, "We want your books here
But not *you!*"
(There was a rumor you'd broken in one night
And rifled the cash register
For the royalties they forgot to pay you
But you couldn't prove it
By me.)
I saw your name in concrete outside Vesuvio's
Meaning you were permanently eighty-sixed
For going up to a cute woman and
Telling her, with an impish grin
"I'd like to eat your cunt!"
One night at Dante's Bar
(how ironic)
When you'd gotten a little rambunctious
They again threatened to toss you out
And you told them that if they did
You'd come back with "a pistola ...

A Roscoe," and teach them a lesson
The barkeep threatened back,
"We got plenty of pistole of our own"
And you told him, "You dummy,
I'm not talking about a real gun,
I'm talking about the hot lead
In my mind!"
Now I hear they're about to evict
Your ashes
From the English Cemetery in Rome
Where I sat on your marble tombstone
And played with the feral cats
Who came by all day long to
Pay homage
To your catlike grace
They say you're not paying
Your rental bill
For the cemetery plot
On time
But who's paying the bill
For Keats and Shelley
Who rest beside you?
Ah, Gregory, I hope those
Small-time thugs who
Shake down the dead
Wake up some night
With the hot lead of your mind
Scalding their dreams
Giving them endless nightmares

And teaching them the biggest lesson of all
That only the truly
And forever dead
Would dream of
Digging up
Someone who is still alive
Underground.

(First published in *Beat Scrapbook* by Gerald Nicosia (Coolgrove Press, 2020). Reprinted by kind permission of the author.)

with Philip Whalen

©Christopher Felver

131

with Lawrence Ferlinghetti

Allen Ginsberg, Gregory Corso and William S. Burroughs

with Bob Kaufman

133

with Alan Ansen, Athens. Photo by Lisa Brinker

© 1967 Gérard Bellart at
Cold Turkey Press

Gregory Corso, Maestro Poet, ancient herald's wand pin, messenger-god Hermes Caduceus near his pen, a quiet afternoon in "The Kettle of Fish," an old bar in Greenwich Village under whose sign Kerouac used to drink. Gregory called me to join him, we spent a few hours talking till supper time, tired he took cab home to Horatio Street, March 13, 1995. I showed him poems by 19 year old new poet, he liked them too., 1995. Photo: Allen Ginsberg, © Allen Ginsberg Estate

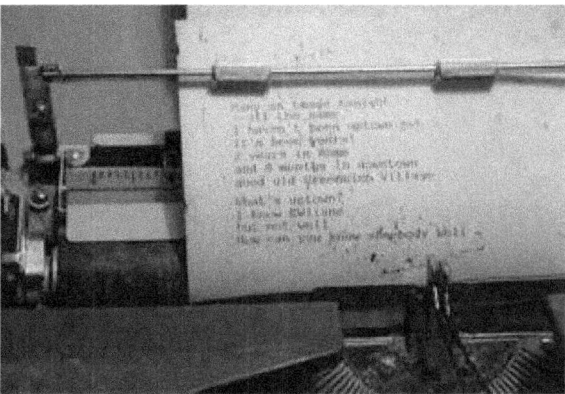

in Rome 1989 with the poet Amelia Rosselli

draft poem on Gregory's typewriter

Gregory at the rare book room in N.Y.

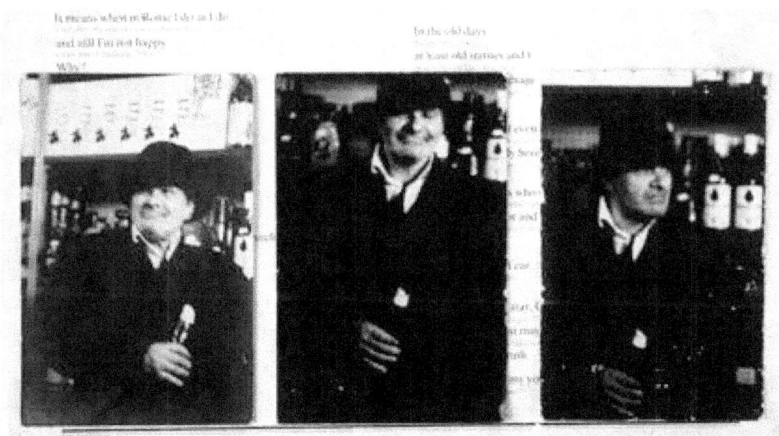

Gregory in the Vineria of Campo dè Fiori, print collage on his poem about Rome

All photos ©Dario Bellini

```
Sicily not Italy
Italy finish,
Palermo tragico
St Stepano bello       knows he
 A young rich man will die
He makes beauty
                ^
        and asks me w hy?
Me, I'm dying too...
In view  of all this
the account of w hat happens in life
        may be possibly true--
I say:: repair your houses
and attend the sow ing of your land
We can sw im the Straits of Messina anytime--
When a guy like me shifts the ground
it's not w ithout purpose--
I'm always getting in trouble w ith the Italians
my w ords do not mean what they appear to mean
                                      cross
Did you ever cross in a boat to Attica?
Who's unable to avoid paying?
The older you are the faster you are getting older
--in your desire to serve your interests
        I shant destroy your cold ovens
from my own coffers
    I give you 3 Darics
and love
```

Draft of poem left behind before Gregory's trip in Sicily to write on the "Room of the golden boat" at Fiumara di Arte (archive Dario Bellini)

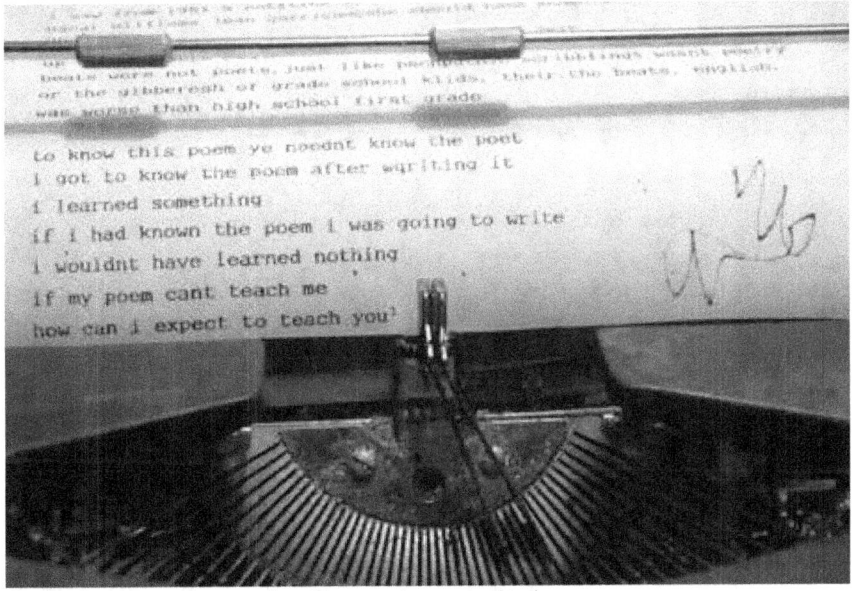

mix of pictures (enlarged contacts) of Gregorio with friends in Rome 1989

draft of poem on poetry (on Gregory's typewriter)

Feelings A Long The Piurara D'Arte

gregorio corso

From the material that doesn't exist

I entered a maze halfway

came out and ran up a blue axe

then ended up descending in a cave--

~~Elsewhere~~ Tired, I passed a hotel unmade

and dreamed a final home there--

The river runs dry to the sea

and a window opens the sky

I wonder if I'll ever see

a purple cow fly--

Here in Sicilia

God, Christ, Madonna,

She the mother of her father

daughter of her son--

Elsewhere; the divine red star of Marx

is dimming--

Long ago Xerxes surveying his vast divisions

cried: In 100 years they'll be no more!

first page of a draft poem of feelings in Sicily

at the Roger Richards rare book room in Greenwich av. N.Y. 1990 (© Dario Bellini)

Gregory Corso with son Max Orfeo Corso and William S. Burroughs. Photo by Ruth Brinker

Typing at Rare Book Room, N.Y. 1990 (© Dario Bellini)

Gregory Corso, Poetus Magnus in his alchemic Attic room 9 Rue Gît-Le-Coeur, dormer window half-block from the Seine; Holbein-Rembrandt postcard faces & Notre Dame stained glass window cards pinned to wall. Gregory half-smiling magician work-mixer with cloak & staff was writing Happy Birthday of Death's "Bomb, "Army," "Hair" & "Death," Peter and I lived in front room downstairs, Burroughs on floor below, Paris 1957. Photo: Allen Ginsberg, © Allen Ginsberg Estate

Gregory in Roma, 1986 © Robert Yarra

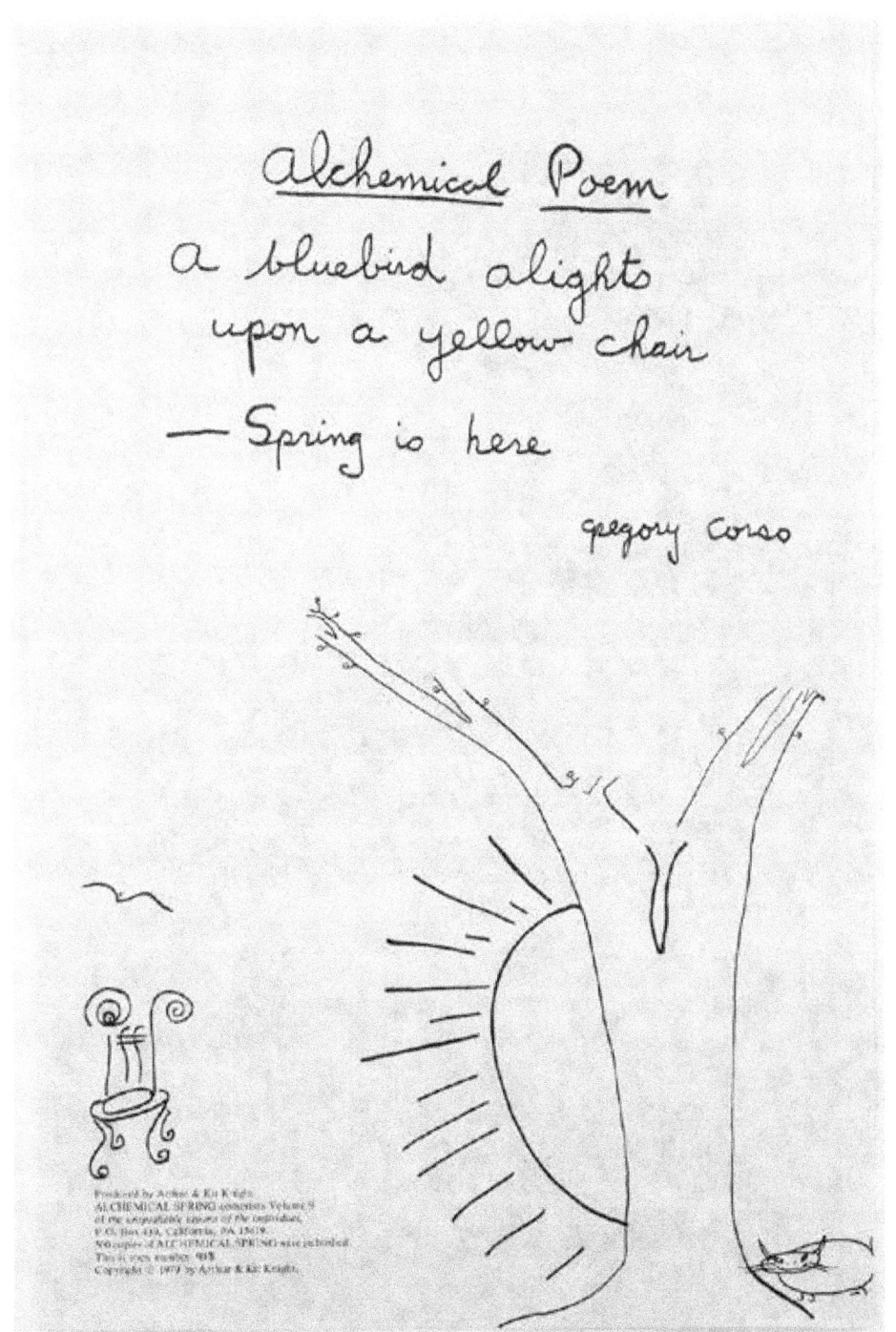

Alchemical Poem

a bluebird alights
upon a yellow chair

— Spring is here

gregory corso

Produced by Arthur & Kit Knight.
ALCHEMICAL SPRING constitutes Volume 9
of the unpublishable works of the individual.
P.O. Box 439, California, PA 15419.
900 copies of ALCHEMICAL SPRING were included.
This is copy number 913
Copyright © 1979 by Arthur & Kit Knight.

Gregory Corso and Max Orfeo Corso, San Francisco, 1979 ©Raymond Foye

This piece appears in its entirety in the *LARB Print Journal: No. 19,* Sept. 7, 2018.

She-Stag and the Tiger of Wanawutu
Remembering Gregory Corso

by Kaye McDonough

Gregory Corso and I met in the fall of 1977 in front of City Lights bookstore, then the hub of North Beach life. Its proprietor, poet and publisher Lawrence Ferlinghetti, asked me, "Do you even know who you were with?" I, a mere mortal, hardly knew how to respond. Gregory himself used to ask me, "Do you know who you're with?" He would answer that question himself: "You don't even know who you're with." Then, in an aside to an invisible audience of his gifted peers, living and dead, he'd add, "She doesn't know." Brutal. Just brutal.

Gregory Corso and Kaye McDonough at the Medici Fountain in the Luxembourg Gardens, Paris 1983 © John Geluardi

Gregory and I lived together off and on, and off again, and on, during the first half of the 1980s. In 1985, I left with our son, Nile, who was then eight months old. If you look at the dedication of Gregory's *Herald of the Autochthonic Spirit*, which came out during those years, he names three children: Miranda, Cybele, Max; and their four mothers: Sally, Belle, Jocelyn, Lisa (Jocelyn, later a suicide, was Max's birth mother, but Lisa Brinker raised him). Gregory was not yet counting his oldest daughter, Sheri, who surfaced as a surprise in 1985, or Nile, who was not yet born. Being the mother of one of Gregory's children was not necessarily a distinction, nor an entitlement to Beat grandeur. I mention it because I have always felt that I was in good company among those women and also because I now understand that I was lucky to have come out of the experience somewhat intact. At the very least, I was mad for Gregory, and I didn't die from it.

I've often been told, and have often told myself, that Gregory—though he certainly did exist—was probably not who I thought he was. The poet Bob Kaufman once called him "The Tiger of Wanawatu" and, less warmly, "The Poetry Mafia." Gregory may, in fact, have been a New York street hustler and con man, though I don't like to think that was the case. Of course, even if that were true, it would be only a piece of it. The Greeks knew. Oedipus himself did his best to be blind. Maybe Tiresias was more on the right track. People tend to be the person we experience them as being—to me, Gregory was my Greek mythology guy, my living, breathing Poet with a capital P. He was better than Byron or Shelley (notice I don't say Keats), I now understand, because he was alive, very much so.

Even years after Gregory and I met at City Lights, I didn't know much about him. In fact, he remained mysterious to most people. My oldest, closest poetry friend Alix and I speculated about where he lived, but no one seemed to know. He'd come out to the cafés first thing in the morning. We'd see him come and go all day and then he'd disappear. I had heard tales though, about his middle-of-the-night visits and alcohol-fuelled rampages. He was periodically 86'ed from many of the bars and cafes in the neighborhood but somehow charmed his way back to all but a few.

Painting by Gregory Corso, courtesy of Kaye McDonough

One day, Gregory wanted to look at the ocean and asked me for a ride. When we came back to North Beach, Gregory asked me to leave the car unlocked—a strange request. Why would I leave my car unlocked on the street in San Francisco? His answer was quite matter of fact. If he wasn't going to sleep in my car—his Pullman for the night— he was going to sleep in someone else's. No wonder he got up early. That night I left it unlocked.

One night at dinner, Gregory turned on me because I wouldn't let him come up to the house to "take a shower" (his usual test—every time I see him we have to go through his will-you-let-me-into-your-house-do-you-really-love-me test and every time I say, "No.") Every time he says, "You'd let George [Scrivani] and you won't let me." He turned to Alix to say, "She's a cunt' (meaning me). Alix answered, 'No, she's a deer," then she spelled it for him, "D-E-E-R"—meaning I was skittish and easily frightened. Gregory answered that I was a "She-Stag." As we parted, he said to me, and to no one present, in that way he had, suddenly taking the conversation into dream realm: "When all the poems are carbon because they've been burned and you're at the Garden, you jump on the She-Stag's back and ride away."

One of our early trysts was not in my Montgomery Street apartment but a different one belonging to another woman he was romancing at the time, someone we both knew. I am glad that I knew none of this. Fortunately, she was at work and remained there, sparing the three of us an awkward encounter. Gregory liked to say that this was "the beginning of our romance." But we actually had many beginnings: there was one at the doctor's office where he pretended to be blind, another at a poetry reading where he spat in his hand, to name a few.

I remember well our discussion of the tattoo on his upper arm. This was the first time I had ever seen it (it was his only one) and, to me, it looked like a stoplight. It was shaped in a rectangle standing on its short end, with two circles inside, one red and one green, with a sort of cord hanging from it.

"A stoplight?" Gregory was aghast at the suggestion he would have anything that banal. "Don't you know," he'd ask rhetorically with that typical inflection of his, the emphasis on "know." "She doesn't know," he'd say again in an aside to that same invisible audience of his same gifted peers, living and dead, "That's the scribe's palette. Thoth's palette. Don't you get it? … Check it out."

During that same encounter, he showed me one of his scars where a bullet had grazed him during a robbery attempt. I also noticed that he had deep claw-like scars on his lower inside arms and on his legs from the knees down. "I had a pet ocelot," Gregory told me, and I was gullible enough to believe him. With Gregory I thought that anything was possible. I can see how some might think I was simply a dope. The truth was that Gregory had collapsed veins from years of drug use.

When Gregory felt well disposed toward someone, that person was "his": "I do so love my George"; "I do so love my Max"; "I do so love my Kaye (me)" and so on. When he saw me washing clothes in the sink or mopping the floor, he would smile and say with great affection, perhaps with a nod to my German heritage, "My Brunnhilde," making us both laugh.

In thinking about his own heritage, Gregory liked to say that poets and writers he knew went to "your Yales and your Harvards" (pronounced "HAH-vahds" in his heavy New York accent), but "your Gregory went to the School of Hard Knocks." Titles were reserved either for those he most revered or for those he most scorned. God he addressed with reverence: "Ah, Miss God!" If he were in a really toxic state, he would sometimes call himself God. "How do you handle being God?" he would ask and then answer, "By being a total fuck-up." If Gregory suddenly addressed someone as "Mister," with the emphasis on the first syllable, let that person beware.

Gregory once described the soul as a "white heart made of air." This is the most perfect description of a soul that I have ever heard.

For most of our years together, we slept separately. Or at least, I slept. I had a job and wanted to keep it. He was up most of the day and night smoking. I would periodically see him with his eyes "closed." He "saw" me but only nodded, then returned to his dream state. The ashtray full of burnt matches and the little blue Mexican glass full of water on the kitchen table were the telltale traces of his habit. When he was in such a state, Gregory would sometimes sit up in his bed, or lie flat with his eyes closed, and slowly wave his arms in the air as he twirled his fingers. At those times, he was completely oblivious to the outside world. His dislocation from reality was sometimes so extreme and shocking that I would feel as if I were out of my own body too, just witnessing the scene.

One of the few times I ever saw Gregory sleeping peacefully was in Amsterdam. Even during that dreamy sleep, he would wake up every two hours or so. Was he human? In *Elegiac Feelings American,* he wrote: "I dream in daytime much too somber / to greet the angels / at my velvet shredded door". One of my light-hearted journal entries from this period reads: "Night flies in on black wings of Terror across the agitated sky."

A recurrent dream Gregory had in prison (he was jailed at Dannemora for theft at 17, though he had lied about his age, claiming he was 18) was of a small girl glowing in a dark hole. The day he was released from jail, he took a train back to New York, and on it was a beautiful little girl, just as if his dreams had made her manifest. He was captivated with her and watched her for his entire journey back to the "real" world. I've often thought that Gregory's vision of the little girl lighting the darkness revealed his own interior radiance—what he was able to preserve, or salvage, from his Dickensian childhood.

Soon after prison, Gregory was seated at his typewriter writing poetry, as he often did then in his Greenwich Village room. This day he was seated with his back to his locked door when he heard someone knocking on it. Without turning or getting up, Gregory said, "Come in," though why he said so was a mystery to him, he told me, because he knew the door was locked. When he heard someone enter, he turned to see a startling apparition: a figure made entirely of light, wearing a black hat and wrapped in a dark cloak. Its face was white and shining and so was its raised hand. The figure pointed toward Gregory with a gesture that both directed and beckoned him. Gregory realized that he was being visited by a vision and that this vision was the Spirit of Life who had come to call on him at the very moment that he was creating a poem. He told no one about this experience but believed from that time forward he had found his own voice as a poet. Never one to sentimentalize an experience, he ended his recollection by saying: "Before that I was a lousy poet."

Gregory often had more than one version of these stories. At another later time, he told me he thought the vision was Shelley's spirit, who at that exact moment had taken Gregory's body as his host. Shelley's spirit would have equated with the Spirit of Life in Gregory's mind in any case, so perhaps the distinction isn't worth quibbling over.

I'm sure those who knew Gregory would be able to share a variety of what he called "takes" on this incident. I can imagine the outcry now: "But he told me…"; "No, no—she doesn't know what she's talking about. He told me…"; "I happen to know…" and so on. I don't know what he told other people.

There were so many questions I couldn't answer then and may never answer now. He died in 2001. I like to think of what Gregory said to me in our first happy days together. "Kaye," he paused before he finished, "do you know how rare this is?" This I did know. Yes.

"Rarely, rarely, comest thou, / Spirit of Delight!" These were some of his favorite Shelley lines after all.

Gregory is buried, not in a pauper's grave as he'd requested on occasion, but near his beloved Shelley in the Protestant Cemetery in Rome. The word "sprit" on his gravestone has been corrected to read: "spirit." I live in a condo in Connecticut at the moment, hardly a pauper's grave, but maybe not a place of illumination either. That needs to come from within. Nile, the joy of my life, tells me he is about to marry someone I like a lot. All's well. But nobody talks to me about She-Stags and the Garden anymore.

Gregory Gave Me the World

by Robert Yarra

The first time I saw Gregory Corso, wandering the streets of North Beach, San Francisco, in the fall of 1983, I was too shy to approach him. I followed him for ten or fifteen minutes until he stepped into Gino and Carlo's Bar on Green Street—and then re-emerged with two big guys. Gregory pointed his finger at me and said, "That guy is following me, man." I quickly split.

Several days later, on the way to my immigration law office in North Beach, I stopped at Caffe Trieste where Gregory was sitting at a table with my friend, poet Rosemary Manno, who invited me to join them. I was still at the table hours later, drinking wine with my new friend Gregory Corso, whose friendship changed the course of my life.

Becoming friends with Gregory was an answered prayer, but Gregory was a heroin addict and always needed someone to look out for him. Gregory wrote in a poem, "I have lived by the grace of Jews and girls" (later changed to women). Gregory and I were friends. During the rollercoaster ride that was our friendship, I learned to take the horrible with the sublime. With Gregory, I never knew how the day or night would unfold; it was always an adventure. He was a naturally great and intuitive teacher, and one of the smartest, most interesting cats on the planet.

I had dough and never turned him down for a fix. I remember walking into the office waiting-room and seeing Gregory among my bewildered clients, head down, sweat rolling off his nose, suffering, junk-sick but very patient. I quickly slid him a twenty and, without a word, he was out the door.

We both loved to walk and lived many glorious days and nights in conversation on the streets of San Francisco or drinking at the Buddha Bar and Li Po, dive bars on Grant Ave in Chinatown where it was unlikely that Gregory would be recognized. He spoke of his painful childhood, how his mother abandoned him when he was an infant, and his father gave him up to foster care. He was locked in a dark room in one foster home where food was tossed at him as if he were an animal. Gregory had another sweet memory of lying in the bathtub next to a foster mother's pussy and finally feeling safe—only to be sent away again.

Gregory lived on the streets for long periods, sleeping on rooftops in warm weather, the subway when it was cold. He was arrested aged twelve and locked up in the Tombs, an infamous, brutal jail in New York City. To escape the Tombs, he faked madness and was sent to the psych ward at Bellevue Hospital where things got even worse. He told me about witnessing countless sexual liaisons and attacks and seeing men pee into each other's mouths—a real horror show.

Gregory told me he had been to Dannemora prison aged seventeen for a robbery conviction. He met an older prisoner who said, "Don't serve time; let time serve you." Following this advice, and with only a 6th-grade education, Gregory read *Webster's Unabridged Dictionary*, the *Encyclopedia Britannica* and most of the books in the prison library, and started writing poetry.

Gregory was twenty when he was released from prison. After his release, Gregory met Allen Ginsberg at a lesbian bar in Greenwich Village and showed Allen his prison poems, which Allen liked. Gregory told me that, in his profound innocence, he asked Allen if he would like to watch a man and woman screw. Gregory told Allen that every day at the same time he watched a man and woman have sex through an apartment window and would masturbate. Gregory suggested that Allen go with him to check it out and masturbate too. By some fantastic twist of fate, it was Allen and a woman screwing that Gregory had been watching! Allen was gay, of course, but he had been seeing a psychiatrist who advised that he could "be cured" of his homosexuality by having regular heterosexual intercourse. By the synchronicity that brought Gregory and Allen together, Gregory first knew Allen through the window.

Gregory invited me to meet him in London in April 1984 for a reunion of sorts at the Royal Albert Hall of the 1965 Wholly Communion International Poetry Incarnation, where Allen, Gregory, and other luminaries read. I arrived in London the week before the event and telephoned the hotel where Gregory told me he'd be staying. The operator put me through to Allen, who said that Gregory's flight had been delayed and to come to his room. We talked for a while; then he invited me to accompany him to Liverpool, where he would read poetry. As Allen was one of my heroes, I was thrilled. Travelling with him for four or five days on our way to Liverpool, with stops along the way to visit Allen's friends, where we were feted like royalty, was heady and glorious. In Liverpool, while friends and admirers surrounded Allen at the Adelphi Hotel bar, he started reciting William Blake's London poem. Blake was my favorite poet, and I knew the poem by heart and spontaneously recited the second verse. Allen then recited the third verse and I the fourth and final verse. We smiled at each other, and I felt a bond was forged. Allen was always so sweet and inclusive to me thereafter.

Upon returning to London, Allen chose me and Alan Wise to cop heroin for Gregory. Alan Wise was a hilarious fellow who managed the arrangements (lodging, transportation, etc) for the poets at The Royal Albert Hall reading. Wise also happened to be the singer Nico's manager. As Nico was a heroin addict, Alan was hip to the drill, but he lacked contacts in London as he and Nico lived in Manchester. We chased down leads all night as we went from one junkie haven to another trying to score for Gregory, who would be arriving junk-sick. We finally copped from a dwarf in a drug den at a seamy housing project as dawn approached and had just enough time to get to the airport to meet Gregory. As soon as Gregory spotted me, he asked, "You got it?" I handed him this stuff, and he strode post-haste to the bathroom and came out a new man.

Allen was waiting for Gregory outside the hotel. When they saw each other, they did something I was to witness often. Allen and Gregory touched foreheads and spoke in hushed tones. "Our friend [Alexander] Trocchi is gone," whispered Allen.

In the autumn of 1983, Gregory and I were in New York City where we spent lots of time together at the Chelsea Hotel. Of all the great gifts from Gregorio, the greatest was my introduction to Vali Myers, the Australian artist and dancer who was to become a beloved friend. Gregory introduced me to Vali at her salon in room 631, a place where I was to spend many blissful days and nights. Vali was magic.

Vali and Gregory were great friends. I started visiting Vali in Positano in the autumn of 1986. While strolling on the beach, I saw Gregory dressed all in white, wearing a white headband, suntanned, looking like a movie star. We had a joyful reunion. Gregory told me he had been sleeping in the backseats of cars. He woke up one day while a woman was driving and frightened them both. I immediately booked him a room in my hotel. Upon waking, we'd go to the cafe and read the *International Herald Tribune* while Gregory had his morning beer and cigarettes. In the afternoon, I would go with Vali's lover, Gianni Menichetti, to their enchanted valley, Il Porto, where they resided with their tribe of over one hundred animals, including Winnie the turtle who was over one hundred years old, Ruby, her eight-hundred-pound pig, and Fanny, a forty-year-old donkey who, Vali proudly proclaimed, had never worked a day in her life. Vali even kept a fox, her beloved daughter Foxy, who lived for fourteen years inside their little home. Gregory couldn't join us as the road to the valley was treacherous.

In the evenings, Vali, Gianni, Gregory and I dined at the best restaurant in Positano, La Cambusa, owned by Vali's great friend and champion Luigi Russo, who treated us with loving generosity as we sat on the terrace in the warm sea-breeze Italian night and drank and feasted and sang till dawn. I know the songs from the 30's and 40's that Vali loved, and I would sing her favorites. Gregory told me I should have been a troubadour. The best time of my life was in dreamy, beautiful Positano in 1986—the sea, Vali, Gregory, Gianni, long nights at the Cambusa and days in the valley, talking, laughing, singing, feasting and drinking. It was heaven.

Gregory loved to push situations way beyond limits. Once, during a bus ride in Positano, I watched as he slid his hand down the pants of an attractive lady whom he knew. She didn't flinch but waited until we got off the bus and turned to him and said, "I don't care, Gregory, if you put your finger in my culo, but if my husband hears about this, he will kill you."

Gregory had received a letter in Positano from Allen [Ginsberg] accusing him of stealing a camera, which Gregory denied. Gregory thought I made a comment in Allen's defense and lit into me, and we had a fierce argument. "Dig the ballgame," he snarled. "I'm the poet. I took the shot. You're nothing. Niente." He started pushing me as a crowd gathered. After the third or fourth push, I cocked my fist and growled, "One more time, Gregory, and I'll lay you out." I meant it, and Gregory knew I meant it, and he backed off. "I just wanted to see if you're alive, Roberto." I was furious and vowed that I would never see him again. After a walk on the beach to clear my head, I passed the Cambusa, where I saw Gregory with two Swedish women we had met previously. Without being seen, I watched in fascination as he pulled out his penis and said to the ladies, "Look at my cazzo. It's not too big; it's not too small. It's just right, don't you think?" And I mused that this would be my last sweet memory of Gregory. Five minutes later, there was a frantic knock on my hotel door. "Bobby, I got these two chicks, man. I can't hold 'em. Come down and help me!" My anger flew away, and I realized how much I loved Gregory. Off we went into the Positano night with the Swedish ladies. Gregory never held a grudge and probably didn't even remember that we had fought.

Gregory wanted to show me Rome, so, after a trip to Sorrento to pick up a nine-day supply of methadone, we took the train to Rome. We got off the train, dropped our bags at the hotel and ran into the streets. Gregory wanted to show me everything! I remember practically running with him to the Colosseum, then to Piazza Navona, then to Campo dei Fiori to see the statue of the brooding monk, Giordano Bruno, who was burned at the stake and fascinated Gregory so much. After the obelisks, he had to show me the old synagogue near the Tiber. We ran towards the temple at around 4:00 a.m. and were immediately surrounded by police and soldiers pointing semi-automatic weapons at us. "E Hebraio! E Hebraio! He's Jewish!" Gregory yelled, pointing at me. It was Yom Kippur, the holiest Jewish holiday, and the police were being vigilant against a possible terrorist attack.

Gregory was well known and beloved in Italy. He would sometimes be recognized on the street and be invited to sumptuous dinners at the homes of his admirers. He held court with friends at Vineria Bar in Campo dei Fiori, where a photo of the young Gregory graced the bar's back wall. We also drank at the San Calisto bar in Trastevere, where we felt comfortable amongst the artists and outlaws. We passed hours at the Keats-Shelley Museum on the Spanish steps, as Gregory revered Shelley above all poets.

Somehow, I became Gregory's aide-de-camp, a gig I never asked for. I had a predecessor, George Scrivani, a friend whom Gregory loved and trusted. George had met Gregory after a poetry reading at the State University at Buffalo. This was Gregory's first return there after refusing to take a loyalty oath during the Vietnam War in 1965. George, Gregory, and Susan Dente, who has been George's best friend since childhood and became Gregory's girlfriend, moved in together to a flat in Staten Island across the street from a brothel. One day, George came home from his work to find the police rifling through their belongings, looking for Gregory's dope. George walked up to the cop who appeared to be in charge and said these magic words, "Excuse me, but do you have a warrant?" George won Gregory's love and trust forever with those words, as the warrantless cops slunk out the door.

In the summer of 1985, at Gregory's invitation, I went to Naropa, The Jack Kerouac School of Disembodied Poetics, in Boulder, Colorado, where we shared an apartment at the Varsity Townhouses. Gregory's teaching assistant had disappeared, so I took his place to ensure that Gregory showed up where he needed to go.

One evening, as I lay in bed with a fever, Gregory came to the apartment with a woman and yelled at me, "Get out, I want privacy!" so I split and passed a couple of blissful hours with Allen Ginsberg and Philip Whalen, who was staying with Allen. Then I met a woman named Sarah, and we caroused the night away. When she and I returned to the apartment the next morning, Gregory met us at the door and moaned to Sarah, "I was mean to my friend. I acted disgracefully." Then he apologized to me and was genuinely remorseful. Gregory practiced true contrition.

I had a rich Serbian immigration client who gave me $25,000 for expenses, a once in a career event. I flew to New York to meet him and booked a suite at the Plaza Hotel for my girlfriend and me. I invited Gregory to dine with us at the Oak Room, where he was given a jacket, and we all dined splendidly on my client's tab. After dinner, we returned to the suite, and my girlfriend and I retired to the bedroom, leaving Gregory watching TV in the living room. Sometime during the evening, I noticed Gregory in our bedroom opening the minibar. The following morning, we found a happily drunk Gregory sitting on the couch watching Russian television with around 40 empty liquor mini bottles spread across the table.

Gregory and I went to midtown Manhattan where we met my sister, Diane, who worked as a bartender. Diane and Gregory hit it off, and hand in hand, skipped off down the street without a word. I met Gregory later that evening at the Museum of Modern Art, where he was to read. We were backstage with Diane, my beautiful sister-in-law Barbara Ann, and a close friend, Tommy Thompson, a two-fisted Oklahoma cowboy sweetheart poet and drug dealer who shared a suite at the Chelsea with Gregory. Gregory yelled to us, "Gather around me!" As we did, he pulled out his works and jabbed it into his arm, probably to get a reaction from Barbara Ann. As the blood shot out of his veins, Barbara Ann fainted. Luckily, I was able to catch her before she hit the ground. She was so shaken that I had to take her immediately to Grand Central and the train back to Connecticut. As Gregory wrote in one of his poems, "I'm rich. I've used my blood like an extravagance."

On my birthday, October 20th, 1999, a bleak, sad, and rainy day, I arrived in New York City from California at the request of Roger Richards to help take Gregory to St. Vincent's hospital. At Roger and Irvyne's Horatio Street apartment, Gregory lay on their couch. When he saw me, he moaned "Bobby, my Bobby, I love you, my Bobby. The machine has broken down, and I'm in the maelstrom!" It was terrible to see him so ill. He couldn't walk, so I practically carried him down four flights of stairs. Roger tried to help, but he was almost seventy and weighed around one hundred thirty pounds, so I had to get Gregory down and later up the stairs on my own. We hailed a taxi to the hospital where I wheeled him into a series of examination rooms and helped him dress and undress, as he was helpless. After many tests, the doctors discovered that he had advanced prostate cancer.

Through the angelic ministrations of his nurse/daughter Sheri, who was the product of a one-night stand and first appeared to Gregory around fifteen years or so before his death, Gregory gained a miraculous half-year of life during which time he became sweet, kind, and gentle. He had had a reprieve and had the blessed opportunity to say goodbye to his family, friends, and the people he loved. Gregory passed away in Sheri's home in Minnesota on January 17th, 2001.

Before he died, I asked him if he wanted to have his ashes buried in Rome. "Yes!" was his response. I had a wonderful friend in Rome, Hannelore de Lellis, who, along with her husband Camilo, gave me gracious hospitality at their villa during my many visits to that great city. Hannelore was a German woman of stout resolve who I had previously introduced Gregory to during a visit by her to New York. I called and asked if she could arrange for Gregory's burial in Rome at the Protestant Cemetery where Keats and Shelley lie. After speaking to the director of the cemetery, Hannelore called and told me that it was not possible. I told her with some urgency how important it was to have Gregory buried in the same cemetery as his beloved Shelley, and could she please try again, at which point she responded emphatically, "It can be done. It must be done. It will be done!" Through Hannelore's great effort, not only did she arrange to have Gregory's ashes buried in the cemetery, she managed to have them buried at the foot of Shelley's grave and at half price! I had to raise the $10,000 for the burial. Patti Smith did a memorial reading and concert for Gregory at the St. Mark's Church, which raised $3,600. I had to badger and persuade others to contribute. I added the final $1,600 myself.

After Gregory died, I enlisted George Scrivani to help me choose an inscription for Gregory's gravestone. Even though Gregory had often said in jest that when he died he wanted the inscription "Oops, I died" we decided on the stanza from the poem "Spirit":

> Spirit
> is Life
> It flows thru
> the death of me
> endlessly
> like a river
> unafraid
> of becoming
> the sea

Even in death, things didn't go smoothly for dear Gregory. I had dictated the epitaph, which was transcribed incorrectly by my girlfriend/typist, and we didn't catch the error. We sent "Spirt" instead of "Spirit." At the cemetery, I was able to add an apostrophe, and the epitaph reads "Spir't" on his gravestone. So it remains.

Speaking about Gregory, Allen, and the rest of the tribe, Raymond Foye once said to me, "Bobby, we walked with gods." And, indeed, Gregory was part of a culture that flourished and then disappeared. Like Rimbaud, Villon, and Shelley, blazing meteors all, poets who "took the shot," Gregory's life was inseparable from his art. Since the caves, the poet has been the one who steps out of the group, who is trying to explain things, and who brings us the message, "Check it out." That was Gregory—Hermes—the messenger.

With Gregory, the good was incredibly good, and I loved his spirit. To me, he was a great lyric poet, a great philosopher, and one who lived a mythic life. He had a wonderful sense of humor, could laugh at himself, and, when on a roll, could make you fall to the floor with laughter and pee your pants. Anything was possible with Gregory, and every day and night with him was an adventure. He kept me on my toes. He could talk with anyone, and his curiosity about what made people tick was endless. Although Gregory looked, acted, and spoke like someone from the streets—which he was—he was also highly sophisticated, a wise and great teacher, an observer of humanity, a raconteur who was always interesting, and a changer of consciousness.

It's been over twenty years since Gregory passed, and it's easy for me to remember the anecdotes, but being Gregory's friend was so much more and was such a blessing.

Ah, Gregorio. Through you, I met the beauties of my life. You gave me the world.

Gregory Corso: An Elder Scamp

by Neeli Cherkovski

Gregory Corso. There are days where I miss him terribly. It is difficult not to think of him as an elder scamp, yes, right out of some topsy-turvy Huckleberry Finn-like American night folded around the streets on both the East and West coast. He was a child of New York and a blessed hellcat of San Francisco. I first met him in front of City Lights bookstore, introduced by poet Andy Clausen. He had his baby son Max in tow. We went up to my apartment on Harwood Alley where I read him my poem, "Oh to Coit Tower". It had been inspired by his own ode to the same monument in his book *Gasoline*.

Gregory listened well, but I was so nervous as to his reaction. Suddenly he rose from his chair and said, "Man, I like it a lot." The next evening, he asked me to babysit for Max. When he came back to get him, he said, "Mr Cherkovski, thank you for taking care of my son." It would be the first of many times that I would take care of him.

On one notable evening, Gregory sat in my cramped kitchen and extolled the virtues of François Villon. It was obvious that his knowledge of the Medieval French poet was extensive. He relished the idea of Villon as an underground figure. "He's one of the daddies," Gregory said, emphasizing the rebellious nature of Villon's poetry. There were other great evenings like one when Gregory read a poem he never finished—"Epistle to San Francisco"—in which he wrote, "Here are your poets but where is your poesy?"

To be with Gregory Corso on any given day in North Beach or elsewhere could be a very exciting experience. He might appear sullen and uncommunicative but he was aware of everything that was going on. It was quite phenomenal. He might be sitting at the table, his eyes cast downward, you talking to somebody about one subject or another. Corso could appear disinterested... then all of a sudden come awake and make a point. I wrote a story once about how he spent other people's money. He had a knack of draining their pocketbooks. I witnessed him do this to a middle-aged beat sycophant

161

who showed up at the Caffe Trieste. Gregory and I spent 12 hours with him as he took us out to a fancy dinner and bought drinks in various cocktail lounges around the city. Money was spent on cabs and money was spent on cigars, and finally the poor guy had nothing left and we abandoned him on a cold street corner. Gregory felt the guy had gotten his money's worth spending all that time with one of the legendary poets of the Beat Generation. Read his poems, as they shine now as much as *he* did in the wild days.

GREGORY CORSO

For Lisa Brinker

when Gregory dies
there is a white butterfly
in the yard taking notes
and talking to the lemon tree
in a low and antique voice

when Gregory dies
the piano players take a bow
in the yard next door
on the day of graduation
and a lone piccolo preaches
to anyone passing

he was born in 1930
in time for the Great Depression
and was passed from
one strange hand to another
he did not know his mother

**

I met Gregory on Columbus Avenue
with the poet Andy Clausen
the hod-carrier, they came to my apartment
and I read my Coit Tower poem in which
the tower is a shadow folded
over a bed of flowers while the sky leaks
and the streets turn into Chinese laundries

he had his own Coit poem
in a book called GASOLINE
an anti vertiginous tower
which struck me as defiance

**

he may have been one of the last bohemian poets
no MFA, no university job, no job at all
except poesy, and the labor of being a drug addict

while he lived and worked
snow fell over his words,
sunlight bore
into his poems, wolves leapt
every chance they had
when he'd turn his neck a moment
to the skylarks escaping
the grip of Shelley,
his master, the always young poet
who wept for the dead

**

when Gregory was
a demonic Huck Finn
he learned how to
proceed down a
zigzag path, in prison
he was handed poetry
and illuminated prose

when he was freed
everything moved poetically
on Greenwich Village's
hometown morning streets and
in the Harvard neighborhoods
where he made his
first book of poems

**

when I met Gregory
he was already a famous poet
of the Beat Generation, he could
quote Poe's "To Helen" and
celebrate "the agate lamp"

Gregory wrote "Marriage"
and "Bomb," he stole my
stereo for drug money,
he left baby Max under my
care for weeks at a time

he spoke of Francois Villon
as if he were a brother, not
a medieval poet of the
dark Parisian colonnades

**

when Gregory lives
a marching band
rises from the garden
and assumes control
of all that is neat

he kept us writhing
for his light, he thought
our country oversimplified
and found a complete
complex of simplicity
in a few well-chosen lines

We Planned Glorious Music

by Francis Kuipers

Wary and streetwise, Gregory didn't give confidence easily and he generally mistrusted artistic collaboration. He suggested that we work together some months after he moved into my place in Rome as he needed money, mentioning that Allen Ginsberg also had a guitarist. Enjoying the attention, Gregory had a great time in front of an audience, but his readings took a lot out of him, as they were likely to blow up into massive marathons of poetry involving exuberant partying and outrageous mayhem of all kinds. Gregory never spared himself. Shows might go on for hours and even days, starting the moment we arrived at a venue.

One of our dreams was to do an opera on Giordano Bruno, the philosopher burned to death for heresy in Rome's Campo di Fiori. Enjoying mellow moments, Gregory liked to sit below Giordano's statue near the legendary Vinaria wine bar, perusing the *New York Times*. We planned glorious music, as well as merry chorus lines of cardinals and nuns.

Like Picasso, for Gregory spontaneity was a discipline. We never rehearsed and our gigs were always different, except that I had to start the show. Then Gregory would start reading and I would play whatever I thought was best. The experience could be fantastic or like walking on a razor. I never knew what was going to happen. Drinking and making love in a dressing room, Gregory might arrive an hour late. Many times, he turned up in extremis accompanied by all kinds of artists, freaks, prostitutes and others he had encountered in bars.

Gregory could be an angel spreading light, full of luminous grace, but he could also become ominous and terrible like a William Blake angel. He believed that poets, like angels, always had to tell the truth. Gregory provided waves of wonderful emotion but he could also provoke rage.

When infuriated audiences wanted to throw things or storm out of the theatre, he would say something so unexpected and so hilarious that it stopped them in their tracks, helpless and almost choking to death with relieved laughter. Like many men and women of genius, he had great comic timing and was incredibly funny. There were of course a few occasions when matters got out of hand, and we had some narrow escapes. "He suffers reverse," William Burroughs said of Gregory. "Like every man who takes chances."

Gregory personally knew Thelonious Monk, Art Blakey and other musicians of his era, but he preferred melodic music. Play it "melodico" he would urge me. He liked the scores of the old movies he never tired of watching and the romantic compositions of Charles Ives. Best of all, he loved Italian opera. At home drinking whiskey, Gregory gladly sang opera all night.

"I don't tell lies because I don't remember them," Gregory once joked to me. Waking at the hour of the wolf, the only way he could keep breathing was by blowing into a paper bag.

I love music, all
ventures of music; from
Couperin to Art Blakey
— Poetry is the estate
of the Muse —
    Eye sounds with words.
ear sights with notes
— Hail Francis K —
    Gregory Corso

Now you see it—now you don't see it
(true account of Gregory Corso)

by Nina Zivancevic

Once I met Gregory in Boulder, Colorado,

showed him my translations of his poetry which he found

beautiful and wanted to try my Taurus ring on,

"Now you see it—now you don't see it," he said.

It took Ginsberg two months to return my ring from him.

Once I met Gregory in NYC after my incredible marijuana arrest,

And having heard my story, he took 400 dollars

from his left boot where he kept money and gave it to me

"take it, kid, you'd need it for the lawyers"; the story of the ring forgotten;

The last time I saw him in New York,

I was with my dad, buying a TV set,

When Gregory jumped on us, out of nowhere,

cursing the commercial habits of high capitalism—"don't you come from Europe folks,"

he yelled "don't you have some taste and elegance?

You don't need this junk to fill your brain with non- seeeense," he said

And then disappeared into Astor place

muggy dust for ever…

Clown of Curation:
Gregory Corso's *Mindfield*

by Ryan Mathews

"No meaning to life can be found in this holy language / nor beyond the lyrical fabrica-
tor's inescapable theme / be found the loathed find—there is nothing to find." [1]

—Gregory Corso "1959", *The Happy Birthday of Death / Mindfield*

Gregory Corso was 59 when *Mindfield*, a curated sampling of his first six books of
poetry and previously unpublished material, was released. We will never know if Corso
saw *Mindfield* as a summation of his poetic career, another mile marker on the poetic
road, a statement of some kind, or whether he just needed the cash to feed his personal
demons. Whichever the case, it remained his last full collection of poetry until the post-
humous publication of *The Golden Dot* [2] in 2022.

One might logically assume *Mindfield* should be viewed as a map of Corso's artistic
career. Each of his major published poetic works is set out in crisp, linear, fashion; suggesting that if you start at the beginning, and read to the end, you would have a more or
less accurate portrait of the development of the artist as a young, middle-aged, and older man. In this case "logical" is the enemy of "actual." *Mindfield* isn't a map, it's a maze.

The reader—and, I strongly suspect, Corso himself—is forced to constantly double
back as they negotiate the book, only to encounter obstacles they are sure they had
just easily overcome, tracing promising routes only to find dead ends, and continuously
moving forward in what becomes an act of pure blind faith. Nowhere near a "Collected
Works," *Mindfield* does offer us the print equivalent of "Gregory Corso's Greatest Hits".
It is a fairly comprehensive selection of his best, or at least most popular, published
work: including selections from *The Vestal Lady on Brattle* (1955), *Gasoline* (1958), *The
Happy Birthday of Death* (1960), *Long Live Man* (1962), *Elegiac Feelings American* (1970),

Herald of the Autochthonic Spirit (1981), and 23 previously unpublished poems.

Originally released with Forewords by William S. Burroughs and Allen Ginsberg by Thunder's Mouth Press in 1989, *Mindfield* was reissued on December 30, 1998 with the two original Forewords and a new Introduction by David Amram. The reissue in particular seemed to promise a reminder of Corso's importance as an individual and not just another generic member of the so-called Beat Generation. Ginsberg's Foreword, "On Corso's Virtues," calls Corso, "… a poet's Poet …," and argues, "He has been and always will be a popular poet, awakener of youth, puzzlement & pleasure for sophisticated elder bibliophiles …" [3] For his part, Burroughs' "Introductory Notes" are a bit more direct. "Gregory is a gambler," he wrote. "He suffers reverses, like every man who takes chances." [4]

One of those reverses is that he and his work often are treated less than reverentially by Beat groupies and some academics; ironic given that Corso always burned hotter if slightly less brightly—or perhaps better said, more opaquely—than his three original East Coast "Beat" comrades-in-arms, Allen Ginsberg, William S. Burroughs, and Jack Kerouac. While *Gasoline*, Corso's second collection of poetry, published by City Lights in 1958, remains a perpetual favorite among Beat poetry cognoscenti, it failed to gain him the sustainable countercultural recognition that *Howl*, *Naked Lunch*, and *On the Road* earned their respective authors.

In his "Introduction" to *Mindfield's* reissue Amram wrote, "In the 70s and 80s, Gregory persevered, and in the 90s the interest by young people in Kerouac's work opened the door for Gregory and his life's work to be rediscovered by a whole new generation." [5] The kind thoughts of a longtime friend proved more fantasy than prophesy. Not only would Kerouac's coattails prove too short to carry Corso to a new generation of readers, in the end, even the publishing market disserted him. When his publisher friends James Laughlin (New Directions) and Lawrence Ferlinghetti (City Lights) passed away, Corso was once more the orphan.

The word orphan summarizes the Corso mythos. Orphaned as a child, he saw children as an idealized perpetual source of power, fueled by purity and innocence. Emotionally orphaned as an adult—often through his own actions—he sought out the sanctifying power of an otherworldly love which manifested itself in a blind devotion to his Muse.

I think a case could be made that—at the deepest, darkest parts of his heart and soul—he wasn't always that sure who he was himself, and so he communicated with the world behind a perpetually rotating series of masks. Among them there is the Clown, who sometimes misses his own punchlines; the Trickster, unable to hold on to an assumed shape even though he desperately wants to; the Holy Fool, incapable of following the wisdom he so freely shares with others; the Street Kid, fated to make juvenile trouble at the worst possible moments; and the Lover, simultaneously drawn to and terrified of love. But one mask never slipped: the Omnipresent; suggesting that perhaps it was not a mask at all, but the face of the Poet. Whatever else Corso may or may not have been, he never stopped being a poet, not for one moment, and it is that Corso we are going to look at.

Given that entire books have been written about the topics we are covering in a short essay, let's start with a with broad overview of *Mindfield,* looking at it as the sum of its piece parts—the selections Corso apparently wanted us to remember, and the others he possibly wanted us to forget. Approached at its highest level, we have to ask whether Corso intended *Mindfield* to be read as a holistic or gestalt collection. In the former case, all the selections in the collection are best understood in terms of their standalone role as a part of a conventional retrospective anthology. In the latter, the act of curation pushes beyond the chronological and interpretative limitations of the holistic approach, revealing a work that is far more than the sum of its parts and advancing a new truth not overtly captured in any of the piece parts. In either case, *Mindfield* captures all the "red threads" running through Corso's poetic weaving—death, love, God, romance, slapstick humor, surrealism, experimentation, derivative efforts, politics, anti-materialism, despair, hope, betrayal, loneliness, and so much more. Our journey begins with selections from Corso's first poetry collection *The Vestal Lady on Brattle.*

Most poets are probably painfully familiar with the intellectual walk of shame that follows giving in to the seduction of going back and examining their earliest work, an experience equal parts nostalgia for lost innocence and passion and visceral cringe of recognition of forced rhymes, derivative efforts easily traced back to the original writers, and mind-numbing naiveté. This may help explain why only 11 of the 36 poems from *The Vestal Lady on Brattle* made their way into *Mindfield*, including two of the best —"Greenwich Village Suicide" [6] and Corso fan favorite "Requiem for 'Bird' Parker, Musician," [7] while the titular piece—a poetic meditation on maternal infanticide—didn't make it. Some of the *Vestal Lady* poems like "Dementia in an African Apartment House" [8] (which isn't included in *Mindfield*) and "The Horse Was Milked" [9] (which is) both rhyme. "Requiem for Bird" is written in almost Bebop rhythms. To characterize Corso's style variations as eclectic would be a gross understatement. Corso correctly curated some of the more marginal *Vestal Lady* poems out of *Mindfield*, but what remains frames much of the decades of work that follows.

I could spend the remainder of this essay exploring how the themes first advanced here are revisited over and over again in the other five volumes and unpublished work represented in *Mindfield*. But, we have a lot of ground to cover, so I'll just touch on just two of these themes with the understanding that we're barely skimming the surface of this foundational work.

The first is Corso's experimentation—or frustration with—the limits of a singular style and / or voice. It's as though he was attempting to work within a system he is fated to destroy. This includes the search for what Miles Davis called "tone"—a signature sound that immediately signals a unique, individual artistic expression. In Corso's case, the components of tone include humor, tools borrowed from the Surrealists' workbench, sometimes absurd juxtapositions, and allusions to other writers, both contemporary and classical. The second is what I think of as Corso's Poetic Manicheism, his positioning of life as a battle between love, beauty, truth, childhood innocence, and art on the one side and death, exploitation, repression, and cruelty on the other.

Three years after he set off down the poetic road walking arm in arm with the child-eating Vestal Lady, Corso was ready to—literally—pour *Gasoline* onto the growing fire of what would become known as Beat literature and, with a nod to Donald Allen, new American Poetry.

If *Vestal Lady* was a declaration that Corso was, albeit sometimes a bit tentatively, "on his way" as a poet, *Gasoline* stands as a huge, flashing, neon "arrival sign" signaling his readiness and willingness to take on the world. Perhaps unsurprisingly, given its popularity, *Mindfield* features 22 of the original 32 poems (69 percent) that make up *Gasoline*. In his "Introduction" Allen Ginsberg tells readers to, "Open this book as you would a box of crazy toys, take in your hands a refinement of beauty out of a destructive atmosphere." [10] It is great advice.

Some of those "crazy toys" were apparently lost or broken in the years separating the publication of *Gasoline* and *Mindfield*. Inexplicably, "Ode to Coit Tower," [11] for example, the first poem in *Gasoline*, is missing. In a conscious act of reverse reification "Ode to Coit Tower" contrasts the Tower (a physical proxy for sexuality, passion, youth, and the human desire to create a beauty capable of challenging the heavens) with Alcatraz. A far different kind of proxy, the prison is a physical testament to the blind and mindless power of law, repression, forced conformity, slavery to the system, and the despoiling of nature. "Ode" seems to advance many of the ideas presented in nascent form in *The Vestal Lady on Brattle*, making its deliberate exclusion from *Mindfield* all the harder to understand.

Instead of "Ode" the *Gasoline* section begins with "In the Fleeting Hand of Time," [12] a not so thinly veiled attack on older, academic poets who can only see the young poet (Corso) as a madman and a threat. He escapes their "bright madhouse" for the safety of a Bleecker Street room and the comfort of an Italian mother's breast which suckles him before the established academics have a chance to "lock away my toys of Zeus." His contempt for the old and established also drives "I Am 25," [13] which proclaims in capital letters: "I HATE OLD POETMEN!" Many of the *Gasoline* poems contained in *Mindfield* contain autobiographical references and / or highly personalized existential questions. In "Amnesia in Memphis" [14] for instance a mummified pharaoh wonders, "Who am I, flat beneath the shade of Isis …", finally conceding, "For what I am; who I am, I cannot regain." In "Uccello" [15] Corso tells us:

> how I dream to join such battle!
> a silver man on a black horse with red standard and striped
>   lance   never to die but to be endless
>   a golden prince of pictorial war

Gasoline is anchored by Corso's standard cornerstones—childhood, death, dreams, beauty, and the poet as victim and victor. These themes carry through to *Mindfield's* next section, selections from *The Happy Birthday of Death*.

In *The Happy Birthday of Death*, *Gasoline's* silver man / golden prince happily riding into battle astride a black horse is replaced by an older version of the poet found in "How Happy I used to Be," [16] who, hearing a sad song, weeps, "… for when had I last imagined myself a king …" Only 23 of the original 51 poems in *Happy Birthday* are included in *Minefield* and one of them—"Bomb" [17]—appears in what amounts to a new form.

A now somewhat dated tongue-in-cheek love note to atomic warfare, "Bomb" was originally published as a four panel, single sheet broadside by City Lights in 1958, in the form of a calligram, a poem typeset in a way that visually reflects its content. If you hang the broadside on a wall and walk to the other side of the room you see the outline of a mushroom cloud. In The *Happy Birthday of Death* the poem appears as a pullout (or a pull-down, depending on how you are holding the book) creating the same effect on a smaller scale. For reasons unknown, and frankly hard to justify other than possibly publishing costs, the calligram effect is lost in *Mindfield* where the poem appears across five conventional pages.

In addition to "Bomb" a number of other landmark poems from *The Happy Birthday of Death* found their way into *Mindfield*. "Marriage" [18] takes a surreal and satiric look at the foibles of modern courtship, social conformity, and institutionalized love. Imagining hordes of newly married husbands and wives flooding into indistinguishable "cozy hotels" in Niagara Falls, Corso conjures up a nightmarish vision of "indifferent clerks," "lobby zombies," a "whistling elevator man" and "winking bellboy"—all jaded at the prospect of so many people rushing to bed their spouses with dreams of eternal bliss the jaded staff know will elude them.

At one point in the poem he suggests that perhaps he should get married and rush upstairs and not make love in defiance of their expectations or perhaps move to a dark cave under the Falls Niagara forever: "I'd sit there the Mad Honeymooner / devising ways to break marriages, a scourge of bigamy / a saint of divorce—" The poem continues as a four-page long internal debate on the pros and cons of traditional marriage. Despite the possibility that he might end up a 60 year old unmarried man, living in a furnished room with pee stains on his underwear while everyone else in the world is married, Corso assures us, "No, can't imagine myself married to that pleasant prison dream."

Many Corso scholars seem to prefer poems like "Marriage." Since I don't carry the burden of academic authority, I'm personally always more drawn to "Clown."[19] I see its nine pages as a platform Corso uses to speak more personally to the reader—human-to-human versus poet-to-audience. Sure, all The Trickster's linguistic talents are on full display, but there is something about "Clown" that seems to more clearly and less defensively articulate the pain in the poet's head and heart. Corso is speaking more directly to the reader, not so much to entertain or shock, but to communicate an honest and profound truth with a minimum of concealment. "And why do they say be a man not a clown?" he asks, followed by the more difficult question, "And what is it like to be a man?" Proclaiming, "It is time for the idiot," Corso explores how he got to where he is, returning to the thickest of the "red threads" running through his work, warning, "Mr. Death has the hero by the balls!" He's not quite willing to concede the fight just yet, admitting, "I still don't know if the clown should die." "If there were no clowns," Corso speculates, "I doubt the reward of Paradise / to be a place where happy old friends meet."

Many of the themes advanced in *The Happy Birthday of Death* continue to evolve in

Long Live Man, published in 1962. *Long Live Man* contains 73 poems, only 21 of which found their way into *Mindfield*, starting with "Man," [20] the original collection's first poem. "Man" covers all of human history and evolution in two pages. In the poem's subhead Corso calls the work a "Prologue to what was to be a long long poem." The poem begins by questioning Creation, suggesting that "Poor cavemen, so scared of the outside, / So afeared of its power and beauty, / Created a limit, and called that limit God—" If man created God, then who created man? Corso speculates: "…Cell, fish, ape-man, Adam; / How was the first man born? / And why has he ceased being born that way?" It's a question that never quite gets answered. A few lines down the poet tells us, "I do not know if he be Adam's heir / Or kin to ape." Nor is evolution guaranteed. The final section of "Man" warns, "The fall of man stands a lie before Beethoven, / A truth before Hitler—"

This is vintage Corso, pitting creativity against repression. Corso's Manichean view of the world sees life as a battle between forces which are life-affirming and those that are life-denying—with humanity occupying a perpetually liminal role somewhere between agent of positive evolutionary force, change and beauty, and co-conspirator and victim of repression, evil and stasis. Curiously, this theme is actually best developed in some of the poems from *Long Live Man* that didn't make the *Mindfield* cut, such as "Greece," [21] "Beyond Delinquency" [22] and "Reflection in a Green Arena." [23] For the most part, Corso remains essentially optimistic throughout *Long Live Man*. In "Greece," for example, he writes:

> I screamed at Death I'm fed up with you! Stupid subject!
>> Old button!
> I unsalute you. On to greater things I go!
>> —the soul's mechanic is done

Was Corso telling us something by dropping works like "By Oscar Wilde's Grave" [24] (where the artist is destroyed by intolerance) from *Mindfield?* And, if that's the case, why did he omit "Saint Francis," [25] where eternal goodness, once again in the form of children, is affirmed as in this passage: "So hail every baby born by every mother / For each child is the second coming, yes! / Welcome new age! New space! New Whatever!"? In the "Full Length Portrait of Saint Francis" section of "Saint Francis" Corso takes stock of himself, noting:

> Francis, I am nearing thirty
> And have not died as I romantically wished
> And I am glad that I will be thirty
> Because I find man indeed life's victory.

A variation of that same perspective is found in "Writ on the Eve of My 32nd Birthday," [26] which *is* included in *Mindfield*. In the poem Corso describes himself as finally looking his age, "if not more," and asks, "Is it a good face what's no more a boy's face?" Saying, "I don't act silly any more," he adds with a hint of sadness: "And because of it I have to hear from so-called friends: / 'You've changed. You used to be so crazy so great.' / They are not comfortable with me when I'm serious."

Even if he feels readers are falling a little bit out of love with The Clown sans bulbous red nose, oversized floppy shoes, and identity-masking makeup, The Poet behind the Clown mask seems to be more at peace with himself—if only temporarily. "I feel I want to be wise with white hair in a tall library," he writes, "in a deep chair by a fireplace."

It would take Corso eight years to publish his next poetry collection, *Elegiac Feelings American*, which forms the next section of *Mindfield*. They were clearly sobering if not sober years, in which the tone is consistent to that of *Long Live Man*, if just a tad more world weary and resigned. Only 8 of the 38 poems that make up *Elegiac Feelings* made it into *Mindfield*. Be that as it may, *Mindfield* does offer us "Elegiac Feelings American (for the dear memory of John Kerouac)". [27] In this 10-page tribute to his fallen friend, Corso asserts that Kerouac was America and that America was Kerouac. Or, as he puts it:

> How inseparable you and the America you saw yet was
> > never there to see: you and America, like the
> > tree and the ground, are one the same; yet how
> > like a palm tree in the state of Oregon … dead
> > ere it blossomed like a snow polar loping the
> > Miami—

The inseparability of the "Beats" and "America" is repeated throughout in lines like, "Was not so much our finding America as it was America / finding its voice in us" and, "Alas, Jack, seems I cannot requiem thee without / requieming America …" Even Kerouac's failed battle with alcoholism is woven into the poem's theme where Corso writes:

> What hope for the America so embodied in thee, O friend,
> > when the very same alcohol that disembodied
> > your brother redman of his America,
> > disembodied ye—

And again, in this passage a few pages later:

> The prophet affects the state, and the state affects the
> > prophet—What happened to you, O friend,
> > happened to America, and we know what
> > happened to America—the stain… the stains…

He restates the interconnection of Kerouac and America over and over again as in the line, "When you went on the road looking for America you found / only what you put there …" The poem ends on a typical Corso note, with Kerouac using the power he possesses to change the world. "And soon … behind thee," he concludes, "there came a-following / the children of flowers." It is doubtful that at the time of his death in 1969, age 47, Kerouac would have wanted to be remembered as even partially responsible for the Hippies, but Corso's point is nevertheless on target.

While it is clearly full of doubts, bordering at points on depression, it's still defensible to see *Elegiac Feelings American* as the culmination of the vision and final clarification Corso had been advancing, to greater and lesser degrees, in all his earlier works. Sadly, much of that work is lost, some of it forever.

Stumbling down his own addictive road, he lost and sold notebooks that—reunited —might give us a clearer picture of Corso's evolution as a poet and a thinker. But it's unlikely that reuniting will ever take place, despite the yeoman archival efforts of people like Raymond Foye (who has done so much to recover and publish the work of a number of Beats, including Bob Kaufman) and his co-editor George Scrivani, the driving forces behind the 2022 release of Corso's *The Golden Dot: Last Poems 1997-2000*. Much of the work has vanished or lies hidden away in the bowels of private collections. Hopefully the Raymond Foyes of this world will succeed in unearthing more of the missing and hidden work, but in any case we'll never know exactly how much of it was simply lost forever.

At the time of *Mindfield* the only other materials available to be anthologized were *Herald of the Autochthonic Spirit* and a few previously unpublished poems. *Herald of the Autochthonic Spirit* appeared 11 hard years after *Elegiac Feelings American*—a tough decade even by Corso's standards. Thirty one of the original 50 poems in *Herald* find their way into *Mindfield*, perhaps because they tend to be shorter than the material that made up some of his earlier works.

In "Columbia U Poesy Reading—1975," [28] the first poem in the book and in *Mindfield*'s *Herald* section, we find a chastened Corso appearing at the university 16 years after his last lecture there. In the Prologue section he recalls that earlier time surrounded by Professor Lionel Trilling and his wife, his own wife and daughter, and his fellow Beats, Kerouac, Ginsberg, and Burroughs. But those days, he admits are gone, and with them so much of his glory:

and good ol Kerouacky… poofed into fat air
Eterne Spirit of the age… a
Monumental loss … another angel
chased from the American door

Ginsberg, who perhaps more than any other individual promoted and tolerated Corso's worst habits, receives this ambivalent assessment:

Al volleyed amongst Hindu gods
then traded them all for Buddha's no-god
A Guggenheim he got; an NBA award;
an elect of the Academy of Arts & Sciences;
and the New York Times paid him 400 dollars
for a poem he wrote about being mugged for 60 dollars

Describing being attacked 16 years previously as, "filthy beatnik sex commie dope fiends," Corso adds, "Now—16 years later Allen's the respect of his elders / the love of his peers / and the adulation of millions of youth …" Is this the language of envy or regret? Turning his attention to Burroughs, he writes, "Bill's ever Bill / even though he stopped drugging and smoking cigarettes." "Me," he confesses, "I'm still considered an unwashed beatnik sex commie / dope fiend"—a charge he accepts with certain minor qualifications.

The body of the poem imagines Corso summoned by the Muse and attacked by Ganesha, Thoth, and Hermes for betraying his calling as a poet while they share a pipe of "Edgar Poe's skullen ash." Addressing Corso as, "O charming poet-stud whom I adore," the Muse asks Corso if he would ever deny her. "Never," shouts Corso. He then offers up a half-hearted, if heartfelt, dissembling defense of his journey into addiction. When she asks the poet, "Do you love drugs more than me?" "Yeah," he screams. Immediately attacked by Ganesha, Thoth, and Hermes for butchering his spirit, bloodying his pen, and failing to deliver the Muse's message, Corso begs for another chance:

> I swear to you there is in me yet time
> to run back through life and expiate
> all that's been sadly done … sadly neglected …
>
> Seated on a cold park bench
> I heard Her moan: "O Gregorio, Gregorio
> you'll fail me, I know."

The theme of youthful talent squandered appears throughout the *Herald of the Autochthonic Spirit* selections. If Corso really curated these poems, what is he trying to tell us in lines like "A poetman / become an olding messenger boy" from "Sunrise" [29] or "I feel like an old mangy bull / crashing through the red rag / of an alcoholic day" from "For Homer"? [30] Death is everywhere in these selections, including "The Leaky Lifeboat Boys," [31] "How Not to Die" [32] and *Mindfield's* second Kerouac poem, "I Met This Guy Who Died." [33] Juxtaposing two of his favorite themes—childhood and death—Corso recalls a time he brought Kerouac back to his place after a night of drinking:

> Happy tipsy one night
> I took him home to see my newborn child
> A great sorrow overcame him
> "O Gregory" he moaned
>   "you brought up something to die"

Taken as a whole, Corso's mood in *Herald of the Autochthonic Spirit* seems to swing somewhere between resignation and acceptance, regret and self-realization, a yearning for the past, denial of the present, and hope for the future. Some read "Getting to the

Poem," [34] for example, and see a mature Corso, at peace with himself and the world because of lines like: "A poet's fate is by choice / I have chosen / and am well pleased". Maybe so, but Corso then acknowledges, "A drunk dreamer in reality / is an awful contradiction," admits "… Loved ones fall away from me …" and describes himself as:

A penniless living legend
needs get the monies
or write more poems
or both.

Whichever side of the resignation / acceptance argument you align with, one thing is clear: *Herald of the Autochthonic Spirit* is some kind of watershed, a poetic plateau that unites all the ideas in all the books that preceded it. But the real question is what did Corso, "the penniless living legend," think was the logical next poetic step? Was it to explore new visions or just "get the monies"? The writing would go on, as we see in *Mindfield*'s "New Poems" section, but the poet had run out of books, publishers and, as it turned out, time.

Mindfield ends with a collection of 23 previously unpublished poems written between 1960 and 1989. The majority (14) were written between 1960 and 1966, the remaining nine between 1980 and 1989. Ordering the poems chronologically, this means 14 poems were written after *Vestal Lady* and *Gasoline* had been published and before the release of *Elegiac Feelings American.* Two of the poems—"The Doubt of Truth" [35] and "The Doubt of Lie" [36]—were written before *Herald of the Autochthonic Spirit*'s publishing date of 1981, and the rest after.

So, the questions we need to ask are: are these works the poetic equivalent of the "outtakes" that often "justify" the re-release of albums by including rejected tracks the musician never intended to be heard? Are they here to justify releasing an anthology of work that was still easily available in more complete forms? Did these "new" poems not find their way into earlier collections because Corso, or Lawrence Ferlinghetti, or editors at New Directions found them unworthy? Or are these poems Corso kept back from the market for reasons known only to himself? Again, it would probably take an entire book to answer all the questions surrounding these 23 pieces of "new evidence" and—given the current market for Beat-related books—no doubt someone someday will write one or two.

But for now, I want to concentrate on the two poems roughly contemporaneous to *Herald of the Autochthonic Spirit* and the seven written after its 1981 publication. "The Doubt of Truth" and "The Doubt of Lie" were both written in 1980, presumably at roughly the same time. In the former Corso describes himself as, "a used-up poet /—what a sweet-sad / demolition is the poet man." He rather ambiguously tells us, "Though truth is no longer my master / I will not entruth lies." He also tells the reader, "I left my chest of poems / forever / but returned the next day ..."

We closed our discussion of *Herald of the Autochthonic Spirit* with a series of questions around whether the plateau Corso seemed to have come to in the book was the end of the poetic road or just a base camp reached in preparation for summiting even higher poetic peaks. "The Doubt of Lie" doesn't help us answer these questions any more than "The Doubt of Truth" does. In it he notes that "humankind" hurt each other and are not reliable, leading him to question whether or not he will ever die, since it was humankind that promised him that death was his inescapable fate.

The reality of death is questioned once again in 1982's "Window." [37] In an apparent reference to some form of perpetual reincarnation—a triumph of the spirit over the impermanence of the flesh—Corso tells us, "The body is but a relay / we are born of ourselves," and, "To believe that life dies with the body is to be spirit-sick." The argument that Corso was getting ready to assault higher mountains gains some momentum in 1982's "Hi," [38] which questions the existence of a traditional god and "Fire Report —No Alarm," [39] written in 1989, which tells us he, "did not adhere to any man's God," and concludes with him describing himself as, "God-free / father of my children / and upon my finger / the ring of poetry—"

The question of whether or not Corso was expressing envy or regret in the discussion of "Columbia U Poesy Reading—1975" surfaces again in "Poet Talking to Himself in the Mirror," [40] which concludes:

> Ain't got no agent
> can't see poets having agents
> Yet Ginsy, Ferl, have one
> and make lots of money by them
> and fame too
> Maybe I should get an agent?
>   Wow!
> No way, Gregory, stay
>   close to the poem!!!

If this sounds like an attack on Allen Ginsberg and Lawrence Ferlinghetti, that's probably because it is. But what are they being attacked for? For selling out, For being successful? For betraying the Muse? Or for not taking better care of Corso? No matter how you look at it, it reads a lot like jealousy.

Mindfield closes with "Field Report" [41]—a monumental epic of a poem that runs from Pages 238-268 and features three full-page Corso illustrations. "Field Report" is an important and complicated poem, one I don't have space or time to begin to do it the justice it deserves.

Corso is sending his "Field Report" on existence to the Muse. "I see all the wonders," he tells us, "and weep for my life still in pawn." Describing himself as, "just a little orphan boy gone old," Corso tells us: "Some think I'm after the answer / (you know, the when what who why bit) / No way, I'm no mouse chasing its tail." Longing for a "truer Godness / one of hope beyond futility / beyond pain, fear, ignorance," Corso tells the Muse, "Indeed life indicates more than living." A little further down the same page he returns to one of his perennial themes, writing, "Why children? / There is no forever child / there is but constant childbirth—"

Page after page he wanders along through the Summer of Love to Charles Manson, stopping to mourn the loss of the San Francisco of his youthful triumphs, a city that betrayed its promise, saying: "The sins of the land are expiated here / This city of Francis" and "This city of Athenians and poetry / aids and Ferlinghetti / are all what's left of it."

Age, death, beauty, history, music, art, places, and people swirl about for pages, the first part of the poem ending:

> I do take little walks from myself …
> at the moment I see myself
> coming down the street
> And as always
> I patiently wait on some corner
> For me to rejoin me
>
> One day I just might
> up and walk away

The next section "DISPATCH DISPATCH DISPATCH DISPATCH DIS-PATCH" is a 14 page surrealistic, nightmarish trip on a Mad Hatter's party ride of language and imagery. It begins in:

> …the draught of a spokeless space …
> …a point perfectly arching toward itself …
> …the workings of the wheel
> flows from the wheelwright
> all in slow steady pace
> what comes first in the circle
> comes last in the circling
>
> … in an avalanche of small dyings

This isn't some religion's version of reincarnation, It is the eternal return of an individual indomitable spirit—immune to the conventional confines of death—moving through eternity, body by body, poem by poem. Politics, social criticism, police brutality, poverty, Hedda Hopper, Clarke Gable, Jim Jones, Joan Crawford, Shelley, Socrates, Rimbaud, and current events are blended together here n a hallucinogenic smoothie of images, autobiographical notes, puns, world play all race recklessly against each pitching headlong toward the end of a poem that seems like it will never arrive. And then the mind numbing procession begins to slow. Corso notes:

> Something has lost itself
> it was in me perhaps part of me
> now it's gone
> gone and I don't know where
> don't even remember what it was
> all I know is I suffer the lack
> It's like if I died and returned
> not to see anything familiar …

The houselights dim. The curtain falls. Old age is coming, accompanied by its handmaiden, mortality. Noting their arrival Corso says, "yeah, sure, we're going / you didn't believe you'd remain here, did you?" "Three powers we got;" he adds, "Here and now; / what's imagined, and what's dreamed—/At least, that's the extent of my power…"

The Clown, masking his tears, worries audiences don't laugh as much as they used to at his jokes. His final trick is to disappear right before their ideas, perhaps to hide his spirit in a newborn child. The poem ends with a single all-capitalized word: "STOP."

But this final note begs one final question: Is Corso talking to us, the Audience, or to himself the Poet?

Source Notes

(1) Gregory Corso, "1959," *Mindfield: New and Selected Poems* (New York: Thunder's Mouth Press, 1998), pp. 97-98.

(2) Gregory Corso, *The Golden Dot*, ed. Raymond Foye & George Scrivani (Colorado: Lithic Press, 2022).

(3) Allen Ginsberg, "Foreword" to *Mindfield*, p. xii.

(4) William S. Burroughs, "Introductory Notes" to *Mindfield*, p. xvii.

(5) David Amram, "Introduction" to Mindfield, p. xx.

(6) Corso, "Greenwich Village Suicide," *Mindfield*, p. 3.

(7) Corso, "Requiem for 'Bird' Parker, Musician," *Mindfield*, pp. 8-11.

(8) Gregory Corso "Dementia in an African Apartment House," *Gasoline & The Vestal Lady on Brattle* (San Francisco: City Lights Books, 1958), p. 64.

(9) Gregory Corso, "The Horse Was Milked," *Mindfield*, p. 7.

(10) Ginsberg, Allen. "Introduction" to *Gasoline & The Vestal Lady on Brattle*, p. 13.

(11) Gregory Corso "Ode to Coit Tower," *Gasoline & The Vestal Lady on Brattle*, pp. 17-19.

(12) Gregory Corso, "In the Fleeting Hand of Time," *Mindfield*, pp. 21-22.

(13) Gregory Corso, "I Am 25," *Mindfield*, p. 35.

(14) Gregory Corso "Amnesia in Memphis," *Mindfield*, p. 23.

(15) Gregory Corso "Uccello," *Mindfield*, p. 29.

(16) Gregory Corso, "How Happy I Used to Be," *Mindfield*, pp. 48-49.

(17) Gregory Corso, "Bomb," *Mindfield*, pp. 65-69.

(18) Gregory Corso, "Marriage," *Mindfield*, pp. 61-64.

(19) Gregory Corso, "Clown," *Mindfield*, pp. 76-84.

(20) Gregory Corso, "Man," *Mindfield*, pp. 101-102.

(21) Gregory Corso "Greece," *Long Live Man* (New York: New Directions, 1962), pp. 20-27.

(22) Gregory Corso, "Beyond Delinquency," *Long Live Man*, pp. 16-17.

(23) Gregory Corso, "Reflection in a Green Arena," *Long Live Man*, pp. 28-29.

(24) Gregory Corso, "By Oscar Wilde's Grave," *Long Live Man*, p. 31.

(25) Gregory Corso, "Saint Francis," *Long Live Man*, pp. 36-40.

(26) Gregory Corso, "Writ on the Eve of My 32nd Birthday," *Mindfield*, pp. 120-121.

(27) Gregory Corso, "Elegiac Feelings American (for the dear memory of John Kerouac)," *Mindfield*, pp. 125-134.

(28) Gregory Corso, "Columbia U Poesy Reading—1975," *Mindfield*, pp. 161-165.

(29) Gregory Corso, "Sunrise," *Mindfield*, p. 166.

(30) Gregory Corso, "For Homer," *Mindfield*, pp. 172-173.

(31) Gregory Corso, "The Leaky Lifeboat Boys," *Mindfield*, p. 175-176.

(32) Gregory Corso, "How Not to Die," *Mindfield*, p. 177.

(33) Gregory Corso, "I Met This Guy Who Died," *Mindfield*, p. 169.

(34) Gregory Corso, "Getting to the Poem," *Mindfield*, pp. 187-188.

(35) Gregory Corso, "The Doubt of Truth," *Mindfield*, p. 222.

(36) Gregory Corso, "The Doubt of Lie," *Mindfield*, pp. 223-224.

(37) Gregory Corso, "Window," *Mindfield*, pp. 225-227.
(38) Gregory Corso, "Hi," *Mindfield*, pp. 228-229.
(39) Gregory Corso, "Fire Report—No Alarm," *Mindfield*, pp. 234-235.
(40) Gregory Corso, "Poet Talking to Himself in the Mirror," *Mindfield*, pp. 236-237.
(41) Gregory Corso, "Field Report," *Mindfield*, pp. 238-268.

A Road Trip to Lowell with Gregory Corso: Rolling Papers, Pipes, Bongs, Roach Clips

by Ron Whitehead

Part 1: How IT Started

We'd finished our 2nd 5th of Southern Comfort and the Mescaline was kicking in.
Jimi Hendrix crosses borders, threatening to ascend towards heaven. With lightning

and thunder he plays Bob Dylan's "All Along The Watchtower." Stereo loud as it will go.
Here in the only underground bookstore in Kentucky: For Madmen Only.

Shelves and bins stocked with books and records from City Lights and bookpeople
in San Francisco and from Atlantis and Alligator in New Orleans Teas and herbs and candles

from mountain communes. Turquoise blue Spiritual Sky incense. And next door in The Store,
our Head Shop, paraphernalia: rolling papers, pipes, bongs, roach clips, water beds, posters,

GROW YOUR OWN: How To Pamphlets, blankets and clothes from India, Native American jewelry,
and we're serving the new consciousness. Inspired by the one and only King of The Dharma Bums:

Jack Kerouac, and Lawrence Ferlinghetti, Gary Snyder, Richard Brautigan, Ken Kesey, Neal Cassady,
Allen Ginsberg, Gregory Corso, William Carlos Williams, William Blake, Hermann Hesse, Knut Hamsun,

Dostoevski, Nietzsche, Bukowski, Thomas Merton, The Dalai Lama, Gandhi, Burroughs, LeRoi Jones,
Diane di Prima, Hunter S. Thompson, Ralph Steadman, with Robert Johnson, Hound Dog Taylor,

Howlin' Wolf, Jimi Hendrix, Led Zeppelin, and always Bob Dylan, Bob Dylan, Bob Dylan on the stereo.

But we're Down and Out in Kentucky, failing like no others dare fail. And we're always on the outside,

outsiders, outlaws, being told "You don't fit! You ain't shit! What the fuck you doing here!" And so On The Road is where we live, traveling traveling traveling. A band of gypsies in search of IT.

Headed out of Kentucky, across the USA: coast to coast, ghost to ghost. Down to Mexico. determined to keep on keeping on, trucking till the wheels fall off and burn. Just passing through. Searching,

searching. Yes, after all these years still searching for IT. And yet somewhere, somehow, one day, one moment, at the heights of Machu Picchu, we went further in, traveled deeper on the inner road. We

entered The 3rd Kingdom, The 4th Dimension where lies the synthesis of apparently irreconcilable differences. And in the heart of The Big Bang Epiphany we discovered that the power and the glory

of IT is bound in the grace of forgiveness, of Beating Karma through love and compassion by persevering through desperate circumstances. So now we GO GO GO. We Never Give Up, We realize

Now that The Road, Jack Kerouac's Road, our Road always leads On so ever Further we GO GO GO. And I was gone baby gone.

Part 2: On The Road with Gregory

Years later, still on the road:

In 1993 I was invited to read with Gregory Corso

at the Lowell Celebrates Kerouac Festival. So I rented a big passenger van and loaded up my kids,

who went on so many adventures with me, and friends and posters and chapbooks and books and albums

then drove fast all through the dark night to New York City arriving at dawn to Allen Ginsberg's apartment.

We visited with Allen and Diane di Prima, who was staying with Allen for a few days, then I called

Gregory to let him know I was on my way to pick him up. Gregory said, "No, I can't go. Not without a

hundred dollars so I can buy some necessary supplies." I said, "Gregory, I don't really have the money but

okay I'll find it. We've got to get on the road." He said, "Come on. Let's go. It'll only take me a few minutes

to gather what I need for the trip." I knew what that meant. On the four hour drive from New York City

to Lowell Massachusetts Corso asks questions and tells stories. When we walk into the Lowell hotel lobby

Michael McClure and Ray Manzarek yell and wave for us to come over. Corso, McClure, and Manzarek all

knew each other so I introduced myself and let them know that Gregory and I were reading that evening.

Manzarek asked me where I was from. I said, "Kentucky." McClure said, "Diane di Prima speaks highly of

you." Then I quickly shared with them a little of my own history. And I preached some of the Global Literary

Renaissance Gospel. We all talked for a few minutes then Gregory said, "I've got to get up to my room and

take care of some business." When I turned to leave with Gregory, Michael said, "Ron, wait.

Let's talk some more." When Corso was out of ear shot McClure said, "I'll give you a hundred

dollar bill if you keep Gregory

away from our performance." I looked at him then laughed and said, "I don't have any control over Gregory. Nobody does. But I'll do what I can." Gregory had a reputation of hatefully heckling other performers. Ray

Manzarek was a nice guy, a gentleman. Later in the afternoon I gathered everyone for a visit to Kerouac's grave, before our reading. On our way we drove by the club where we'd be performing. Corso yelled, "Stop!

I've got to have a drink." I said, "Gregory, we don't have time." Gregory said, "I'll hurry. I'll be right back." I said, "Okay. I'll go with you." The place was packed. As we entered everyone turned and, seeing Gregory

Corso, grew quiet. A path opened for us to get to the bar. As the bartender came over to take our order, a guy at the bar said, "Hey, you're Gregory Corso. You heckled Diane di Prima at her reading. I'm gonna

whip your ass." Corso turned white as a ghost then he started growling. Corso didn't take shit off anybody. I stepped between Gregory and the drunk at the bar. I looked at the bartender and said, "Hey, this idiot wants

to fight Gregory Corso. He needs to get the hell outta here!" In a heartbeat two bartenders grabbed the guy and tossed him out. Folks said he should've been thrown out earlier. We ordered our drinks. John Sampas

and his brother yelled at us to come over to their table. They offered to buy us drinks and dinner. I thanked them but told them I had a van load of folks and we're headed to visit Kerouac's grave before the show.

Corso accepted their offer and stayed. At Jack Kerouac's grave I called on his spirit inviting him to join our performance offering him Southern hospitality in Lowell, Massachusetts. As I summoned Jack's spirit I felt

the wind pick up and orange and yellow October leaves began to dance and swirl about and with us there at Saint Kerouac's grave. Back at the club I felt his spirit grow stronger as I presented my reading to a

packed house. When I was done I introduced Gregory Corso. No sound. When I looked over to his table Corso let out a pleading moan saying, "I can't. I'm too fucked up. I've got to go back to the hotel." I asked

two friends to help Gregory back to the hotel.
The room was silent as Corso stumbled away.

Gregory Corso As a Werewolf, Moreso: An Imperfect Slice of Memory

by Kyle Roderick

Date: July 3rd-6th 1994.

Scene: The Arapahoe Lodge Motel, Boulder, Colorado, and the Naropa Institute.

The motel stands a few doors down from the Naropa Institute and the Jack Kerouac School of Disembodied Poetics, which was founded in 1974 by Allen Ginsberg, Diane di Prima and Anne Waldman. Gregory taught poetry during the Kerouac School's first summer sessions in the mid-1970s.

Naropa has rented the Arapahoe Lodge to house Gregory and fellow poets like Gary Snyder, Amiri Baraka and Ed Sanders, plus composers and musicians like Hal Willner and David Amram. Everyone is here to participate in and attend readings, concerts and plays in celebration of the 20th anniversary of Naropa's founding.

Why Gregory Corso is in Boulder: Along with Ginsberg-Burroughs-Kerouac, Corso rounds out the Beat literary Foursome. Gregory is here to read his works in public, hang with his lifelong poet friends like Allen Ginsberg and Anselm Hollo, who translated some of Gregory's books into German. Gregory is also here to submit to questioning for documentary film, television and print interviews. At age 64, he continues writing fine poetry and reading his work in public with dignity and grace. Blessed with a silver-gray mane of straight hair that almost grazes his shoulders, the private poet is also a toothless, long-term heroin addict who tells me that he reads Emily Dickinson, Plutarch and the Marquis de Sade because, "My life depends on it." He supplements his heroin injections with Jose Cuervo Especial Gold Tequila, Coca Cola and cigarettes.

Why I Am in Boulder: I have been working on a Corso biography for over a year. Corso is the poet whose lines offer infinite riches. I am enchanted by his conversation, his brutal humor, honesty, frequently easy-to-spot lies, his roaring laughter, strange kindnesses and furious self-destruction. We get on and laugh like loons because... I never know why. The fact that I am a 34-year-old woman with blonde hair and olive green eyes who wrote her thesis on Louis-Ferdinand Céline's novels seems to help smooth the way. All the Beats admired Céline, especially Corso, Kerouac and Ginsberg, whose winding, visionary and baroque sentences echo Céline's disabused voice and elliptical, maximalist narrative eruptions. Gregory confesses that when he and Ginsberg were invited to visit Céline at his house in Paris, Gregory chose to romance the U.S. actress Jean Seberg instead. "Céline... for me that was one of the greatest miss-outs of ALL TIME!" Gregory laments.

I am also in Boulder because Gregory has supplied me with signed letters of introduction naming me as his authorized biographer. I use these to gain access to literary archives and obtain interview appointments. I know that the existence or absence of a biography ranks way lower on his hierarchy of needs than do his drugs and his poetry. Knowing my book may never get into print, much less get finished, I soldier on, however, because I am an Andrew Mellon Literary Fellow at the Harry Ransom Humanities Research Center at the University of Texas, Austin. I am what they call "an independent scholar" and they are paying me to research and write about Corso's poetry and the Beats.

JULY 3, 1994: I spend the day herding Gregory to and from interviews with television and print journalists. Gregory looks great in the long-sleeved, green linen shirt I gave him to cover the bruised and scabby needle tracks on his arms. The gold-mirrored sunglasses he borrowed from me hide his dilated pupils. Photographers from around the world snap us together and separately and then we head over to the Naropa Institute press conference. After a few minutes, Gregory nods out. Although I respect his utter lack of interest in capitalizing on these PR and photo opportunities, I fear that if he dies here, right now, dozens of culture vulture photographers and filmmakers will document his very public death. I don't like the way people criminalize drug addicts. I believe all drugs should be legalized.

After the press conference, Gregory wakes up and we walk back to his motel room. "Knock five times whenever you come so I'll know it's you," he instructs. "I won't open my door to just anybody." I amble off to speak with composers David Amram and Hal Willner, and then I'm going to try and schedule an interview with Gelek Rimpoche, Allen Ginsberg's Tibetan Buddhist teacher. Allen introduced me to Rimpoche earlier that day, explaining that he is here to embody Tibetan Buddhist spirituality during the celebrations. Because one of the magazines I write for is spiritually oriented, I trust that I can sell an interview with Gelek Rimpoche to help fund my Corso research.

Let's be clear: at this point in my life, I am a journalist who has interviewed everyone from Prime Ministers to poets to Super Bowl-winning quarterbacks to Nobel Prize-winning researchers. I never assume that anyone, even a religious leader, possesses more wisdom than I do.

One of Rimpoche's attendants ushers me in to a room that is triple the size of Gregory's room. The stocky tulku is sitting in the middle of his bed reading Tibetan prayers. He looks up in surprise and puts the papers to one side. When I mention that I know some Tibetan Buddhist monks in Los Angeles that he has known for decades, I immediately sense a shift in his energies. UGH.

I ask him if he has a few minutes to tell me about his Jewel Heart center in Ann Arbor, Michigan, because I'm going to try and sell an article on him to a spiritually oriented magazine. He nods in the affirmative and as I sit down on the furthest end of his bed, closest to the door, he tells me, "The Jewel Heart Center is shit, the stupa is shit, all of the jewelry you are wearing: it's all shit," he tells me. "You can come back to my room anytime, even after midnight."

As I am trying very hard not to laugh in the face of this revered Tibetan Buddhist scholar and teacher, I cover my mouth and fake a cough as I rise and head toward the door. "This has been most enjoyable, thank you Rimpoche," I tell him with the neutral tone of a therapist. I scamper out of the suite, past the monk's attendant and stomp back to Gregory's room, knocking five times on his door. After he lets me in, his toothless grinning face fairly shouts, "You are just in time, my Kyle, we got the movie shot, tonight, Lon Chaney as "The Wolfman" is coming on next!" I tell him about the Rimpoche's proposition while I light up an *American Spirit* cigarette. "That guy may be devout but what a sacred and profane lamebrain," I say. "I don't have rich donors like he does, I have to sell stories to stay alive. He'll never get that women like me have to work and have zero interest in his wisdom, even if Gelek's uncle was the thirteenth Dalai Lama."

"Buddhists are sexy people, too," Gregory says with a raucous laugh. Lounging shirtless on the bed and sporting baggy navy blue boxer shorts printed with white line botanical renderings of wispy alpine flowers that my father handed down to me, Gregory continues, "You want to fuck a guru, go and fuck a guru. It's an opportunity that doesn't come along often in life." He shrugs casually, as if suggesting I try a rare fruit that's now in season.

"But he's revolting and a total drag, I'd rather watch werewolf movies with you."

The black and white 1941 film *THE WOLFMAN* starts and Gregory pours himself a tequila and Coke. I wonder idly how drunk he is, how high on heroin is this guy?

"Are these really your father's undies?" he asks.

"Yes, indeed."

"Too fuckin' much! Thank you, Daddy and Kyle!" he exclaims.

We settle into the film. Later, as villagers on the TV screen discuss the werewolf in their midst, Gregory begins speaking in unison with the characters. Together, they recite this poem:

> Even a man who is pure in heart,
> And says his prayers by night,
> May become a wolf
> when the wolfbane blooms,
> And the Autumn moon is bright.

"Just like the Buddhist who put aside his prayers to flirt with me," I tell Gregory.

"You got it, that's it. You're not scared of that Buddhist wolfman and neither am I."

"Why would I want to fuck a guru when I can watch werewolf movies with you?"

Gregory never answers. Later in the film, as Lon Chaney starts sprouting werewolf hair on his palms and head, Gregory lunges toward me on the bed, roaring like a werewolf and holding his hands up like clawing paws. He looks so adorably toothless, I am giggling uncontrollably, and Gregory is soon laughing so hard that he is drooling.

When the movie is over, Gregory announces, "Time for another shot," and heads toward his bathroom with the blood-speckled mirror.

Poets Don't Snarl: Gregory Corso at the University of Connecticut, 1996

by Kurt Hemmer

No one wanted me to do it—not even my mentor at the University of Connecticut, Ann Charters. When I had brought Herbert Huncke to UConn the previous December, Professor Charters was happy to have the storyteller junky, who had given William S. Burroughs his first taste of morphine, in her house. But she drew the line with Corso. They'd recently had a confrontation—Ann didn't want to talk about it. Even Huncke warned me about Corso; they'd been feuding for years over a drug deal gone sideways. So, I'd been warned. He's a sexagenarian barbarian liable to pull down the panties of any co-ed he could get his dirty old poetman hands on. I'd heard stories of him signing contracts to read at other universities and not showing up. Or maybe he would show up and throw up on the dean. Or maybe he'd get drugged up and start yelling at the librarians, "Penguin dust, bring me penguin dust, I want penguin dust!" Some UConn professors were sure that they'd heard of him standing up in the middle of a reading, walking to the back of the stage, and pissing in plain view. He was notorious for heckling other poets. But this time he'd be by himself. Maybe that was the break I needed.

Corso left a message on my answering machine the night before I left to pick him up. It was his sixty-sixth birthday: "Happy birthday! It's a fucking beautiful night! Tomorrow for lunch at eleven is great. Maybe we can see my kid in New Haven on our way to the college. I haven't seen him in years. His mother is keeping him away from his old man . . . yeah . . . maybe we'll try to see him." He blew a party horn into the phone and hung up.

Earlier that week, he told me he was considering making this his last reading at a university. He really didn't like these gigs—too stuffy and contentious. His friends, the filmmakers James Rasin (*Beautiful Darling*, 2010) and Laki Vazakas (*Huncke and Louis*, 1999), who had helped me get Huncke to UConn, had put in a good word for me. Every week they all watched Monday Night Football at Roger Richard's, the former proprietor of two famous bookshops that had been the gathering spots for New York's avant-gar-de: Greenwich Books near 14th and 8th and The Rare Book Room on Greenwich Avenue. Roger's wife, Irvyne, had produced a cable access show in the '70s called *Greenwich Books Presents*. James was working with Robert Mapplethorpe's ex-lover, Jack Walls on a screenplay about Mapplethorpe's early romance with Patti Smith, which would also be the focus of Smith's *Just Kids* (2010). Laki was still working on his Huncke documenta-ry, but he wasn't going to be able to make Gregory's reading. Maybe he knew something was up. Maybe he thought I shouldn't invite the dean.

The English Department at the University of Connecticut didn't want me to in-vite the dean. They wanted little to do with Corso. They were willing to give me some money to get him to the school, but they wanted me to take care of all the details alone. That way when the puke hit the dean, they could say it wasn't their fault. One profes-sor recalled seeing Corso read at some Ivy League school in the '60s. He described the event as if fondly reminiscing about seeing Papa Wallenda just before the tightrope fall. He didn't plan on coming to the reading I'd started planning in February, when I'd first spoken to Corso on the phone. Even the hip New York people were full of trepidation. Maybe, if I was lucky, he would pass out on the stage and the police wouldn't have to be called in. Driving down 95 South, I felt like the only one who believed this reading could be pulled off. But maybe I was delusional.

Over the years Corso gained the respect of many poetry enthusiasts and scholars and was even touted as the descendant of European traditions as much as being a Beat bad boy. His poems were published in major anthologies and his name was frequently en-countered in magazine articles examining the Beats, though the type of fame achieved by Kerouac, Ginsberg, and Burroughs eluded him—partly the result of a drug addiction that had begun as early as the late '50s. Nevertheless, he had written some of the best Beat poetry. Even Ginsberg believed Corso was the best of the Beat poets. As I merged with the city traffic, the realization hit me. I was soon to meet the *enfant terrible* who had named the rundown hotel at 9 rue Gît-le-Cœur in Paris the "Beat Hotel" and magically seduced dozens of women in the claustrophobic confines of his attic room with talk of graveyards, Rimbaud, and Chatterton.

I arrived at the Horatio Street apartment early, so Roger told me to have a drink around the block at McKenna's. I wondered if the furtive men and women sipping beer realized a famous poet lived right around the corner. Maybe Corso came in here and gave lectures on *Gilgamesh*. The locals didn't look too friendly. They were a beaten group drinking before noon, trying to figure out, while looking at me askance, why a young punk like me was in their midst drinking too.

I finished a couple of beers and went back to the apartment. Roger Richards and his wife, Irvyne, were taking care of Corso. I had heard that Ginsberg helped out from time to time and had found Corso a patron. Roger met me outside and told me that we were to go to the local market to pick up some lunch. I was willing to spring for food, but Roger would have none of it. I was the guest, and they would provide. We strolled down the street getting to know one another. Roger had operated the hippest bookstore in the Village. He'd been in New York since the '50s when he came down from his family farm in New Hampshire after serving in the Army and transferring to Columbia from the University of New Hampshire. One of the first people he befriended was an un-known writer named Hunter S. Thompson. After letting several transvestites crash at his place on 28th Street out of sympathy, he became part of the Factory scene, getting close enough to Warhol to have the balls to ask the pop artist to sign a copy of *SCUM Manifesto* by Valerie Solanas, the woman whose bullet ripped through most of Warhol's body. Later Roger published a chapbook by his friend Henry Miller. The customers at his bookshops included Nelson Algren, Robert Frank, and Robert Mapplethorpe. In the '70s he started becoming friends with a number of the Beats, including Ginsberg, Huncke, Carl Solomon, Lucien Carr, and William S. Burroughs. He was closest to Corso, who moved in with Roger in the mid-'80s, when Gregory was homeless, and stayed for over a decade, only leaving their care when his health pushed him to move in with his daughter, Sheri. Roger believed that the only true Beats were Huncke and Corso. Roger and Irvyne were the closest thing Gregory had ever had to a stable family, and a great deal of credit should be given to Roger for the more affable person Corso became at the end of his life. Roger told me how excited Gregory was about the UConn reading. By the time we entered the market the subject had turned to Ginsberg, whom Roger told me bought cannoli in this West Village neighborhood.

"You know the fucked-up thing about Allen," Roger told me, "is that whenever you're in a room with him and some famous person enters, it's like you disappeared. He's always got one eye over your shoulder looking to see who's just arrived. He's got to be in all the pictures. But you know when I'm alone with him he cries and whines and says he knows he's just a fake. Really, it's terrible. But Gregory owes a lot to him. Allen created the Beat Movement."

Roger ordered some smoked salmon, which was weighed, priced, and wrapped in plastic, and we walked down the aisle looking for some bread and condiments. As he walked slightly ahead of me, still talking about Ginsberg, he stuffed the salmon into the front of his pants. Maybe this was some hip way of carrying food to the checkout. I knew in suburbia, where I was from, I could never pull this off. As soon as I tried to go through the electric doors the alarm would sound. I knew I had to get out ahead of him before he tried to go through those doors. I'd pretend that I wasn't with him. Roger picked up a few more things, which he didn't stuff into his pants, and waited in the checkout line.

"What does Gregory like to drink?" I asked.

"Vodka," he said. "There's a liquor store across the street."

This was my chance. I would run across the street for booze. As I approached the electronic doors, I gave one last look back at Roger hoping that he had removed the salmon from his pants. But rather than seeing him pull a fish out of his pants I saw him pull a small vial out of his pocket. He unscrewed the top, which had a small spoon connected to it, and took a quick snort while nonchalantly waiting in line. As I made my way out into the street, I nearly knocked over a cop.

"Excuse me, sir," I said.

I was certain that Gregory wasn't going to be the only one drinking, so I found a big bottle of vodka and paid for it, anticipating the bust of Roger across the street at any moment. But when I turned around there he was smiling and talking and ready for lunch.

As we walked back, he said, "We got the salmon for free. I swiped it."

"Yeah," I said.

"You saw that? Well don't tell Gregory. He'd be very upset. But we're low on money and salmon is so damn expensive, but Gregory loves it."

I agreed that it would be our secret and we made our way back to the apartment.

As we entered the apartment Corso came out of the living room bouncing and smiling, inviting me to have a seat on the couch next to him. He was no longer the taut demon lover with curly, dark hair and the intense glare. His wild hair was white, pulled into a frenzied ponytail, much longer than how he wore it in the early Beat days. He had a lot more flesh on the chin, his nose seemed to have grown longer, and his eyes looked tired behind glasses that I hadn't recalled seeing in any photos. The black turtleneck sweaters and long black overcoats had been replaced by a wrinkled, loose buttoned-down shirt over a beaten t-shirt. He looked like, as his friend the poet Neeli Cherkovski had said, an inspirited gargoyle from the Notre-Dame de Paris, portly and animated. His movements were quick and spontaneous, not stylized and cool, and he seemed to be having more of a monologue with himself than with anyone else in the room. I began mixing the vodka with apple juice for myself. No one else was drinking. I mentioned that I had recently read Richard Holmes's *Shelley: The Pursuit.*

"Shelley was a saint," said Gregory in his endearing nasally whine that seemed to fit how he looked now more than it did when he was a handsome hooligan in the 1950s. We talked about William Godwin and Mary Wollstonecraft, about what a coquette Claire Clairmont was and what a piss poor father Byron had been. We talked about the mind of Mary Shelley and how it might not have been Shelley's child that Harriet was carrying when she drowned herself. We began exchanging our favorite anecdotal stories about Shelley. "Shelley loved the Irish," explained Gregory. "He'd write pamphlets about the emancipation of the Catholics that really stuck it into the English arses." I recalled how a copy of Keats was in Shelley's pocket when he washed up dead on the shore after his boat, the *Don Juan*, flipped over in a storm.

Kerouac had pissed off Corso by basing the character Yuri Gligoric, the friend who steals the girl in the novel *The Subterraneans* (1958) on him. Defending himself, Corso told me, "Back then everyone was fucking everybody." In December 1956, Randall Jarrell, then Consultant in Poetry to the Library of Congress, what we now call Poet Laureate, had thought enough of Corso to let him stay with him and his wife in Washington, DC until Kerouac visited and Corso was not invited back.

Later the talk moved on to William S. Burroughs, who had shot his wife in Mexico City in 1951 while playing William Tell drunk on gin. Burroughs had claimed that the incident was the result of being possessed by something he called the Ugly Spirit. I asked Corso what he thought about it.

"Bill never forgave himself for that," Gregory told me. "Here was a man who prided himself on being the most intelligent, the most rational man in the room, and then he goes and does something just plain *stupid* like play William Tell while he's drunk. He invented that whole possession by the Ugly Spirit bullshit because he couldn't face the fact that he had just done something fucking stupid."

We talked about Gregory's visit to see Burroughs in Tangier, where Corso also spent time with Tennessee Williams. "Tennessee was one of the kindest men I ever met. I wasn't queer, but I was much better looking back then. We were drinking at a table, a whole group of us. Someone had told him that I was broke, and, while we sat there, he slipped me some money under the table. He didn't want me to pay him back. He was taking care of one of his own."

Suddenly, Gregory demanded silence. Kato was on *Geraldo* and Gregory had to hear what was going on with the O. J. Simpson civil suit.

"I hope they nail that fucker," said Gregory.

At the end of the show, Gregory told me it was time for his nap. I said OK and expected him to go into his room. But he just sat there and stared at me. Eventually it occurred to me that his bed was the couch we were sitting on.

I sat with Irvyne just outside the kitchen and watched Gregory sleep. Drunk and

glowing after my afternoon with Corso, I thanked her and Roger for having me over. I
left a handful of books for Gregory to sign.

On March 28, 1996, the morning of the reading, I was feeling a bit sour after spending the night, after visiting Gregory, carousing on the Upper West Side. We didn't
have time to stop and see his kid in New Haven on the ride up to UConn. Gregory was
nervous about the reading and drinking vodka from the bottle I'd bought, spilling some
of it in the back of my car. We had to make a few piss stops before arriving at the university. I put him in my dorm room with Roger, had some vodka myself, and made sure
everything was going well at the Doris & Simon Konover Auditorium, where he would
read at 4 p.m. When I got back, I found Gregory sitting on the bed trying to look nonchalant, like I wouldn't notice that the room reeked of cologne. He had helped himself
to a bottle of Obsession by Calvin Klein, which I kept on the dresser, but he was trying
to distract me by looking at books on my shelves.

"You got us all up there," he deflected, looking at my collection of Kerouac, Ginsberg,
and Burroughs, and probably happy to see most of his books up there, too, which he
had signed the night before. At least he'd smell good for the dean. I showed him a poem
I had written, "An Unpublished Poet," inspired by his poem, "I Am 25." In his poem
Gregory goes to the homes of old poetmen and "rip[s] out their apology-tongues /
and steal[s] their poems." He looked at me like I had asked for his last line of coke, his
hands clenched the bed sheets, and his eyes bulged. Didn't I know how uncouth it was
to force my drivel, like so many other hacks, on his poem-wary eyes? But he sat on the
edge of my bed and read it, probably figuring that he owed me as much for the cologne.
"You go much further than me. I only steal the old poetmen's poems, you murder them,"
Gregory observed. "But I like it anyway. It's good."

Waiting outside of the auditorium he paced with nervous energy. Flapping his arms,
running his hands through his hair, talking to himself incessantly, and swigging from
the bottle of vodka, he looked like a man psyching himself up for a brawl. "They won't
like me," he said. "Do these kids even know who I am, Kurt?" All the self-doubt was
creeping back into him, even after all these years—not wanting to be rejected, not want-

ing to be abandoned. Out in the audience over one hundred people waited for him.

I finally got him onto the stage, and he immediately began to speak. "You can hear me back there?" he asked the audience.

"Can I introduce you?" I asked him.

"*Pardon*," he said with a French accent.

"Don't let it happen again," I said, feeling by this time that I could joke around with him. "Please welcome my friend and poet, Gregory Corso."

But he really wasn't my friend. Excited by our time together, happily surprised by his politeness, his humor, and his charm, I wanted to be his friend. But I wasn't. Introducing him after all the planning and organizing, and bringing him from New York, was a thrill and a relief. I had done it. The highlight for me came just before he read "I Am 25," when he told the audience, "This is one Kurt likes, I didn't like it because I used the word 'hate.'" But he read it anyway, and I thought it was just for me—though I was twenty-six.

"I HATE OLD POETMEN!" Corso yawped.

During the reading, Gregory said, "I wouldn't even call myself a poet. I don't know what the hell I am." He said that when he was younger that he played the fool because he was too shy to read his serious poems, which he wanted to do this late afternoon. He read his first poem, "Sea Chanty," about his mother, whom he had not found yet. He said he tried to do on one page what others did in epics. At the end of "The Whole Mess ... Almost" he changed the ending: "Why don't I throw myself out already and get done with it." He criticized himself for promoting drugs. He told us, "If you see a poet snarl, I don't think he is a poet." His performance inspired cheers.

At the end I gave Corso a hug, but he tightened up, not feeling we were that close yet. I was happy that the dean didn't need to go to the cleaners (as a matter of fact, the dean hadn't shown up at all). Ann Charters, gracious as always, had shown up.

People lined up to get books signed.

One young woman came up with a napkin. "I won't sign a napkin," smirked Corso. The young woman's heart sank. I felt bad for her. "But I will sign a poem," Corso said as his smile stretched across his face. He was flirting and probably reminiscing about the times when he used to get laid after gigs like this. He read out loud as he wrote, "I want to stick—" I started to sweat, looking around to see if the dean had showed up after all; the place seemed to have gone suddenly silent. "My rose—" Gregory continued, to my relief and apparently to the relief of a few others in line, as well. "Into your—" Gregory began again. I could feel a collective holding of breath as the tension became taught. "Heart," Gregory concluded, as I looked for the vodka bottle, despite my relief, and secretly wished I had been the one asking him to sign a napkin.

After the book signing, someone brought their four-year-old cherub, a little blond girl in white, who looked up at Gregory in disbelief, the old poetman, as if she had been enchanted by the gargoyle. She gazed at him in amazement as he recited lines from memory: "BOOM BOOM BOOM BOOM BOOM / BOOM ye skies and BOOM ye suns / BOOM BOOM ye moons ye stars BOOM / nights ye BOOM ye days ye BOOM / BOOM BOOM ye winds / ye clouds ye rains / go BANG ye lakes ye oceans BING / Barracuda BOOM and cougar BOOM / Ubangi BANG orangoutang / BING BANG BONG BOOM bee bear baboon / ye Bang ye BONG ye BING." I was ready for him to double snap, clap, slap his head, and go "woob woob woob" like Curly, the Stooge. His screwball antics had the cherub laughing sweetly, and maybe we got a glimpse of how he survived the prisons he was in.

With a friend, I took Corso and Richards to Hartford for their train back to New York. I played pinball with Corso before the train came. He asked me if I wanted something to eat. I was too juiced up and excited. "I don't like it when people don't eat," he said solemnly to himself. We shook hands good-bye, and he waived from the train. Though we spoke a few more times, it was the last time I ever saw him.

More than fifteen years after I had met Corso, I visited his grave on May 23, 2011 in Rome at the Cimitero Acattolico, one of the most beautiful cemeteries in the world, where Keats is buried. Corso's pal Bobby Yarra, who now helps artists through The Golda Foundation, had convinced a friend, Hannelore Dellelis, a famous German model, to pull some strings to get Corso's ashes buried at the foot of his beloved Shelley's grave. Corso had wanted "Oops! I died," but thankfully the epitaph was Corso's poem "Spirit," chosen by Yarra and George Scrivani, who had first seen Corso read as a student at the University of Buffalo in 1970. By accident, Yarra's girlfriend at the time did not put the second "i" in "Spirit," which was not caught by anyone in time, so an apostrophe was used in its place. Corso would have been just fine with it. Patti Smith raised some money for Corso's grave at St. Mark's Church and Yarra paid the remaining funds out of his pocket. I left a red poppy on the flat ashen stone.

Gregory Corso and the "Rogue Archive"

by Dick Ellis and Hugo Frey

Although best known as a poet Gregory Corso consistently worked in the field of the visual arts—both sketching and painting for their own sake, but also, especially later in life, to finance his addictions. It became a more extensive part of his practice than is usually recognized—say, as in the illustrations in his only novel, *American Express* (Paris: Olympia, 1961), and for the long visual narrative "Earth Egg," published as an issue of the little magazine *The Unmuzzled Ox* (1974). As with his writing, Corso had received no formal training and his work was often naïve, even cartoonish, although always expressive and often drawn with a deft felicity. In the drawings his work tends towards the grotesque, frequently portraying the human figure and face as twisted and misshapen, yet retaining a sense of the struggling human beneath. As with a lot of untrained outsider art Corso's aesthetic is hard to pin down, shifting between styles and genres, yet it can communicate with a vibrancy not always found in more conventional work. His drawing is figurative, detailed, yet at times surrealistic. Pieces were created impromptu with the aim of being quickly sold on. Unlike, say, Ginsberg's photography, the resulting visual work never coheres into a single project, but rather offers playful interventions, explorations and ad hoc creations. Yet the idea of working with the "space on the page" to express an idea is a consistent trope, and in his best known text-image work, the concrete poem "Bomb," and the carefully designed panorama created by the nine feet long "Earth Egg," a poetic force emerges. And in both these, and often in other works, there is a sense of energy, a desire to communicate quickly visually or in dialogue with language and, perhaps above all, a wittiness or a sense of the comedic.

For a couple of decades increasing attention has been paid to the Beats not only as writers but also as visual artists, although much work remains to be done here. Corso's work has been shown at several of the major exhibitions, including the Whitney show "Beat Culture and the New America" (1995) and the Centre Pompidou's "Beat Genera-

tion" exhibition (2016). So too American University archive holdings of Corso's work now increasingly acquired visual materials alongside literary manuscripts. There is no catalogue raisonné of his art, and perhaps there never can be as Corso's drug habit and alcoholism repeatedly led him to toss off visual work to acquire money. There is therefore almost no way of knowing its full scope. To borrow from the literary theorist, Abigail de Kosnik, Corso's art belongs to the space of the "rogue archive." Quite beautiful and fascinating items appear and disappear at online auction sites (for example, his painting "W.S Burroughs at home in Kansas"); more informally his work turns up within e-bay digital thrift sales and seemingly are sold and/or acquired by collectors all over the world. Value seems undetermined by any market measure other than the online "trade" that sets a price on a given day, although the Paris Centre Pompidou show has probably raised prices considerably. Across North America, the extended world of Booksellers and Antiquarians periodically and increasingly list works by Corso, but much more rarely than one would anticipate. Sometimes relatively high sums are set for small drawings or very informal sketch work, and authenticity and provenance are often left entirely open. In fact, there is some scholarly pleasure in the detective work involved in rethinking Corso not only as a writer but also as an artist. All the more so because of the mixed quality and sheer variety of his work. Items of real importance have been found, including original works that fetched up in the backwash of the British Beat scene through the later 1970s and 1980s.

   The two works reproduced to accompany this short essay seem typical of the "rogue archive" and some of Corso's interest. Both are portraits of a kind but neither conventional. One is a sketch of Peter Orlovsky from the early 1970s probably made "live" as Corso listened to a reading. Its last home a North American high-end book dealer after being auctioned years earlier. The second a small oil painting copy of a WB Yeats poetry collection dust jacket that was sold on by a Syracuse "beat" book trader online after it was framed up by Ricky Clifton.

   Neither is that typical of Corso's work in *American Ex-*

press or "Earth Egg". Instead they evoke two different Corsos, one engaged as a witness and recorder of three of his fellow Beats and one paying homage to a Romantic poetic tradition he felt a part of (he requested he be buried at the foot of Shelley's grave in Rome).

Down the Line

by Anne Waldman

Patti and I went to see Gregory a few months from the end, west village. Apartment of complicated friends. Complicated truths.

He was gleefully abed. Seemed people could visit bearing gifts of inebriants, elixirs, smuggling the goods in.

And flowers and elegant stuff too…

We walked together with some urgency.

His oldest daughter, a nurse, staying there with him, wasn't having it. With the drugs or alcohol. There were slippages. She'd chase people out down the stairs.

Prognosis was in any case dire. Gregory was watching TV—a generous screen of baseball. I remember that bright clarity of muscle, energy, and force of game sound, aggressive, hyped, but not who was on base. I was distracted waiting for the oracle to speak.

I was worrying about his scattered poetry, who would look after because he was so very scattered in poetry keeping, every which way. Mislaid, misplaced, forgotten, sold for a pittance, sometimes more. He had exquisite taste in jewelry. Raymond Foye would surely "do it" for him? Take care. Make the book. But where would the poetry be? Others might steal, sell it etcetera but I knew there was a pattern to all this. I just wanted his poetry safe and there was the promise of a new book.

Talk of this book a long time. *Down the line.*

He was pleased to see us, amused, we'd brought ourselves and maybe brought an arrowhead something from that cool flower shop close by. I was waiting for a way to read onto the situation and forgetting to just be with the space as they say. Dissolve into his space. No projections. I was at the TV, a bit glazed. Trying to see through his gaze, notice what to notice.

Patti was sweet with him, matter of fact, a buddy, they had some close history, the Chelsea. She and I were being lovingly nonchalant. Both thinking: could be the last time although prostate cancer could be slow.

Both of us had history. I saw him as a kid, Bleecker Street. I'd followed his poetry forever. At Naropa it was like being with family. And as gatekeeper. And attending to whims. Trying to keep him like everyone from doing harm. Heh poet, do no harm. She was in the ranks with him too, and steady. Eye to eye.

Gregory Corso, Anne Waldman, Gary Snyder, Allen Ginsberg

Throat felt tight, burning & stress in chest. Tongue tied. Too many deaths, the old timers. Old souls before their time. Is it allotted? I remembered that phrase: *"a-lot-id"* *A death sentence. Also* something bountiful: A LOT IS. Buddhism speaks of "adisthanas"—blessings—showering down.

Never too late to feel the rain of blessing. Maybe Gregory Nunzio Corso was feeling it.

I remembered the plane travelling with Reed Bye first leg from Colorado, a few years back, heading to a festival in Rome. And Allen & Gregory and Scrivano and the emergency landing and Gregory calling out:

"Ginzsy? Ginszy? How about that red plaid shirt? Can you leave it to me? I want that shirt, Heh Al! Leave it to me in your will!"

He was bothering some of the people on the plane, demanding another drink maybe vodka/tomato juice and people quite nervous it was to be a fast steep landing he was sitting behind Allen and Allen mollifying… fasten up…

And Gregory here now with some excellent art supplies and he drawing… figures faces some words cartoons. Not funny, not urgent. I wasn't registering details.

I also can't remember much but of mood, but tone, his mumbling preoccupation with the drawing that wasn't forced. And you know when someone is following a game, their mind is strongly on the game. No one's clown. *Thought of the word: ameliorating.*

That he could be amusing, That he could be a terror. He knew that, and he was amused…could it be the pills? *Probably. I was always naïve.*

It went beyond pills. He was razor sharp much of the time.

That he was not having to play for anyone, or score or manipulate the frequency.

How sweet he'd become. I'd hope maybe for transmission from the wise fool. He'd done it before; tell me what to do.

This was it: an elegant poet deal with mortality.

No fuss today.

Sherri was sane. Patient, tough too. A daughter's skill, late to the task—could feel her heartbreak—all of it—command the room, puttering in the kitchen, keeping it ordinary.

A wager for the *magus Gregoire.* Magic of the ordinary magic mind.

The following is the elegy Rosemary read at Corso's San Franciscan memorial service in January 2001.

Memories of Gregorio

by Rosemary Manno

In dark overheated Chelsea room
we share dead Bob Kaufman news
get high again
then Chino Cubano airstream trailer comida at noon
on sunny 8th Avenue…
we talk about Bobby's wife's stolen jewels
you said no one could blame you here
safe in New York City

We drink in your room
we drink in mine
we stop in another bar
then a Chelsea bodega
we pour out half the coke in the can
to make room for the rum
for the walk
O playmate

One night with flickering votive candles
in Grant Avenue hotel
you talk about the Italian broccoli farmer
in snowy white tee shirt
somewhere on Long Island
This is the mafia you solemnly say

You drag me to City Lights
to share the book on your early life
and your mother Michelina

before she left you to save herself
to escape the bully Fortunato
in New York City…
when we leave the store
you tell Suzette at the counter *I'm clean*

You gave me your Italian ring
tricolored gold of white, yellow and rose
banded by links many years ago on my birthday
in the Caffe Trieste…
you said *I own nothing this year that I owned last year*
Moon said it was my best thing, my poet's ring
Last Wednesday morn I put it back on
as I do each day and it broke…
you died that night
thanks for saying goodbye

Briefly today it felt like spring
the kind of day we'd wait for when first we met
through *Marriage* and *The Happy Birthday of Death*
Your special fatalism went so far back all boundaries were lifted
The waitress in Yuet Lee missed you right away
"Where's the funny man?" she asked after you left
Peggy wanted you to dance on her grave so she could come back
I know you're still making everyone laugh
tonight you would've noticed my winter fat
you always said what you saw

Now we say goodbye in your public way
on the corso
at street corners
bellisimo de la strada
tumbling poesia
ciao Gregorio

24 January 2001
New College Memorial

Keep This Generation Honest:
An Interview with Raymond Foye and George Scrivani

by William Lessard

The Golden Dot: Last Poems, 1997-2000 is a white-hot summation and extended last word of a poet who was most alone in the company of others and frequently his own worst advocate. The Shelley-infused lyricist, familiar to us from more than a dozen books across forty years, is still in evidence, but there is a newfound clarity and urgency to the work, which is like meeting a long-lost friend after decades apart. Long-time Corso compatriots and editors Raymond Foye and George Scrivani have accomplished the heroic task of transforming the fluid manuscript Corso left into the poignant collection we now have. Like many folks from NYC's poetry community, I knew Corso had a final great book in him, but I doubted the unrepentant hellraiser would ever pull it off. To hear Foye and Scrivani explain it, Allen Ginsberg's death in 1997 and his own approaching demise in 2001 were the catalysts. Following is our exchange, which took place via email somewhere between Greece and the Hudson Valley.

WILLIAM LESSARD: For anyone who is coming back to Corso after reading him a while ago or experiencing him for the first time, what would you say are the biggest misconceptions about him and his work?

GEORGE SCRIVANI: Just the whole mythology of him as the bad boy of poetry, the *enfant terrible*. Gregory never wrote poetry about his mythology: the mythology was to help him get through the day, or to get through the poetry reading. It had nothing to do with those moments when inspiration struck. The myths and stories about Gregory get in the way of appreciating his work.

RAYMOND FOYE: The mythology was part of the man; he was a mythic figure. He was playing with archetypes and enduring ideas within the grand sweep of history. When you met Gregory, it was like meeting Keats or Byron, he was a poetical force of nature. Having acknowledged that, I would say in the end the only thing one should trust is his work.

LESSARD: You're talking about received notions about the Beats. Do you think the term is still useful?

FOYE: For me the term Beat Generation meant quite a lot in its inception. When Ginsberg and Kerouac meet Herbert Huncke on 42nd Street in 1948, and he used the word "beat," a light goes off in their heads. This was a new sensibility, and a new vocabulary to go along with it. Today it may be too broad a term to mean anything outside the historical context. But it was a great label, like Abstract Expressionism—which means quite a lot when applied to a de Kooning from 1953, but practically nothing when applied to a de Kooning from 1986. Stylistically they all outgrew the phrase.

SCRIVANI: Beat was about a new consciousness, a new way of looking at life. Gregory more than any of them fit the bill of the Beat Generation writer. He lived the spirit in ways truer than any of the other ones, but Gregory himself didn't like the constraints of the term. He had an on-again off-again relationship with the term. He either liked it or hated it depending on the day. The problem is the mass media jumped on the Beats from day one and tried to make a caricature of them, largely to undercut their message. If the reader is still going to buy into the stereotyped notions about the Beat Generation, it's going to keep them from doing the reading they need to do to understand what these people were thinking and feeling.

FOYE: My definition of Beat is broad. I would include Joanne Kyger, Diane DiPrima, Amiri Baraka, John Wieners, Bob Kaufman, Philip Whalen... all remarkable writers.

There are many more. We are now at an interesting stage with the Beats, where a lot of ancillary writings are coming out. Importantly, I would point to Allen Ginsberg's *Deliberate Prose: Selected Essays 1952-1995*, and his *Spontaneous Mind: Selected Interviews, 1958-1996*, both are essential. Jack Kerouac's *Some of the Dharma* is the best guide to the "spiritual" side of the Beats; I think it's an extraordinary book. I would also recommend *Preserving Fire: Selected Prose* by Philip Lamantia, and *There You Are: Interviews, Journals, and Ephemera*, by Joanne Kyger, and all of Amiri Baraka's prose. Many of the poetics classes from Naropa Institute are online at archive.org—that's an essential resource. I don't know any other group of writers who have left such clear instructions to young people about how to negotiate the perils of power, political propaganda, and media brainwashing. I wouldn't much bother with the biographies.

LESSARD: In your introduction, you write about Corso's public persona as a jester. You explain it as a way of protecting himself from other people, but also himself. I agree with you 100%, having seen Corso in action. To me, it was all about the shame he felt about his early life.

FOYE: Is it shame, or is it the very natural sensitivity that comes from having to expose your deepest feelings in public? The poet is naked in that respect, far more than a painter or a musician, who can still hide behind their paintings, or their instruments. When you saw Gregory read his poetry in public you saw the raw nerve. The tragedy of his childhood is always there, but I don't know if shame is the right word. Actually, I think he overcame that shame. At a certain point he realized he had to move past that, and he did. Not to say that it ever goes away. You do not get over your mother and father.

LESSARD: It's striking how precarious his life was, all the way through. Today, many writers are academics. But Corso was an unrepentant old-school bohemian, and he often paid the price for that freedom.

FOYE: That is certainly true. He never compromised his values, ever. Think about his refusal to sign the loyalty oath upon arrival at SUNY Buffalo in 1965, and being dismissed on the spot, when he was about to begin a very comfortable job in academia.

SCRIVANI: I remember when Allen Ginsberg offered to nominate Gregory for the American Academy of Arts and Letters. He said, "No, not me. I'd rather not be part of this. Somebody has to stay outside the Academy and keep this generation honest."

LESSARD: The poems in *The Golden Dot* are both familiar and strange. Corso's voice is unmistakable, but I feel like I am discovering a totally new poet. Was that your reaction when you first read this manuscript?

FOYE: Yes, absolutely. His honesty amazed me. I once said to Gregory, unkindly, "It's always special pleading with you." Drug addicts and alcoholics have a lot of excuses. There are no excuses in the late work. It's a philosophical and karmic reckoning, and it's *total.* Also, the level of skill amazed me, technically speaking, although I suspect many won't see that.

SCRIVANI: I felt like I was discovering a totally new poet. This was a new voice for Gregory, but it isn't *not* Gregory. You can recognize Gregory in his last book just as much as in the first one, but there's a clarity of address. He's hell-bent on making the situation clear and dispensing with the verbal pyrotechnics and the rhetorical flourishes he once revelled in—he keeps some of them but he's using them very sparingly. Because he has a point he wants to make. Either he wants to clear up a misconception or make a confession. We all knew the public Gregory as an arrogant fucker, but he wants to tell you that that is *not* who he is.

LESSARD: In one of the finest moments in this collection, Corso writes: "What I don't know / I know well." People make a lot of his Buddhism, but he seems like a Catholic to me—or Christ surrendering to the inevitable.

FOYE: He's Catholic *and* Buddhist. He says in *The Golden Dot* that he accepts Christ and Buddha as his teachers. His Buddhism is the Zen of the koan [a paradoxical anecdote or riddle without a solution]: "What I don't know / I know well." That's about dwelling in the mystery. But I really don't think theology was important to him in any significant way.

SCRIVANI: Gregory accepted the Buddha, but as a person he was branded with the Catholic nightmare. The indoctrination of children by the Catholic Church—particularly the pre-Vatican Council church, was terrifying and absolute, and his relationship with Catholicism was conflicted and antagonistic. Which is not true of his relationship with the Buddha. His relationship with Buddha was not ambiguous. He had a Buddha in his mind, and he liked the Buddha that he had in his mind, and he took it with him to the very end.

LESSARD: Many of the poems are about saying things left unsaid with friends, lovers and other people in his life, from Ginsberg on down. That many of the people he knew were no longer around seems to have freed him up.

FOYE: Yes, there's this feeling that he's been going through life blindly, striking out at everyone and everything and now there's a new piercing clarity and focus to his life. Throughout this book I kept thinking of Allen Ginsberg's line to his mother, in "Kaddish": "Now I've got to cut through to talk to you as I didn't when you had a mouth." What's remarkable is that he was given the time to write this book, he had three and a half years in this modality of Death. Allen only had two months, at the most.

SCRIVANI: Old friends and lovers populate this book, but mostly he is writing to himself, and the reader. In *The Golden Dot* he's looking for the original connection, he's coming full circle. Other aspects of being a poet took the lead in the glory days of his youth, but now he's come to this wizened old understanding, and he wants to set down in the poems all the things that came out of being a poet. The message, the communication, is what it's all about. It's about him connecting with the reader. And: *Can he do it?* He's put everything in his life through the grinder and there's not much left, but the song is still there and it's very simple and sometimes sad but often exalted, and it's about a few things that he's come to understand about the life that he's lived. He evolves from the lyricism of his youth, into basically a pre-Socratic philosopher. And if you look back on those pre-Socratic philosophers, and Socrates himself, they were all poets who then turned to philosophy, and that's what happened to Gregory. Gregory understood there was a natural progression there, if you stay alive long enough, you're going to become more philosophical. So then, it became, "OK, what is the wisdom that I have to impart?" And that becomes the subject of the last book. He becomes a part of wisdom literature. During the time I hung out with him I felt like this guy was pure gold, and nobody could see it. He was not recognized; all people saw, if they saw anything, was the problematic person, not the truth or the poetry or the pure gold that was there. Thus, the golden dot at the end.

LESSARD: My understanding is that this manuscript was still in a fluid form when he died. How much work did it take to get it into what we have now?

FOYE: It was far from a clean manuscript, but on the other hand we were not altering the poems in any way. We were going through the manuscript poem by poem and trying to get at the essence of what he was saying, trying to allow enough repetitions for the themes to cycle back, without it being tedious. As an editor you are not just thinking about individual poems, the book itself must have a form. It was clear he was struggling with the book, although it was full of gems. There was a fair amount of deciphering because pages were torn or stuck together. In some cases, his typewriter ribbon ran out, but he continued to type, so the lines appeared to be blank. I took a soft lead pencil and gently rubbed it across the surface of the paper, and those lines suddenly appeared, because the typewriter keys were striking the paper and making a faint impression. Some important poems were recovered in that way.

SCRIVANI: We worked toward letting the manuscript have a voice. That dictated how we edited it. We worked to free the manuscript of the confusions, while leaving the imperfections to the reader's discretion.

FOYE: I had a working friendship with Gregory more than twenty years, as editor and publisher, and George was with him for over thirty years, as best friend and translator and editor. We both helped him prepare manuscripts for publishers, so we had first-hand knowledge of his editorial process. There were plenty of times where we had to stop and think, what would Gregory do in this instance? We were evoking him, channelling him, having arguments and playing out the discussions. We were asking him to answer the questions we had. And I know we both had some very intense dreams of him during this period—not to get too weird about it.

SCRIVANI: I felt closer to Gregory during our work on that book than I had since his death.

FOYE: More than in his lifetime even, in many ways. Because this was a Gregory we hadn't seen—or had rarely seen. And it's the true Gregory.

SCRIVANI: That manuscript brings the presence of the man and the whole complex of what he was into palpable form. It's hard to fathom the meaning of another person, especially *his* person. I feel like he went a long way towards helping us try to do that.

FOYE: What was interesting was the fact that the manuscript came into our hands not the year he died, but 20 years later. His friend Irvyne Richards kept it locked up. Then suddenly it appeared when we're in the middle of a pandemic, and the life-and-death nature of what was taking place outside in the world lent a real drama to what we were doing in private. It made it seem like the most important thing in the world at that point for both of us.

SCRIVANI: (Laughs) It certainly did. I haven't quite gotten over that feeling. It was exhilarating. And hopefully soon we're going to see this thing, unless there's a new plague, or a new war.

LESSARD: What has been the reaction to the book so far?

SCRIVANI: For me the great thing was how the young ones are all getting it. It seems like they are looking at the poems for what they are. They're free of the Beat thing, in a way.

LESSARD: Where would you place Corso within the tradition? Between Shelley, Catullus and his countless other influences, it's no secret where he placed himself.

FOYE: He never claimed to be on that level, but that's what he aspired to: Shelley, Vermeer, Mozart, Emily Dickinson: pure spirit.

SCRIVANI: Gregory's poetry is about the weird and it's about the true, and it's about the beautiful on the simplest plane imaginable. That's what I am seeing of what he accomplished in the last book.

Woodstock

IN THIS ISSUE

Journal

September 1-15, 2000   VOL.6, No.18   FIFTY CENTS

The Woodstock Journal: working for an organic food supply, safe air, nonpolluted water, a total end to poverty, national health care, personal freedom and fun.

The Journal is distributed at many locations in New York City. At galleries & at bookstores, at NYU, at Gem Spa on 2nd Ave., on the Staten Island Ferry and other places.

A Salute to Gregory Corso
Poet Among Poets

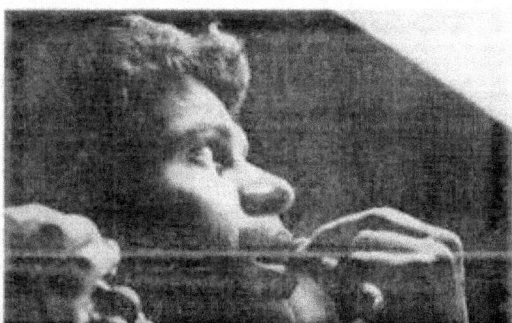

BY EDWARD SANDERS

Few have lived the life of a poet with more energy than Gregory Corso. He seems to have experienced about twenty lives from a hyper-energy source that must lead directly out of ancient Parnassus. Fearlessly he has thundered through the decades, going back for more than 60 years, beginning his poetry writing even before he met Allen Ginsberg in a bar in Greenwich Village in 1950. During

sation, yields gist-phrasing, extraordinary mind jump humor. Clown sounds of circus, abstracted from plethora are reduced to perfect expression, "tang-a-lang boom. Fife feef! Toot!" Quick sketch, sharp mind scissors."

Gregory Corso's at home now, in a nice apartment in Greenwich Village, on Horatio Street, and he's ill. A few weeks ago it looked as if he would pass into the beyond fairly soon, but, thank God, his condition has improved, and when I visited him a few days ago, he was full of good

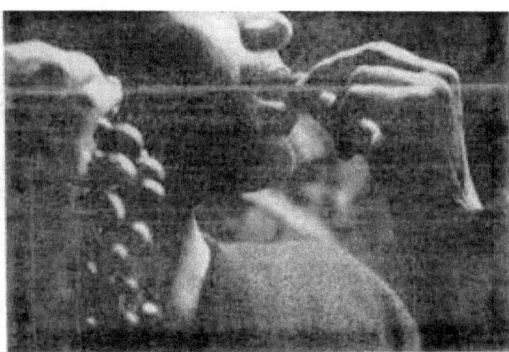

Gregory Corso in a photograph by Allen Ginsberg, Paris, 1967. Used by permission.

Public Rejects Comeau Pool

BY TINKER TWINE

A standing-room-only crowd at the Woodstock Community Center this week rejected an anonymous offer of $100,000 to build a swimming pool at the town-owned Comeau property. Only four people of the 37 who expressed their opinions to the town board favored the idea of accepting the gift and its stipulations.

Suspicion provoked by the would-be donor's anonymity was amplified by his/her insistence (in writing) that the bucolic Comeau property is the only acceptable site for a pool. Other conditions include the town's

commitment to "commence construction" by September, 2002, as determined by the donor's representative--the law firm of Wapner, Koplovitz and Futerfas--or to pass the money on to Marist College.

Town board members will vote on the question by September 30. That's the date by which the donor wants a written commitment from the town.

The people were eloquent in addressing the issue of a swimming facility. Some suggested removing fallen trees from the Sawkill Creek and providing a lifeguard at the Big Deep swimming hole, which the town owns and is open to the public. One resident suggested acquiring a former reservoir from the City of Kingston for recreation purposes.

Many people said Andy Lee Field, where a children's pool provides the

Continued on page 11

have experienced about twenty lives from a hyper-energy source that must lead directly out of ancient Parnassus. Fearlessly he has thundered through the decades, going back for more than 50 years, beginning his poetry writing even before he met Allen Ginsberg in a bar in Greenwich Village in 1950. During those fifty years Gregory Corso has become world famous, and he has thrilled generation after generation with his poetry.

Miriam and I first saw Gregory read at the Gaslight Cafe in the Village in early 1959 when we were still in NYU, and subsequently we have been onstage, backstage and on the poetry circuit with him on many occasions during the last 30 years. He's one of a kind, as they say; a legend; a man of a million anecdotes; virtually every well-published poet in America has a few Gregory Corso stories they cherish to tell.

He's the real stuff. I've seen him pull a crumpled note sheet from his pocket just before heading out to a podium to thrill a crowd with a few hot-off-the-mind lines. I've seen him at a packed Town Hall in NYC literally being begged by the audience to read his famous "Marriage," hesitating for a few seconds, then reciting it as freshly as if it had been just written that morning.

In his essay, "On Corso's virtues," Allen Ginsberg went to the heart of Corso's verse: "Gregory Corso's an aphoristic poet, and a poet of ideas. What modern poets write with such terse clarity that their verses stick in the mind without effort?.... As poetic craftsman, Corso is impeccable. His revision process, which he calls "tailoring," generally elision and condensing of mind scisors."

Gregory Corso's at home now, in a nice apartment in Greenwich Village, on Horatio Street, and he's ill. A few weeks ago it looked as if he would pass into the beyond fairly soon, but, thank God, his condition has improved, and when I visited him a few days ago, he was full of good talk, while watching a Cocteau Movie, though pausing now and then when a jolt of pain would hit. His daughter Sherry, a cardiopulmonary nurse who lives in Minnesota, has taken a few months off to live by his side, and caring for him around the clock. She is an angel from the Heaven of Poesy, as all who have seen her in action will testify.

Of course, in the presence of a remarkable person when they are ill, you recall all the instances of interaction, conversations from Naropa 23 years ago for instance, or the time he

Corso in 1981.

Continued on page 5

Woodstock Journal *September 1-15, 2000*

The Catholic Woodstock

BY ANDREI CODRESCU

I missed the first Woodstock, but I felt that I was there anyway because I got the crabs from a virgin who went. I hate crowds. They are all like that. You go there an idealist and a virgin and you come back with a social disease. I've never been to a Dreadful Dead concert and I never stood in a mob with a lit match in my hand. I don't ride the New York subways at rush hour and I stay out of Bourbon Street at Mardi Gras. I've been to sparsely attended baseball games, but never to a series, and I prefer minor leagues to major. Any room with more than a hundred people in it makes me nervous because they can turn into a blood-thirsty mob just like that. My idea of hell is a packed disco.

So, imagine how I felt when I got to Rome and I found out that two million youths were there for the Pope's Jubilee Year. As the cabdriver drove slowly past mobs of flag-waving, sandal-wearing pilgrims, he told me that most of central Rome was closed to traffic. From the hotel window I saw the Colliseum completely surrounded by young Christians. They streamed endlessly along the Via Crucis, singing and cheering in the stifling heat. Now and then a nun or a priest would appear amid the shorts-and-sandals crowd. Water trucks parked at intersections kept the pilgrims from fainting. The huge newspaper headlines touted this as "The Pope's Legions," and "The Catholic Woodstock."

At dusk I decided to brave the street. A magnificent sunset of the kind that props up the heavens in Renaissance paintings was drenching the Roman ruins in gold, purple, mauve, and magenta. Candles were being lit. Angelic voices came pouring out of loud speakers. The police closed the center of the

Corso

Continued from page 1

recited Shakespeare's "Under the Greenwood Tree" during a chat. But it was so good to see him talking, eating a hotdog even, and coming up with the pithy sentences and insights for which he is so renowned.

Lawrence Ferlinghetti and I decided to publish a tribute to the great Gregory in the *Journal*. Here are many of the responses to our call.

LAWRENCE FERLINGHETTI

Gregory Corso is the last great *voice* of the original Beat rebellion. Never derivative, never literary, never anything but his own raw self, Gregory is the true American primitive, made of mouthfuls of mad language, his poetry cast on the world like a roll of loaded dice. Gregorio of Horatio Street, *ave, ave ...*

ROBERT CREELEY

"Short and Clear"

for Gregory, who said it

Short and clear, dear –
short and clear.

No need for fear.
All's here.

Keep it
short and clear.

*You are the messenger,
the message, the way.*

Short and clear, dear,
all the way.

to me and pointed to my leg and demanded, "Why do you shake your knee?" I was dumbstruck. Before I could think, he whirled to Peggy, "But it works! That was it. I had passed the test.

We took Peggy and Gregory to the restaurant near the theatre. While we were there, Ralph Mills, a poetry professor of mine at University of Illinois, came over, hand extended and introduced himself to Gregory by saying, "Hello, I am a good friend of your friend, Allen Ginsberg." Gregory looked at him and politely asked, "Would you mind if I don't shake your hand." Prof. Mills gave me a glance of sympathy and walked off.

The Body Politic was packed that night. It was the first reading that we had charged admission. The crowd expected something special. Gregory was completely drunk. Chicagoans are predisposed to dislike New Yorkers and Gregory made it sublimely easy. He staggered over the stage repeating that he would only read "The Hits." Just "The Hits." He would read one line from the middle of a poem and then mumble. The audience starting calling out quickly, "You suck." "You're Stupid!" Gregory shot back, "I know everything! Ask me anything!" Everyone started yelling. Gregory kept talking and challenging till he couldn't stand. Afterwards he said, "Man I loved that. Those people really talked back! That was so great."

The next day, the angelic Gregory woke up in our home. He needed a clean pair of dress socks and traded his Christian Dior knee-highs for one of my more pedestrian pair. Gregory was scheduled to read at the University of Illinois. There was a small midday audience in a sterile lecture hall and Gregory sweetly, without a fuss, read his poetry for an hour and was stunningly good.

Gregory and Peggy were with us for a few more days. I remember Gregory listening to an extended Lenny Bruce performance. He talked to Lenny the whole time agreeing and having further thoughts. I thought I was in heaven. Gregory talked to me and encouraged me to move to New York for Poetry but not for a career. He was supportive and friendly. He didn't rip off any of Ted's paintings yet I did move Gregory and Peggy out onto the stoop after a few days. The last I saw of them, they were seated on the stoop waiting for a

Pope's Legions," and "The Catholic Woodstock."

At dusk I decided to brave the street. A magnificent sunset of the kind that props up the heavens in Renaissance paintings was drenching the Roman ruins in gold, purple, mauve, and magenta. Candles were being lit. Angelic voices came pouring out of loud speakers. The police closed the center of the road from the Forum to the Collisseum and the candle-holding pilgrims lined up on both sides.

They looked like good kids. They had come to Rome, heeding the Pope's call to show their support for social justice and to make a stand against consumerism. The hundreds of churches, monasteries, and convents of Rome had thrown open their doors and hosted the young pilgrims. Lines of showers had been set up in the their courtyards and they all showered together.

As evening fell, thousands of robed nuns, monks, and priests proceeded up the middle of the Via, singing hymns. Huge television sets relayed the ceremonies taking place all over the city. The kids, who came from over a hundred countries, waved their flags and cheered. Now and then the syrens of an ambulance could be heard, headed for some heatfelled jubilant. I was touched. I decided to convert. I decided to sleep on the floor of a convent.

Have intense discussions about the future. What kids! What a Pope! This had to be the largest concentration of virgins on earth. Good virgins. No bad acid. No crabs. Revolution without insanity.

Meanwhile, I was getting kind of sleepy so I decided to cross the street back to the hotel. That couldn't be done. Italian police didn't let anyone across. The only way back was around the ruins of the Baths of Caracalla, the Trajan column, the Temple of Saturn, and the Vestal Temple. I had to circle all of pagan Rome before I could get away from the Christians. I fell asleep just as the Pope showed up on the huge TV screen. "How do you like it?" he asked me in Polish. "It's great," I said. "You can cross yourself but you can't cross the street." He ignored me completely after that and started blessing the virgins.

short and clear.

You are the messenger,
the message, the way.

Short and clear, dear,
all the way.

Robert Creeley received this year's Bollingen Prize in poetry.

BOB ROSENTHAL

Gregory's Sox

In 1972, I was part of a group of Chicago poets who presented poetry readings weekly at the Body Politic Theater. Rochelle Kraut and I were housesitting Ted Berrigan and Alice Notley's large flat on Waveland Avenue (one and half blocks from Wrigley's Bleachers). Ted's only house rule was: "Don't let Gregory Corso stay here."

We already had invited Gregory and he was coming. We made hotel reservations at the North Park Hotel at the foot of Lincoln Park. Ginsberg and Burroughs had stayed there before. Gregory was traveling with a friend, Peggy Bederman. Peter Kostakis, Richard Friedman and myself piled in my car to pick them up at O'Hare. As we drove into the city, Gregory drunkenly and aggressively quizzed us. Someone made a comment like, "There goes my career." Gregory jumped on him and mightily exclaimed that Poetry is not a Career. The word soul was mentioned and Peter K. said, "There is no soul!" Gregory turned to Peggy and said, "See, he knows!" I was glad that I was driving and not likely to be quizzed. We had reserved a room with separate beds for Gregory and Peggy. In the lobby, Gregory loudly declared that he did not fuck Peggy. The Management decided to withdraw the room. And so I broke Ted's rule.

Gregory shared some grass which turned out to be very "trippy." A lot of Chicago poets were hanging out in our living room and sparing with Gregory. Lots of booze flowed. Gregory was wearing bell bottoms and blue suede shoes that Marty Balin had given to him. I sat in the circle and jiggled my knee in caffeine abstraction. All at once Gregory turned

thoughts. I thought I was in heaven. Gregory talked to me and encouraged me to move to New York for Poetry but not for a career. He was supportive and friendly. He didn't rip off any of Ted's paintings yet I did move Gregory and Peggy out onto the stoop after a few days. The last I saw of them, they were seated on the stoop waiting for a new friend to come by and pick them up. I never knew when or how they got back to New York. I kept those socks and wore them to my wedding. I still have them. Thank you, Gregory, for all the permissions.

—poet Bob Rosenthal was for many years Allen Ginsberg's secretary

Continued on page 7

Figured from the Staples Center. My co-panelists included Paul Krassner, Tommy Smothers, a man from *Time* magazine whose name I forget, and with Al Franken as my immediate neighbor. I didn't care much for Franken and the antipathy was evidently mutual. Franken's an ardent supporter of Al Gore. In this undignified posture it's hard to be a comedian and Franken certainly didn't meet the challenge. After I'd made a few disobliging comments about the Clinton-Gore record the *Time* man glared at me from the other end of the panel and said something to effect that "In other words, everyone else is wrong and you're right" – an unusually accurate statement from an employee of the Time-Warner company.

worth of Bill Bradley declaring his allegiance to re... Gore?

I passed up Lieberman on Wednesday night in favor of a trip to Simon Rodia's Watts Towers, now in the final months of a five-year rehab program. The five towers (though spires is a better word), two of them soaring a hundred feet into the air over the indigence of Watts ghetto in south-central Los Angeles, are as glorious as ever. I'd never fully appreciated that one of the main railroad commuter lines from Long Beach to Downtown LA ran along the west side of Rodia's property line and that therefore in the thirty-four years that Rodia worked on his towers between 1921 and 1955 his was most certainly one of the best attended artistic projects in

[illegible] his wildest eye[illegible] to [illegible]. That would have been a declaration of faith in the human spirit. But they sat in the Staples Center and listened to Al Gore giving his dull imitation of Bill Clinton's State of the Union addresses as devised by Dick Morris. Gore trudged his way through the laundry list of items designed to appeal to the middle class, and scored big. The joke came when the commentators termed this a "populist" oration. Gore's poll-driven rhetoric had the same relationship to populism as water to Chateau Lafite. At least he had the sense to kiss Tipper properly before he began, though I'm sure some of his advisers worried that even a good kiss might be dangerously reminiscent of Bill's illicit passion.

Corso

Continued from page 5

STEVEN TAYLOR

For Gregory

It's hard not to sound presumptuous when speaking of (and in the virtual presence of) a magnitude 1 star. Then again, Gregory put the whammy on me twenty-four years ago—as was his habit upon meeting young poets—he absolutely demanded that we declare ourselves. I met Gregory in Allen Ginsberg's living room office at 437 East 12st., must have been the summer of 1976, the time of my first gigs with Allen. Later Gregory joined AG, Peter Orlovsky, and myself in Amsterdam where we read with Andrei Voznesensky at the Kosmos. We then joined with Judith Malina and Julian Beck, their young daughter, and Hanon Reznikoff for a string of gigs in France and Italy, where we were joined by the great, long-time translator of American literature Fernanda Pivano. What a company! I have many treasured memories of that tour. It was a magical time. I remember sitting with Gregory and looking at the moon over the hills near Bergamo and him saying it looked like a sail and myself wondering why the simple simile rang so.

It's no mystery. In "I Held a Shelley Manuscript" he declares his company. *Saluto Maestro.*

—poet Steven Taylor is also a composer of note, a teacher, member of the Fugs, and for many years played guitar and sang with Allen Ginsberg in hundreds of performances.

SHIV MIRABITO

Carousing with Corso

A few years ago I took the bus to NYC to attend an art book party eulogizing Allen Ginsberg & benefiting Naropa University. Dozens of artists donated signed art & photos which filled each oversized book, & sold for 5 or 10 thousand each. Eugene Brooks (Allen Ginsberg's brother) kiddingly said to me "Howmany are you buying?".

It was way uptown, next to the Cafe Carlyle- everyone in suits & ties- no freaks in sight. Suddenly Gregory Corso glides into the stuffy rare book shop hosting the event, & the room lights up like lightning was about to strike.

I said hello & he was warm & friendly- I handed him some of the complimentary champagne & he saluted everyone with gusto. He sat down, dressed in the softest brown velvet three piece suit I had ever seen, in the most comfortable chair in the room. I

sat at his feet as we laughed, drank, & gobbled huge ripe red strawberries. He reminded me of my Sicilian grandfather & great-uncles jokingly downing as much liqueur & meatballs as they could before Christmas midnight mass. The happier we became- the more he transformed into Bacchus- toasting, boasting, & giggling- eyes glowing- wrapped in ermine furs.

As the party moved into the bright dining room for the $100 a plate dinner, Corso put his gentle hand on my shoulder & dragged me in saying " there's always room for one more..." & as we sat & ate he asked me if I had a joint. I stuck one into his deep pocket (along with a book of my poetry) & lit another for him, obviously ignoring the no smoking sign. He puffed & puffed- surrounded by sweet smoke- creating an oasis of Bohemian open-mindedness amid a desert of shocked conservatism (& flustered waiters). He stood his ground well- happily surrounded by pointless rules & adversity- a solid satyr focal point among waivering public opinions- the Beat queen bee amid a swarm of busily anxious American drones.

Long live gregarious guru Gregory Corso!

—poet Shiv Mirabito lives in Woodstock and produces a good series of Saturday night readings upstairs at Joshua's on Tinker Street

Continued on page 9

Woodstock Journal *September 1-15, 2000*

9

Corso

Continued from page 7

JOANNE KYGER

Gregory Corso

The next morning I think, did I dream all this? Returning late night from the party to instant sleep waking and talking with Ed on the phone. Gregory...

Hark to the Herald. A Bolinas Beach morning early autumn 1977. Billy Burroughs Jr., Tasha Robbins, Gregory, myself. Just after 9am the market has opened and Gregory has bought a can of pineapple and a bottle of champagne. Just us on the beach. Look at him says Billy Burroughs Jr. He is the absolute greatest, we have to take care of him.

We are looking at my photo album from India. Hope Savage! (note from editor, Hope Savage was a very early girlfriend of Corso) She was my early mentor! Out comes the picture, a memento.

He said I was 'a good sort' in a letter I carried later to the mother of his daughter in Santa Fe.

It's a Naropa summer. It's Sunday morning and everything is closed. Here's a glass of orange juice for you he says kindly. After I drink I find it's dosed with mescaline. A floating day, look look at those clouds. We are watching a grand and formal Japanese archery display. We go to Trungpa's house for cocktails and a talk. I'm standing by a pillar listening and I drop my glass. Oh look what boo boo you did Joanne, says Gregory loudly. You didn't have to answer him says Allen later. I said something foolish like 'I support my corner of the house'.

Gregory can read minds. He knows who's outside the door. Where the stash is hidden.

And he goes right to the heart of beauty. He's sitting sitting next to her, his arm around her, at home.

Allen asks me to introduce Gregory and him at a Naropa summer reading. I want to give it some Cosmic Sizzle and talk about them as the White Lights of poetry. Gregory is terrifically angry and says white light! That's what you see when you die! I don't do the introduction.

You always know things will be lively, outspoken, truthful, around Gregory, provocative, on stage. Center stage for the muses.

–one of America's finest poets, Joanne Kyger lives in Bolinas, California

---

MICHAEL MCCLURE

Saluto!

Only one poet in all the realms that exist, that have ever, or will ever exist, could write these lines:

....Poor little Bomb that'll never be
an Eskimo song   I love thee
I want to put a lollipop

Senior Notes

BY MESCAL HORNBECK

We note that the eligibility requirements for the State's EPIC program which eases the cost of prescription drugs for Seniors (those 65 and over) have been eased. The income limits have been raised to $ 35,000 per year for couples. The deductible amounts have also been eased. The new plan will go into effect Jan. 1, 2001 but applications can be made as early as October this year. The big idea to note is that this program could help seniors very much. BUT is not well known and many who need it do not take advantage of it. Please also note that Gov. Pataki wanted to cut appropriations for this program but a bipartisan support in Senate and Assembly overcame his idea. Do two things: enroll for EPIC if you are eligible AND tell your friends about it. Information can be obtained from U.C.O.F.A. at 845 340-3456 and EPIC 1 800 332-3742.

Programs such as EPIC are wonderfully helpful for segments of the population who can take advantage of them but they leave the vast majority of us in the dilemma of being as badly off as ever. It is the opinion of groups in the medical and pharmacological field as well as other groups studying the situation such as Merrill Lynch, to name one, that the only solution to the dilemma is a Universal or National health insurance program which would have the capability of requiring policy changes of the drug companies.

We have just learned with sorrow that Gertrude Williams died August 21. She has been a staunch supporter of and worker for the elderly population in Ulster County and she will leave a heritage of caring behind her. Her pleasant personality and boundless energy will long be remembered.

Only one poet in all the realms that exist, that have ever, or will ever exist, could write these lines:

> ....Poor little Bomb that'll never be
> an Eskimo song   I love thee
> I want to put a lollipop
> in my furcal mouth
> a wig of Goldilocks on thy baldy bean
> and have you skip with my Hansel and Gretel
> along the Hollywoodian screen...
>   "Bomb"

Gregory Corso is the golden leviathan of imagination, who with rampaging behemoth thundering and with zingers of flashgenius, exploring the caverns of his cell walls captured with grace, and wrote down another of his genius poems from the airy universe: *"Rembrandt — Self Portrait"* which begins:

> When I draw the magnificent Dutch girl
> When I unshackle the peachwolf from browngold air
> When I have the shepherd foxglove the chin of an angel...

Without lines and poems like these, Poetry would be a poor thing.
"Let me lightdrench the saddest of men," is what you said, Gregory.
My love and thanks to you and to those who are yours.

–Michael McClure's recent books include *Rain Mirror: New Poems* and *Huge Dreams: San Francisco and Beat Poems*.

ROGER RICHARDS

For Gregory

Great poetry and great music have at least one thing in common. What can you say about them? Can they be explained? "If I could paraphrase Ulysses," Joyce once snapped at a critic, "I wouldn't have had to write it."

All the exegesis in the world isn't going to add or take away one whit from Corso's work. The best thing you can do is pick up a copy of "Gasoline" and be astonished at the precocity of this self-taught young poet. Gregory wrote poems before he had heard the word or knew the concept of poetry. "Gasoline," in my opinion, is the most extraordinary collection by a young poet in our time. Then go on to "The Happy Birthday of Death," "Long Live Man," "Elegiac Feelings American," which has the long elegy to his friend Jack Kerouac, one of the most tender and poignant poems ever written, an invocation to America to recognize one of her most loving sons. His last books have not lost any of his humor, irony, or wit.

There was a brief moment when poetry was actually popular. Young people and college students knew great pieces of Ginsberg's "Howl," and Gregory's "Marriage," "Bomb," and "Power."

With Gregory, the last of the great "Beats" still alive, and still close, I am reluctant to do anything but respect his ferociously guarded privacy. His poetry speaks for him. All you have to know is that behind that curmudgeonly exterior is a beautiful, loyal, generous, sensitive, truthful and extraordinary human being. Like Huncke, you can't fool him – he knows. He is a wise, spiritually profound man; in Nietzsche's words, "Human, all-too-human."

–Roger Richards and his wife Irvyne are long time friends of Gregory, live in the same building on Horatio Street, and have provided a good portion of his care during his illness.

PATTI SMITH

Plainsong

Alas, your sleep seemed to span
an air too sweet to wake again
once more to sup from mortal plate
etched with daisyboy charades

As petals closed we wove a chain
chanting 'round this refrain
l'auntleroy no longer lord
pull upon the golden chord

Sing for us all that you've seen
of your long and distant dream
drop by drop word by word
the velvet tome the twittering bird

–poet/singer Patti Smith is a long time friend of Gregory Corso

Continued on page 10

Woodstock Journal *September 1-15, 2000*

Corso

Continued from page 9

ANDY CLAUSEN

We Were in Port Authority

It was a couple weeks before Christmas, it was in the first half of the eighties, waiting for a bus to New Brunswick, New Jersey. Gregory says, "Watch this." His eyebrows conveying stealth, reaches in his coat gets a dollar bill and lays it flat on a homeless sot sleeping on his side on the floor of the upstairs Port Authority Terminal concrete for a mattress, stubble & spittle. Then Gregory has us wait silently in the wings. A young woman pushing a baby carriage starts to go for the dollar. The bum is dead to the world, has no story to be told. The fabric the bill rests on is rotting tweed. The young mom's young man holds her back, tells her not a good idea. Gregory whispers, "He's telling her it's back luck." No one took the dollar. People looked but no one took. Our bus came.

-poet Andy Clausen lives near Woodstock. This piece is excerpted from King of the Gargoyles.

OLIVER RAY

I saw a positive Gregory Corso
sitting at the Slaughtered Lamb
talking with a broad
his hair falling down on each cheek
like silk marble
and tied back in ponytail white—

Last night in the rain:
"If you're gonna dig some body's grave
make sure you dig two:
one for theirs and one for yer own,"
slumlord freedom fighter
(Orchard St. Jew)dog lonely-izer

DIANE DI PRIMA

July 28, 2000

so I am printing out poems to send to the 26 magazines who want them
or say they do
I figure I'd better get on it while I have the time
my book is done
at Viking even now getting messed with in unthinkable ways
and I have the time and I better use it
yesterday I went to visit a friend who's dying and that always reminds me
get the poems out while you can, youknow
and everything else for that matter
not to mention I had a dream last night that wasn't so good

so I am printing out poems and the phone rings and it's someone from the
     Examiner
and only this morning I read the *Examiner* will soon be extinct so I wonder
how the guy feels about that and I pick up the receiver
he says he heard Gregory Corso died last night and he wants a quote
they always want a quote and usually I ignore them
but this time I say he had the greatest lyric gift of any of them
Allen, Jack
and the greatest innate genius

yeah says the guy but you know genius and discipline don't often go together
I have discipline the guy says but no genius
I am finished printing a poem to Sharon Doubiago and want to get on with it
before we all drop dead, you know? so I tell him to call Allen's office
Allen will still have an office after we're all gone
and that office will always have quotes for everything I am so grateful
and he wants to know about Gregory's time in San Francisco
and I tell him to call City Lights and then I hang up

by this time my printer is spitting out old haikus
I only have 68 poems and 25 magazines want them or say they do
and I want to send at least three poems to each, so they'll have a choice
and I'm trying to figure this out when the guy calls back
he says he got thru to Allen Ginsberg's office and the woman who answered
said only "He Breathes!"
that's good I said and I thought about Ray Bremser
and Jack Micheline, and my friend in Mill Valley and all the rest
me too, soon "She Breathes No Longer" they'll say and somebody
will mention my lyric gift but no discipline
and what a bitch I was   so I get my sweater

and tied back in ponytail white—

Last night in the rain:
"If you're gonna dig some body's grave
make sure you dig two:
one for theirs and one for yer own,"
slumlord freedom fighter
(Orchard St. Jew)dog lonely-izer
says to me after I go too far
after I "blame the victim"
his poor dog staring at me with swollen red eyes
mad with it's solitary confinement in the house-
hole
abandoned on the corner all windows boarded
against neighborhood and world
He holds the leash with two hands
steps between us each time the dog
alludes to my direction
like he knows it would
plunge its fangs in my heart
just because it's so lonely
"You were being a gentleman about the rats
but you went too far with the dog and crack-
heads."

I cast no stones at Gregory
who sits already on Horatio
taking care to keep the world
safely outside his door
while he inside semi satiated
with talaria torn.
No I cast no stone at his mobile-dream
of Polybius and Pliny
and Tacitus and Suetonius
and Catullus and nothingness
spinning in the clogged destiny of crown
trapped beyond cognition
but not mine to shine
the sad old myth.

Not to compare
having seen his doppelganger
the illumination of the possibility of
another side of Gregory.
Why should he want to come out?
after they beat the world (then beat it)
the whole world beat now
for forty years plus
poetry gone
the poems cold
wet black ashes at the bottom

and I'm trying to figure this out when the guy calls back
he says he got thru to Allen Ginsberg's office and the woman who answered
said only "He Breathes!"
that's good I said and I thought about Ray Bremser
and Jack Micheline, and my friend in Mill Valley and all the rest
me too, soon "She Breathes No Longer" they'll say and somebody
will mention my lyric gift but no discipline
and what a bitch I was   so I get my sweater
and go to the Asian/American Restaurant, it's Chinese/Peruvian actually
but suddenly I decide I don't want to leave the house
so I cook some pasta and think about Gregory breathing and I write this
while the pasta is getting cold
and I can't help it I wish I could give him some ziti with summer sauce
and Sara Raffetto my friend breathing not so good
Allen too
and he wasn't even Italian

—the poet Diane Di Prima lives and teaches in San Francisco

of trash cans
no longer burning beneath abandoned tressel-
work
nor upon the banks of the Bouwerie
nor along the concrete banks of the rivers
meandering like old men
through the shackles of the City···

They're all dead your friends
and you left alive
with this tawdry new millennium
lost in pasts not your own you believe
still hold pieces of your soul.
The true solitude of man is everywhere
sitting on rainy stoops
standing with face to wall
divided   conquered
eyes fixed on pervasive emptiness—
Nothing—
your childhood
your children
your children breeded
the Via del Corso continues
Vodka- nothing

Gregory
Slumlord of Poetry
Laureate of Languor
got all the Poems boarded up
against time
and with 'em

the Soul chained
and if you listen close
you can hear
pariah dog
howling
inside.

I saw a positive Gregory
sailing against the clouds
arms outstretched like Christ
illuminated by the glow
of below city
sailing with cathedral spires
in ecstatic comatose-levitation
Am I supposed to write your history
in a poem—
or call beneath your window
Gregory Gregory you motherfucker
let down your hair
lift me up from this land of dead poets
and dead poetry
I am nothing compared
to the times gone...
lift me above this...
above beyond myself
you are positive
Gregory

—Oliver Ray is a musician who works with Patti
Smith; his poem was written a few weeks prior to
Gregory's illness, but in premonition of it.

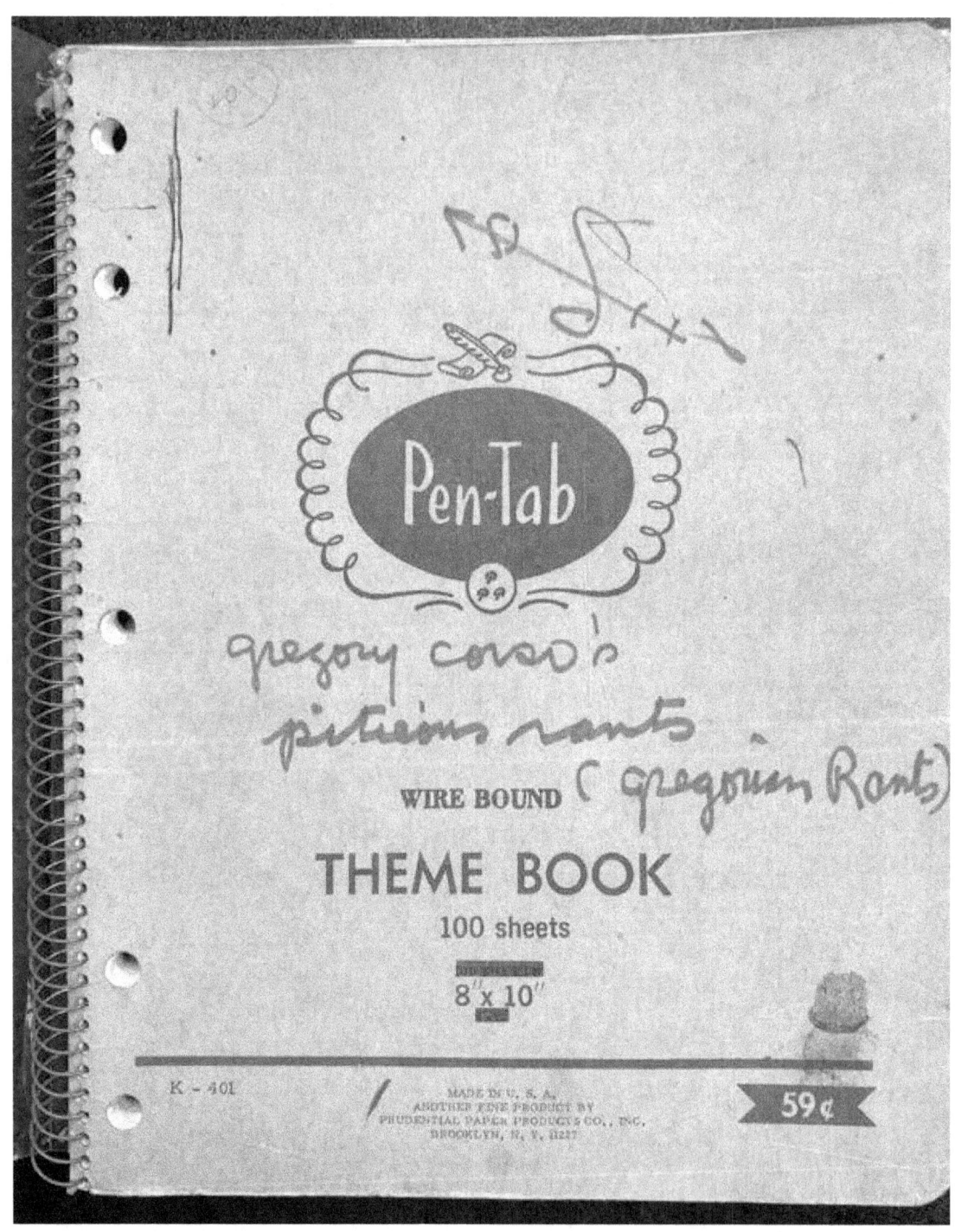

From an unpublished & undated notebook (late 90s) in the collection of Donna Lynn Stillo, with kind permission.

Gregorian Rants

by Gregory Corso

60 billion trillion
miles of Kosmos

*

from your focal point
the galaxy you see /
In the human there is no sound
nor in the mind

It does not exist this evil
there is no sin
because there is no free will
Only good emanates from me
the bad I encounter
comes from thee

What is what is not?
(essence, like Hamlet)
We know what evil is

and yet evil exists not

What is sinful
without free will

Existence as seen & felt by godhead
manhead analogous to it—
i.e., each part reflects the whole
god mind the mirror-man mind the reflection
each mind is like a cell in god mind
each cell of man mind

The whole can never be given whole
part cannot give whole

the act is evil, evil is an act—before the act
wherefore the evil? The cause

The object is the cause
To kill without cause is evil
Evil is illogical
no thing in itself is evil
a thing can cause evil
no logical cause is evil

evil is an essence—a quality—

a quality which is negative and limited—

Only in the mind is time real

the sight of a tree
        is real to the mind
not to the tree—

most distinguish between evil as it is
perceived by us, and as it is in itself—

see & feel, light & heat.

the complex factors of the equation
:—the associations of these interrelated
factors—

the revolution shall not be tested in blood—
a revolution where none lose—

***

Is the Kosmos infinite
or finite? Does Time exist or not
exist? Does the Kosmos have a beginning
or was it always?

If there is a choice between two
things and the mind cannot decide
between the two—the best thing is to choose them both.

_____

Man reflecting. As it was in the
beginning so it is now—and the end
is not anywhere near. "Man is a God
when he dreams. A beggar when he reflects."
  Long has he reflected: (above)

Self-conscious is man and it
has made him unnatural. Nothing of
nature questions nature. The animal already
knows the answer—instinctively.

For that which exists a reason must also exist. What
is the reason for man's self-consciousness?
That he seek the reason (cause) for being? the reason why
nature?

Zero
0 desires / one
0 is that from which all things come
  and that to which all things go

0 contains infinity

0 is absolute

0DAM

To see the Kosmos

Like a galaxy seen as a star

is the distance man must go

to know god

Time cannot tell

as can eternity

the changes there are

covered the earth with stone

filled the air with stone

abolished the sea with stone

1 am without trees

All are buried with their gods

Where are they of once great nations

where are all the priests

In eternity there is a time for gods

About the Contributors

Dario Bellini is an Italian photographer and cinematographer. He has worked for numerous magazines, including *The Economist* and *Time* (cover, 1976). He moved into cinematography in the seventies, working on feature films and documentaries, and is currently working as a cameraman for Radio Televisione Italiana. In 1989, he made the short documentary *Gregory Corso Talks and Walks in Roma*. In 2023, he organized a celebration of Corso in Rome, which included film presentations, music and live readings.

Neeli Cherkovski was an internationally renowned poet, biographer and memoirist. He published 14 books of poetry, including *Animal* (1996), *Elegy for Bob Kaufman* (1996) and *Elegy for My Beat Generation* (2018). He wrote biographies on his friends Charles Bukowski and Lawrence Ferlinghetti, taught literature and philosophy at the New College of California, and produced the first San Francisco Poetry Festival. In 1989, he published *Whitman's Wild Children*, a collection of essays on the poets he knew, including Philip Lamantia, Gregory Corso, Jack Micheline and Harold Norse.

Dick Ellis is a visiting Professor in American Studies at the University of Chichester. Dick has published widely on the Beats and throughout his career has pioneered American Studies in the UK.

Christopher Felver is a photographer and filmmaker. His distinctive visual signature offers a lasting contribution to the legacy of our national cultural community. Felver's films and photographs read like a roster of American mid-century avant-garde.

Raymond Foye is a writer, publisher, and curator based in New York City. In 2020, he received an American Book Award from the Before Columbus Foundation for his co-editing of *The Collected Poems of Bob Kaufman* for City Lights. He is currently editing *The Collected Poems of Rene Ricard*. He is a consulting editor with *The Brooklyn Rail*.

Hugo Frey is a Professor of Cultural and Visual History at the University of Chichester in the UK. His work includes writing and art curation on graphic narrative, the 1960s, and personal collective memory.

Westley Heine is the author of *Busking Blues: Recollections of a Street Musician and Squatter* (Roadside Press, 2022), a short story collection *12 Chicago Cabbies* (Newington Blue Press, 2021), and a volume of poetry *The Trail of Quetzalcoatl* (Scars Publications, 2016). A regular contributor to the literary journal *Beatdom,* he has twice featured at the Green Mill Poetry Slam in Chicago, and is the host of the poetry open mic night at The Gallery Cabaret. His second collection of poetry *Street Corner Spirits* was published by Roadside Press in 2023.

Kurt Hemmer is Professor of English at Harper College in Palatine, Illinois, and the editor of the *Encyclopedia of Beat Literature.* With filmmaker Tom Knoff he produced several award-winning films: *Janine Pommy Vega: As We Cover the Streets; Rebel Roar: The Sound of Michael McClure; Wow! Ted Joans Lives!;* and *Love Janine Pommy Vega.* His essays have appeared in *Naked Lunch@50: Anniversary Essays* (2009), *A History of California Literature* (2015), *Beat Drama* (2016), *The Cambridge Companion to the Beats* (2017) and *William S. Burroughs: Cutting Up the Century* (2019). Kurt is currently working on a biography of Gregory Corso.

Kaarina Hollo is a scholar and translator of Irish literature (both medieval and modern) and an occasional writer of Irish and English poetry. Her translation of Derry O'Sullivan's "Marbhghin 1943: Glaoch ar Liombo" ("Stillborn 1943: Calling Limbo") won first place in the Stephen Spender Prize for Translation 2012, the first poem by a living author and first poem translated from Irish to do so.

Leon Horton is a countercultural writer, interviewer, and editor. A regular contributor to *International Times* and the literary journal *Beatdom,* his essays and interviews include

"Hunter S. Thompson: Fear and Loathing in utero," "Keeper of the Sacred Scrolls: An Interview with Bill Morgan," "The Beaten Generation: Burroughs, Ginsberg, Thompson... and the Battle of Chicago," "Turning the Tables: An Interview with Victor Bockris" and "Charles Bukowski: Only Tough Guys Shit Themselves in Public."

Mark Ilott is an artist and illustrator based in the UK. He studied Illustration at Bournemouth College of Art and Design, and Drawing at the University of Central Lancashire. With his brother Richard, an animator, he started the Hand of Brothers Creative Studio (www.handofbrothers.co.uk) - a partnership born from their mutual passion for imaginative art and animation.

Jay Jeff Jones was an American essayist, poet and editor who lived and worked in San Francisco, London, British Columbia and Manchester (UK). He was the editor of the quarterly *New Yorkshire Writing* and author of the play *The Lizard King*. With Douglas Field he co-curated the exhibition *Off Beat: Jeff Nuttall and the International Underground* for the John Rylands Library in Manchester and co-edited the fiftieth anniversary edition of Nuttall's classic book on the 1960s *Bomb Culture*. Sadly, Jay passed away during the production of this book on Sunday, May 21, 2023.

Francis Kuipers is an Anglo/Dutch singer/songwriter and guitarist resident in Italy. He has composed for film and produced radio series on music and on the sound environment for Rai and NZBC. For 4 years, he directed the music and sound department of the multi-media school Fabrica. Collected during his lengthy travels, his archive of ethnic world sound and music is unique. In the 1980s he performed and collaborated with Gregory Corso on numerous ventures.

A. Robert Lee, formerly of the University of Kent, UK, was Professor in the English Department at Nihon University, Tokyo (1996-2011). His books includes *Multicultural American Literature: Comparative Black, Native, Latino/a and Asian American Fictions*

(2003), which won the 2004 American Book Award; and *Gothic to Multicultural: Idioms of Imagining in American Literary Fiction* (2009). His work on Beat writings includes *Modern American Counter Writing: Beats, Outriders, Ethnics* (2010); *The Beats: Authorships, Legacies* (2019); *Neal Cassady: The Joan Anderson Letter* (2020); and the edited collections *The Beat Generation Writers* (1996), *The Routledge Handbook of International Beat Literature* (2018), and, with Douglas Field, *Harold Norse: Poet Maverick, Gay Laureate* (2022).

William Lessard is the author of *instrument for distributed empathy monetization* (*KERNPUNKT Press*, 2022). His work has appeared or is forthcoming in *American Poetry Review, Best American Experimental Writing, Fence, The Laurel Review*, and the *Beloit Poetry Journal*. He is Poetry and Hybrids editor at *Heavy Feather Review*. Read more of his work at: www.williamlessardwrites.net.

Michael Limnios is a journalist, blues music aficionado and a collaborator with the Museum of American Poetics (NYC). He has written extensively about the Beat Generation and their connection to blues and jazz music and was a contributor to *Bukowski: An Anthology of Poetry & Prose About Charles Bukowski* published by Silver Birch Press. In 2014 Limnios was inducted as Greek Ambassador to the Blues Hall of Fame.

Rosemary Manno (1949-2022) was a poet, artist, and lover of the natural world. Born in Buffalo, New York, she spent many hours in the company of Corso - who stimulated her to read and write aphorisms - while traversing the streets, cafes, and tavernas of New York and San Francisco. She developed much of her poetic vocation through reading Corso's work, notably *Mindfield,* and told wonderful stories of his humor and provocative spirit. Rosemary passed away in December 2022. Her final collection of poetry, *El Sol*, was published by the Golda Foundation in 2023.

Ryan Mathews is a poet, essayist, and non fiction best selling author as well as an artist, philosopher, and futurist. His essays on both better known and more obscure Beat figures have appeared in *Beat Scene* magazine and the literary journal *Beatdom*.

Kaye McDonough is a poet, publisher, playwright and teacher. After gaining a degree in Art History from the University of California, she became part of the North Beach literary scene in San Francisco, working as a publisher for Greenlight Press and as an editor for Alix Geluardi's now classic anthology of San Francisco poets *185*. She is the author of *Zelda: Frontier Life in America* (City Lights, 1978) and *Pagan: Selected Poems* (New Native Press, 2014). She is currently working on her memoir *The Spell of Bohemia: Twenty Years in San Francisco's North Beach 1965-1985*.

Gerald Nicosia has been studying and writing about the Beats for close to fifty years. His renowned biography of Jack Kerouac, *Memory Babe*, is rightly regarded as the definitive critical study of the nascent Beat writer. Gerald also edited *Jan Kerouac: A Life in Memory*, a collection of essays and remembrances about her. His other works include *The Last Days of Jan Kerouac* (2016); *Kerouac: The Last Quarter Century* (2019); and the *BEAT Scrapbook* (2020). A revised and extended version of *Memory Babe* is forthcoming.

Kirby Olson wrote *Gregory Corso: Doubting Thomist* (published by Southern Illinois University Press, 2002). He is a tenured professor at SUNY in the Western Catskill Mountains of NY State. He studied with Gregory Corso and Allen Ginsberg at Naropa University in 1977 and 1979.

Dan Richter is best known as Moonwatcher, the man-ape in the opening sequence of Stanley Kubrick's iconic masterpiece *2001: A Space Odyssey*, which he also choreographed. Dan has had a long career as a mime, choreographer, actor, director, producer, memoirist, and for two decades a Hollywood executive. His book *Moonwatcher's Memoir* is about working on *2001*. His recently published memoir *The Dream is Over* describes the years he lived and worked with John Lennon and Yoko Ono from 1969 to 1973.

Kyle Roderick studied French language and literature at Institut Catholique de Paris, graduated from Sarah Lawrence College and has worked as a journalist, author, ghost writer, book editor and photo editor. Roderick abandoned a Corso biography project in 1996 when her research fellowship finances were depleted and the poet lost interest in the endeavour.

Ed and Miriam Sanders have led the rise of the counterculture from its earliest days. Ed achieved fame as a poet, political activist, publisher and member of the satirical rock band The Fugs. He founded *Fuck You / A Magazine of the Arts* in 1962, and two years later opened the Peace Eye Bookstore in the Lower East Side of New York. Miriam studied at the Catan-Rose Institute of Art and met Ed at New York University. Married in 1967, they live in the Catskills, where they continue to create glyph-poems (the fusing of text and image) and to produce the *Woodstock Journal*.

George Scrivani studied Latin and Greek at SUNY Buffalo, where he met Gregory Corso in 1970. For the next thirty years he served as Corso's secretary, editor and translator (Italian and German). His translation of Alberto Savinio's *Departure of the Argonaut* was published by *Petersburg Press* in 1986, with illustrations by Francesco Clemente. Between 1986 and 1995 he worked in India as editor for *Hanuman Books*.

Gregory Stephenson grew up in Colorado and Arizona, but has lived in Denmark for more than 50 years. He is the former editor of the literary review *PEARL*, teaches at the University of Copenhagen and has written extensively on contemporary American and English literature. He is the author of *Exiled Angel: A Study of the Work of Gregory Corso* (Hearing Eye, 1989), *Friendly and Flowing Savage: The Literary Legend of Neal Cassady* (Textile Bridge Press, 1987), and more recently *And the Rivers Thereof: Riverine Imagery in the Writing of Jack Kerouac* (Felix Culpa Press, 2023).

Anne Waldman is an acclaimed International poet and an active member of what she terms the "outrider" experimental poetry community. She was instrumental in setting up The Poetry Project at St. Marks Church in New York, and was co-founder with Allen

Ginsberg and Diane diPrima of the Jack Kerouac School of Disembodied Poetics at Naropa University, where she teaches as a professor of poetics.

Ron Whitehead is a poet, author, and activist. He is the author of more than thirty books and 40 albums, has been translated into 20 different languages, and has edited and published numerous works by Gregory Corso, William Burroughs, Allen Ginsberg, Hunter S. Thompson, Diane di Prima, Jack Kerouac and Lawrence Ferlinghetti. In 2006, he was nominated for the Nobel Prize in Literature. In 2021, Whitehead was named Lifetime U.S. Beat Poet Laureate by the National Beat Poetry Foundation.

Robert Yarra is a writer, publisher, founder of the Golda Foundation (created to help artists in need) and co-trustee of the Vali Myers Art Gallery Trust.

Nina Zivancevic is a Serbian-born poet, playwright, essayist, and art critic. She has published 17 books of poetry, two novels and three collections of short stories. A former assistant to Allen Ginsberg, she has worked as both a writer and scholar of experimental literature, is the recipient of many literary awards, and has contributed to *New York Arts Magazine*, *American Book Review*, and *East Village Eye*. She has translated numerous writers into Serbian, including Charles Bukowski and Kathy Acker.

Acknowledgements

By its very nature, a book such as this is a product of creative collaboration. It would not have been possible without the dedication of the numerous contributors who agreed to take part. The publishers would like to extend their deepest thanks and appreciation to the dazzling array of writers, artists and photographers who gave their time and their talent so enthusiastically.

For their general guidance and support for this project, thanks to the Gregory Corso Estate, the European Beat Studies Network, The Beat Studies Association, the Allen Ginsberg Trust, the Beat Museum, and the literary publications *Beatdom* and *Beat Scene*.

Special mention must go to Raymond Foye, whose unerring support and calming influence throughout the development of this project has seen this tribute brought to fruition.

Permissions

Roadside Press wish to extend their deepest gratitude for permission to reproduce the following works:

"A Most Danerous Art" by © Raymond Foye was originally published by Lithic Press (2022). By kind permission of Lithic Press. "Grand Larceny in Vermont: Undisclosed Early Misadventures of Gregory Corso" by © Gregory Stephenson was first published in *Beat Scene* (Issue 105, 2022). By kind permission of the author. "Between Childhood and Manhood" by © Gregory Corso was first published in *Cavalier* (Volume 15, No. 139, January, 1965). By special permission of Raymond Foye. "The Beat of Silence: An Interview with Kirby Olson" (2013) by Michael Limnios first appeared on the website *Blues.Gr.* By kind permission of Kirby Olson and Michael Limnios. "Where Marble Stood and Fell: Gregory Corso in Greece" by © Leon Horton was first published in the literary journal *Beatdom #22* (2022). By kind permission of Beatdom Books. "Poem for Gregory Corso's Ashes in the English Cemetery in Rome" by © Gerald Nicosia was first published in the author's own *Beat Scrapbook* (Coolgrove Press, 2020). By kind permission of the author. "She-Stag and the Tiger of Wanawutu" by © Kaye McDonough was originally published in the *Los Angeles Print Quarterly* (Journal No. 19, July, 2018). By kind permission of the author. "Gregory Corso (for Lisa Brinker)" by © Neeli Cherkovski was first published in the poetry collection *Elegy for My Beat Generation* (Lithic Press, 2018). By kind permission of the author. "Gregory Gave Me the World" by © Robert Yarra was extracted from the Chapbook of the same name (Counter Culture Chronicles / Casioli Press, 2023). By kind permission of the author. "Now You See It—Now You Don't See it" by © Nina Zivancevic was first published in the poetry collection *Roller-skating Notes* (Cool Grove Press, 2021). By kind permission of the author. "Poets Don't Snarl" by © Kurt Hemmer was originally published in *Beat Scene* (Issue 89, 2018). By kind permission of the author. "Memories of Gregorio" by © Rosemary Manno was first published in the poetry collection *El Sol* (the Golda Foundation, 2023). By kind permission of the Estate of Rosemary Manno. "Keep This Generation Honest: An Interview with Raymond Foye and George Scrivani" by William Lessard first appeared on the website *jacket2* in November 2022. By kind permission of Raymond Foye, George Scrivani and William Lessard.

For permission to use photographs, photographic images and artwork, the publisher would like to thank Gerard Bellaart, Dario Bellini, Lisa Brinker, Christopher Felver, Raymond Foye, Peter Hale, Kaarina Hollo, Mark Illott, Greg Masters, Kaye McDonough, Ed and Miriam Sanders, Tate Swindell, John Geluardi, and the Gregory Corso Estate.

MORE ROADSIDE PRESS TITLES:

By Plane, Train or Coincidence
Michele McDannold

Prying
Jack Micheline, Charles
Bukowski and Catfish
McDaris

*Wolf Whistles Behind the
Dumpster*
Dan Provost

*Busking Blues: Recollections of
a Chicago Street Musician and
Squatter*
Westley Heine

Unknowable Things
Kerry Trautman

How to Play House
Heather Dorn

Kiss the Heathens
Ryan Quinn Flanagan

St. James Infirmary
Steven Meloan

Street Corner Spirits
Westley Heine

*A Room Above a
Convenience Store*
William Taylor Jr.

Resurrection Song
George Wallace

*Nothing and Too Much to
Talk About*
Nancy Patrice Davenport

*Bar Guide for the
Seriously Deranged*
Alan Catlin

Born on Good Friday
Nathan Graziano

Under Normal Conditions
Karl Koweski

The Dead and the Desperate
Dan Denton

Clown Gravy
Misti Rainwater-Lites

Walking Away
Michael D. Grover

All in a Pretty Little Row
Dan Provost

*These Are the People in
Your Neighbourhood*
Jordan Trethewey

*They Said I Wasn't
College Material*
Scot Young

Radio Water
Francine Witte

And Blackberries Grew Wild
Susan Mickelberry

Licorice Heart
Miles Budimir

Disposable Darlings
Todd Cirillo

Full Moon Midnight
Belinda Subraman

Innocent Postcards
John Pietaro

Cistern Latitudes
James Duncan

*Another Saturday Night
in Jukebox Hell*
Alan Catlin

Abandoned By All Things
Karl Koweski

Ain't These Sorrows Sweet?
Lauren Scharhag

*She Throws Herself Forward
to Stop the Fall*
Dave Newman

*We Don't Get to Write
the Ending*
Aleathia Drehmer

*These Many Cold Winters
of the Heart*
Ryan Quinn Flanagan

*Things You Never
Knew Existed*
Josh Olsen

Green Roses Bloom for Icarus
Hiromi Yoshida

Let the Scaffolds Fall
Shaun Rouser

MORE ROADSIDE PRESS TITLES:

www.ingramcontent.com/pod-product-compliance
Lightning Source LLC
Chambersburg PA
CBHW081531120626
46550CB00009B/2683